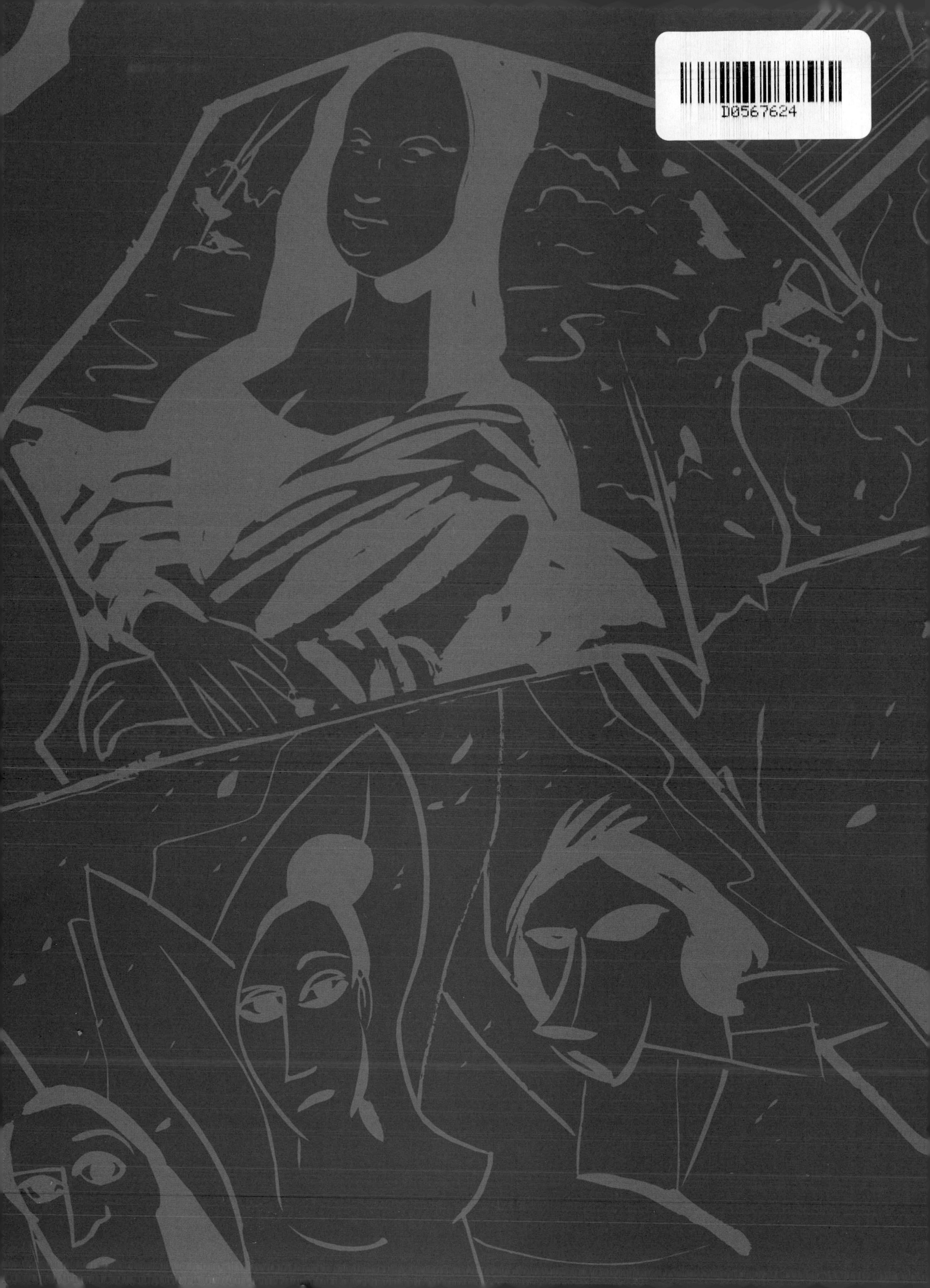

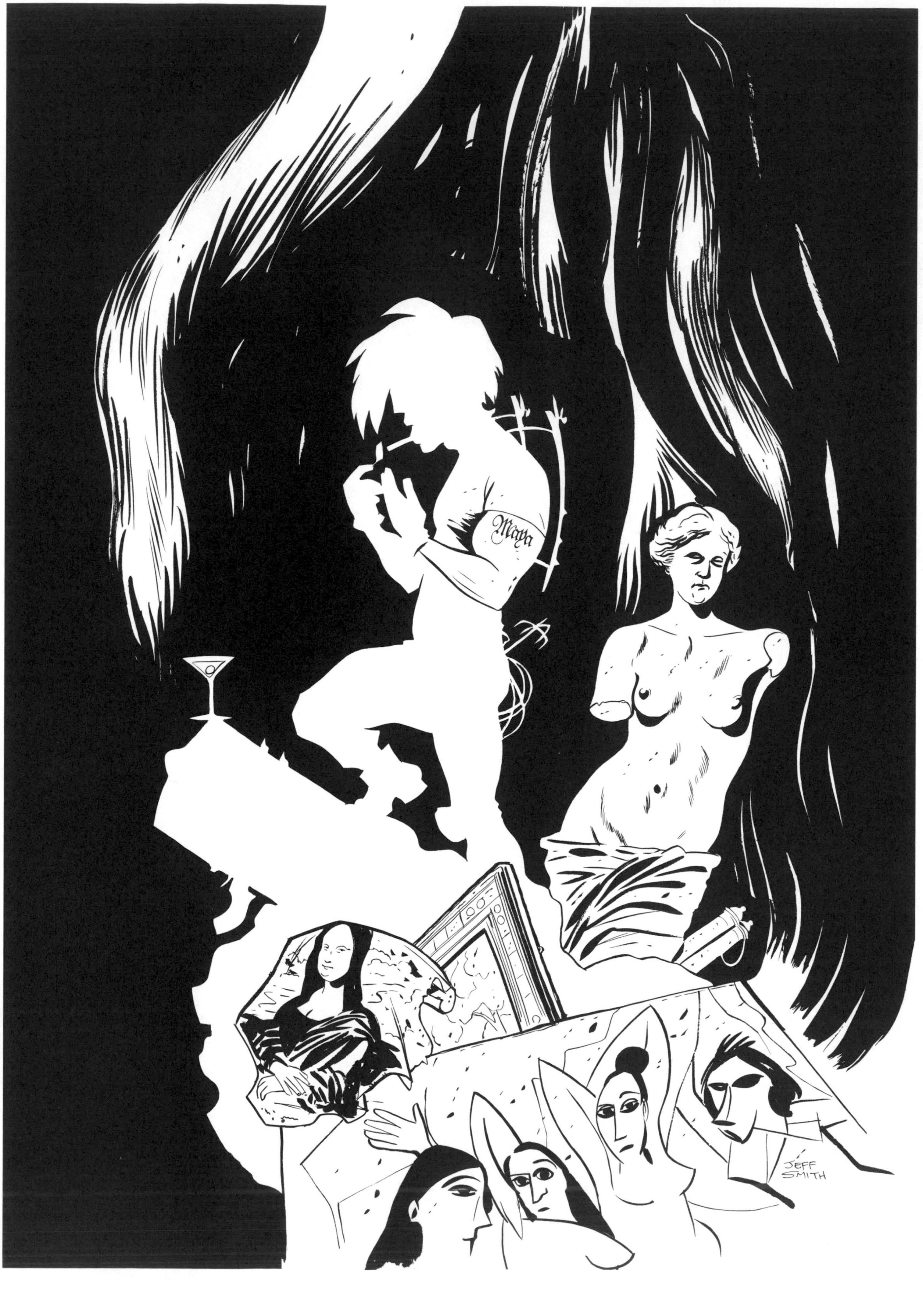
Maya
JEFF
SMITH

RASL

BY

JEFF SMITH

Cartoon Books
Columbus, Ohio

This book is dedicated to
Jennifer Oliver

RASL Volume 1: The Drift

The chapters in this book were originally published in the comic book RASL
RASL™ is © 2008 by Jeff Smith.

For Cartoon Books:
Cover Art by Jeff Smith
Cover Color & Logo/Design by Steve Hamaker
Published by Vijaya Iyer
Production Manager: Kathleen Glosan
PrePress/Design: Tom Gaadt

For information write:
Cartoon Books
P.O. Box 16973
Columbus, OH 43216

Softcover ISBN-10:   1-888963-20-4
Softcover ISBN-13:   978-1-888963-20-5

10 9 8 7 6 5 4 3 2 1

Printed in Singapore

"Throughout space there is energy. Is this energy static or kinetic? If static, our hopes are in vain; if kinetic - and we know it is, for certain - then it is a mere question of time when men will succeed in attaching their machinery to the very wheelwork of nature."

-Nikola Tesla

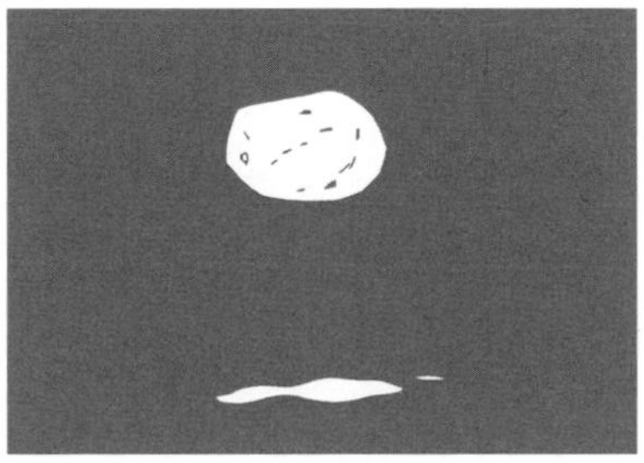

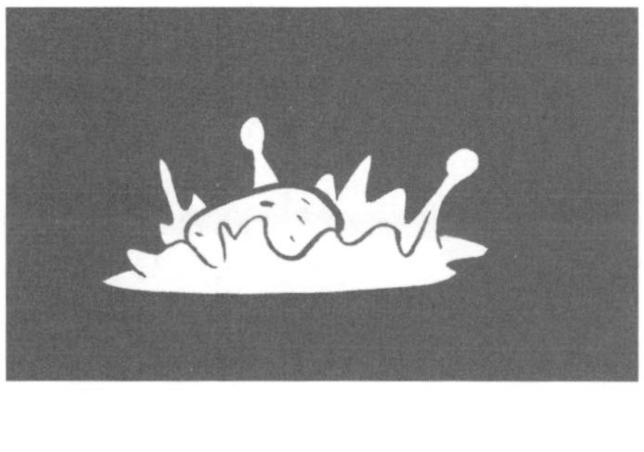

1.
THE DRIFT

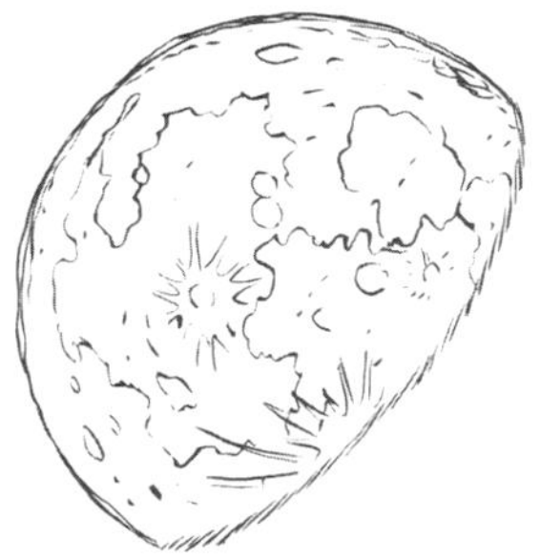

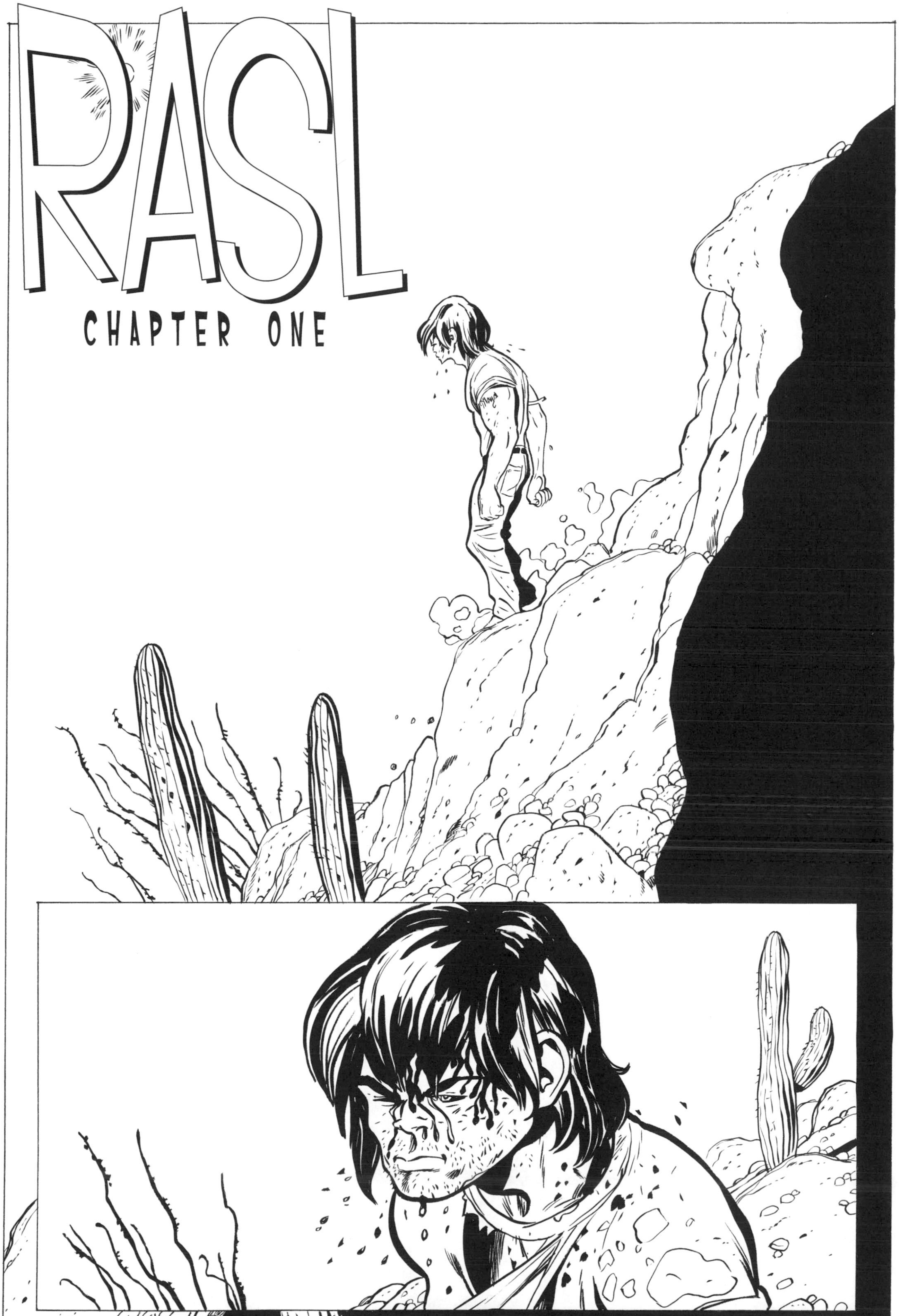
RASL
CHAPTER ONE

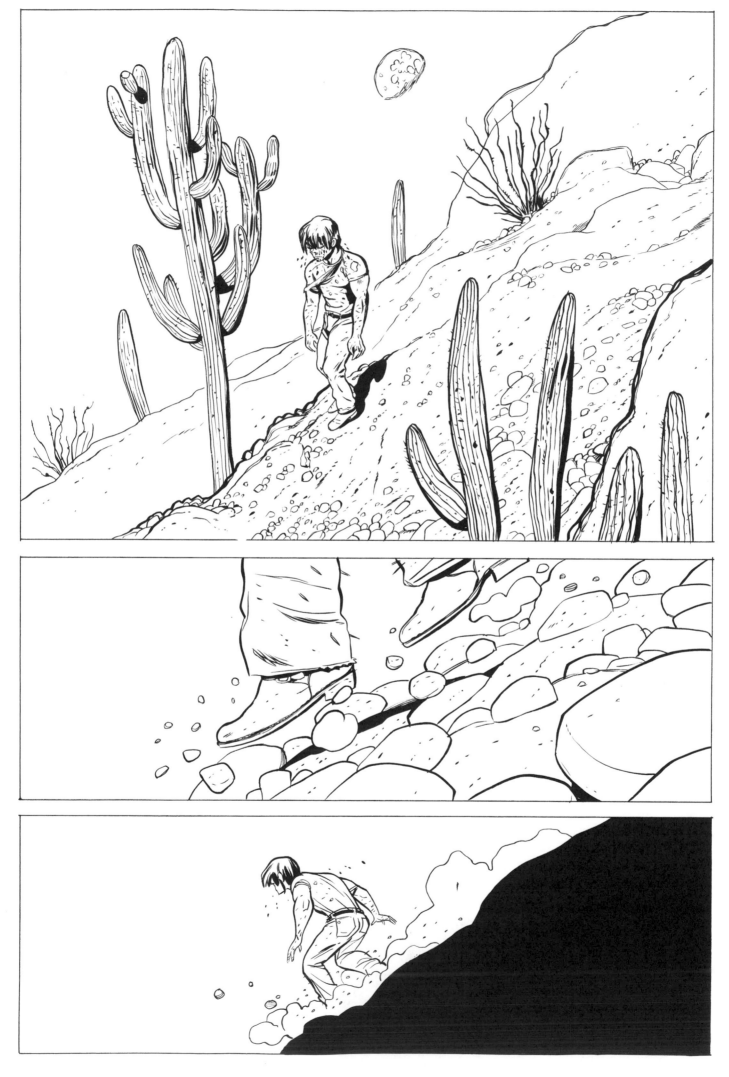

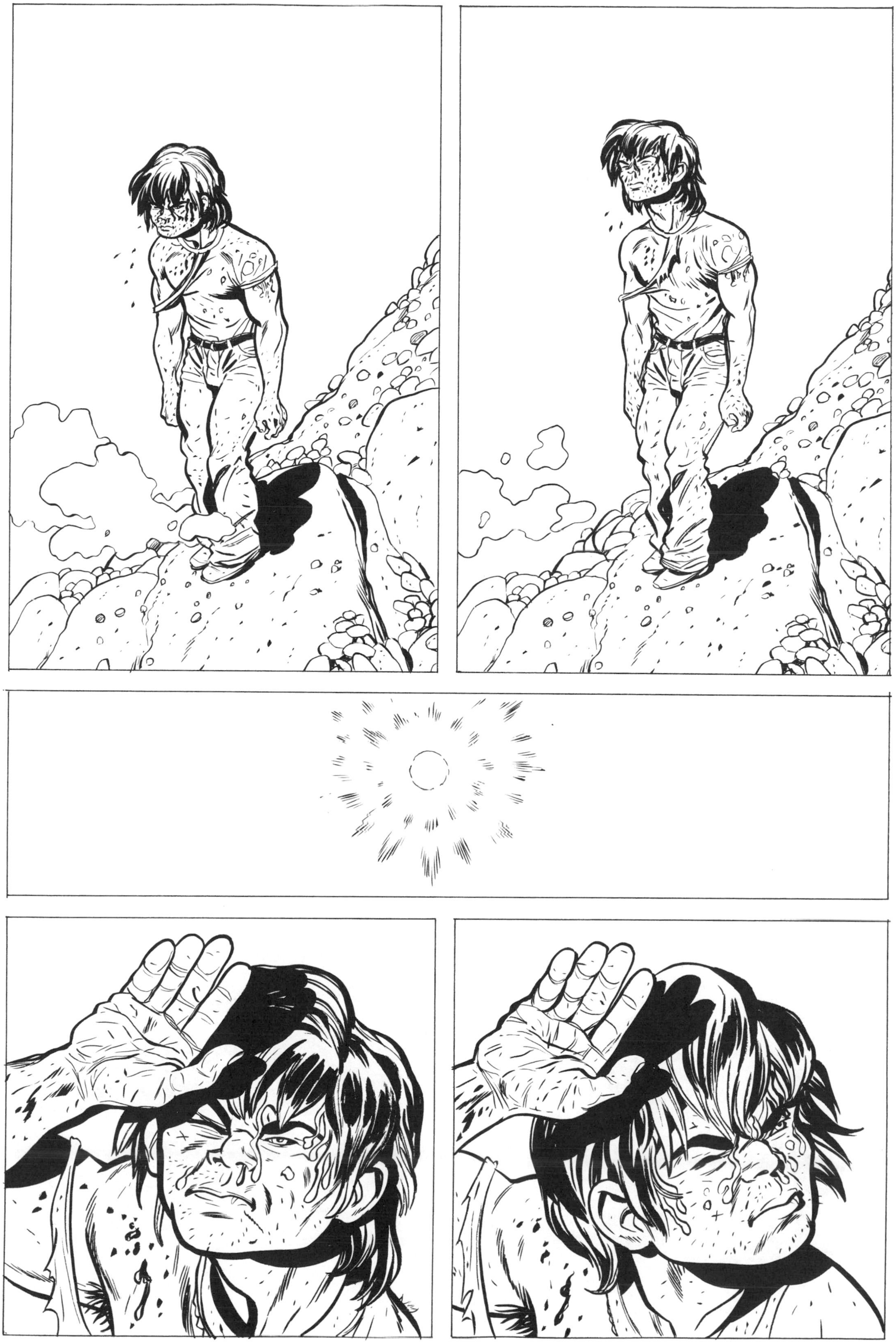

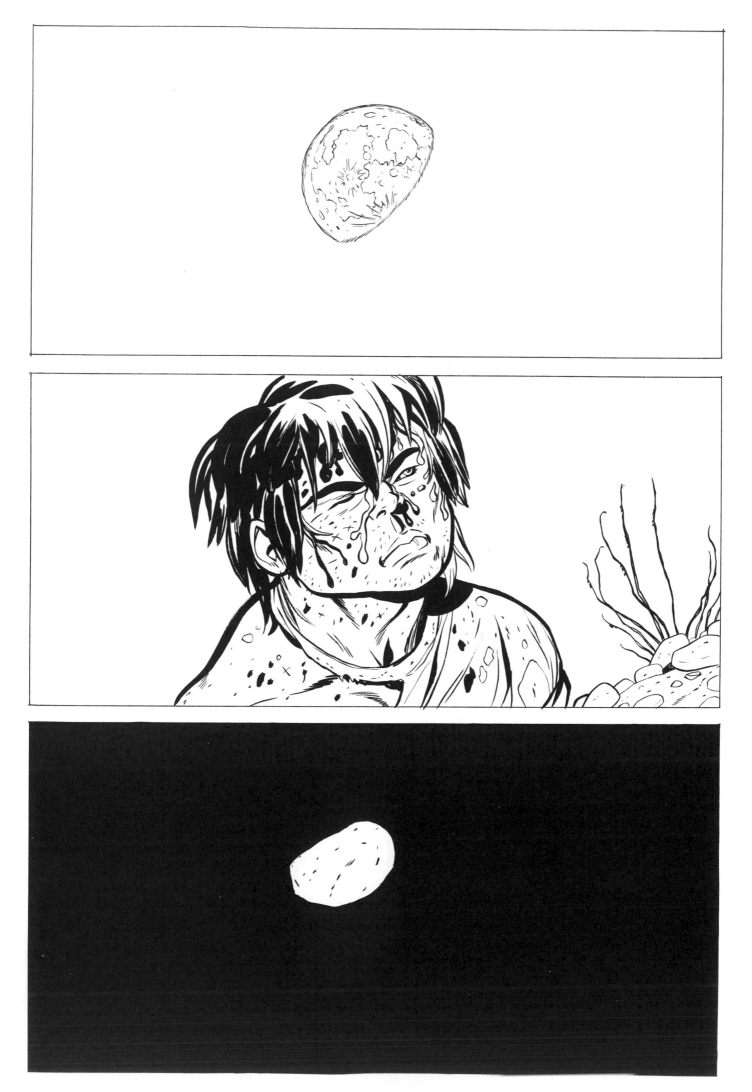

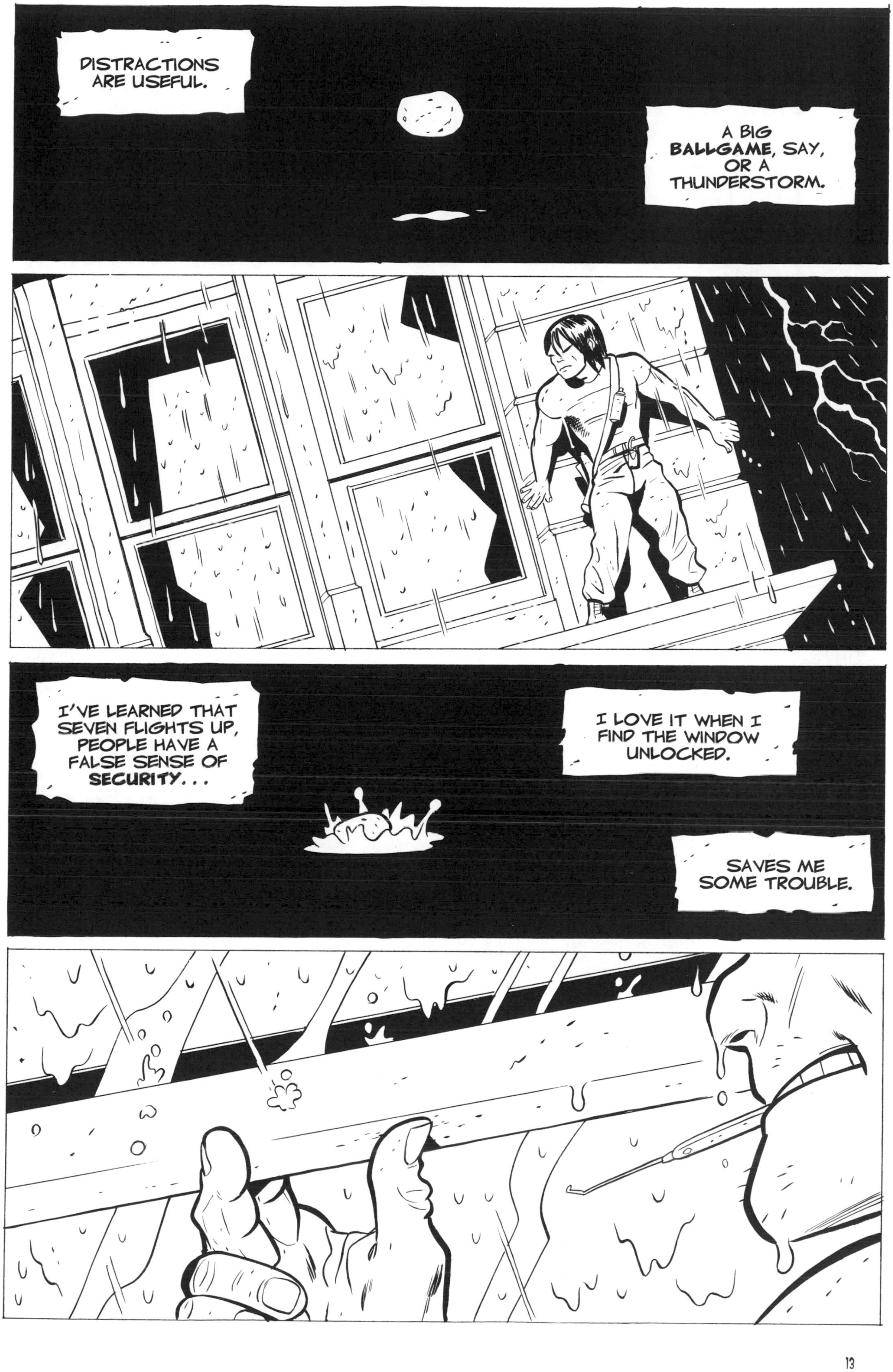
DISTRACTIONS ARE USEFUL.
A BIG BALLGAME, SAY, OR A THUNDERSTORM.
I'VE LEARNED THAT SEVEN FLIGHTS UP, PEOPLE HAVE A FALSE SENSE OF SECURITY...
I LOVE IT WHEN I FIND THE WINDOW UNLOCKED.
SAVES ME SOME TROUBLE.

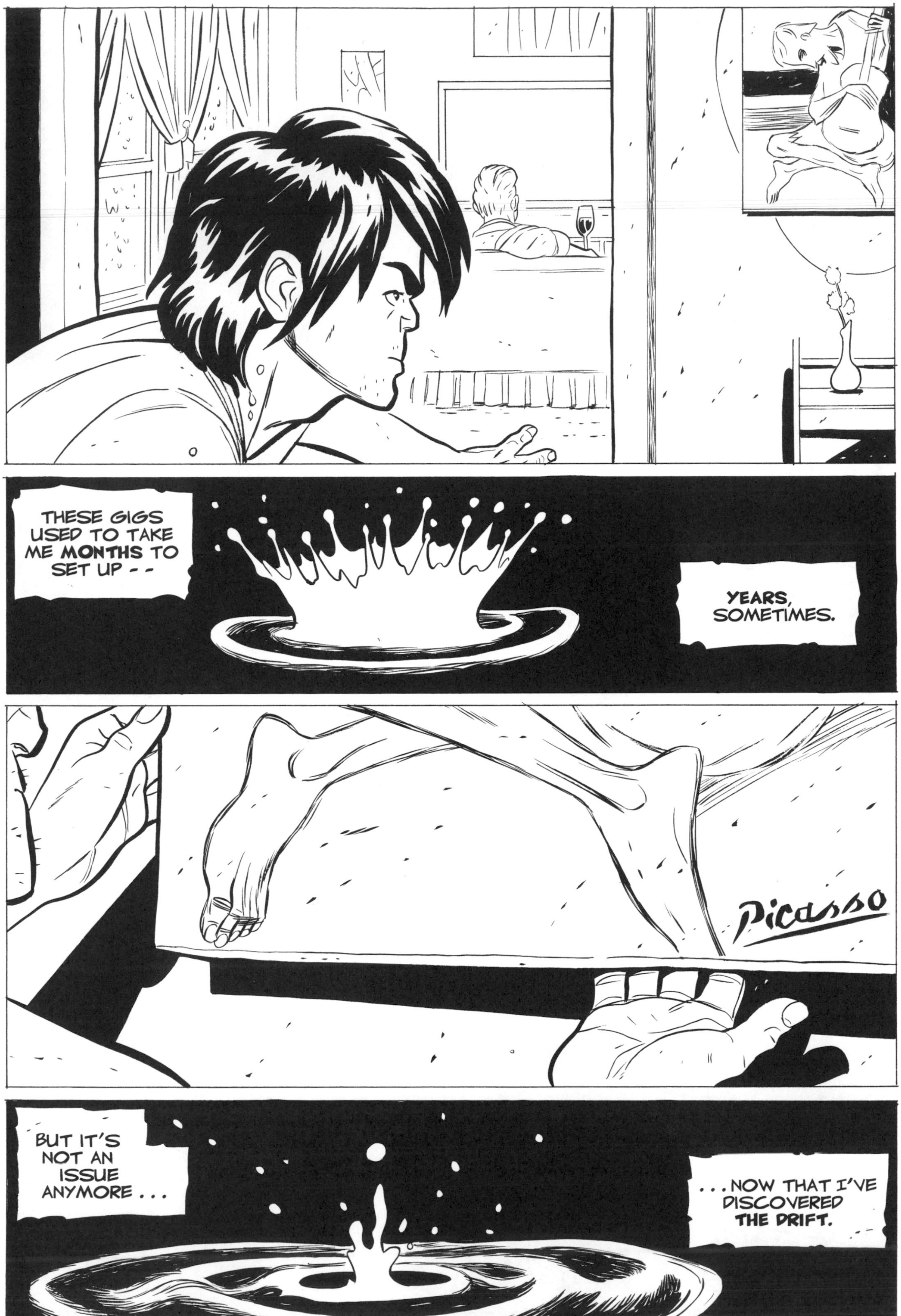
THESE GIGS USED TO TAKE ME **MONTHS** TO SET UP --
YEARS, SOMETIMES.
Picasso
BUT IT'S NOT AN ISSUE ANYMORE ...
... NOW THAT I'VE DISCOVERED **THE DRIFT.**

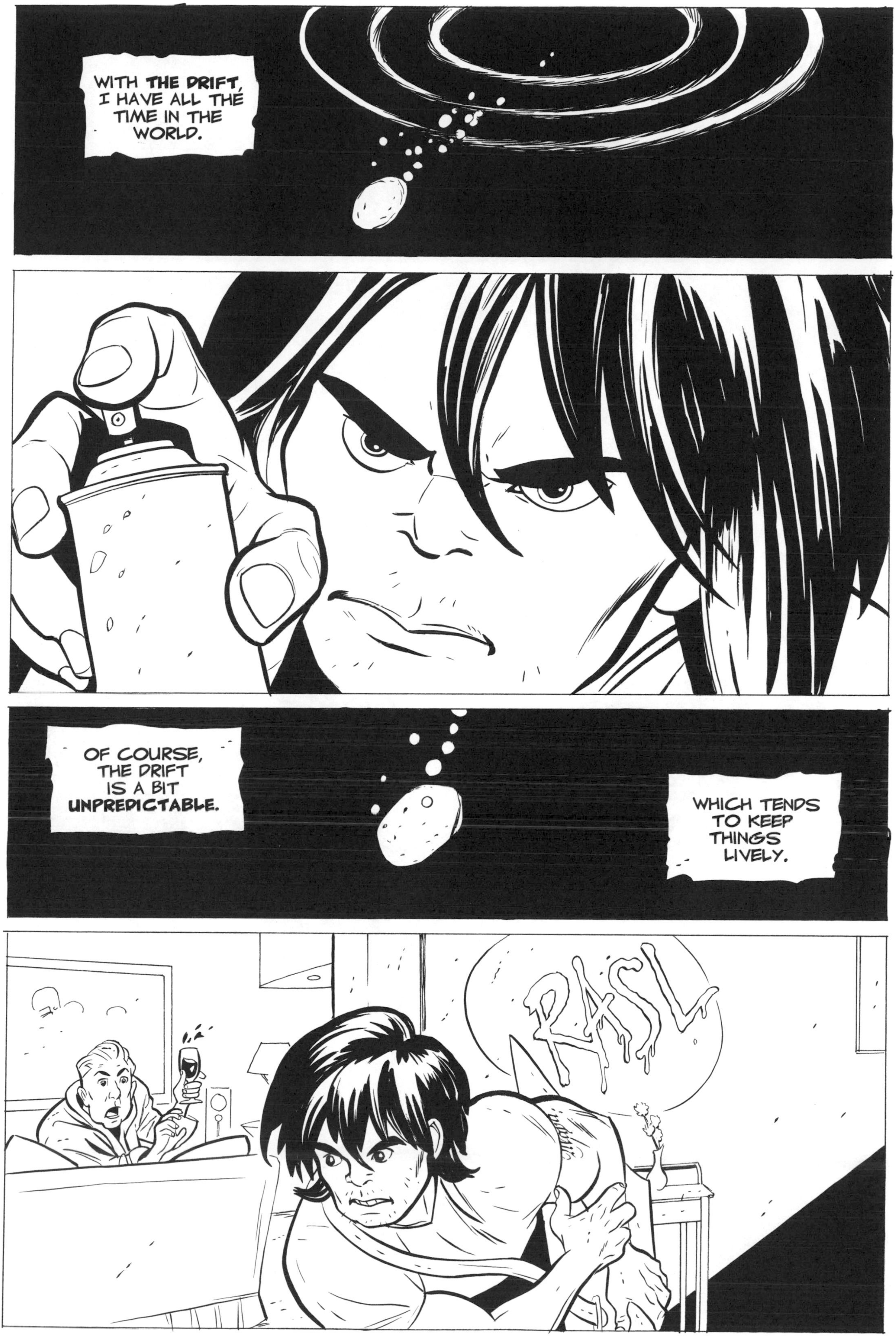
WITH THE DRIFT, I HAVE ALL THE TIME IN THE WORLD.
OF COURSE, THE DRIFT IS A BIT UNPREDICTABLE.
WHICH TENDS TO KEEP THINGS LIVELY.
RASL

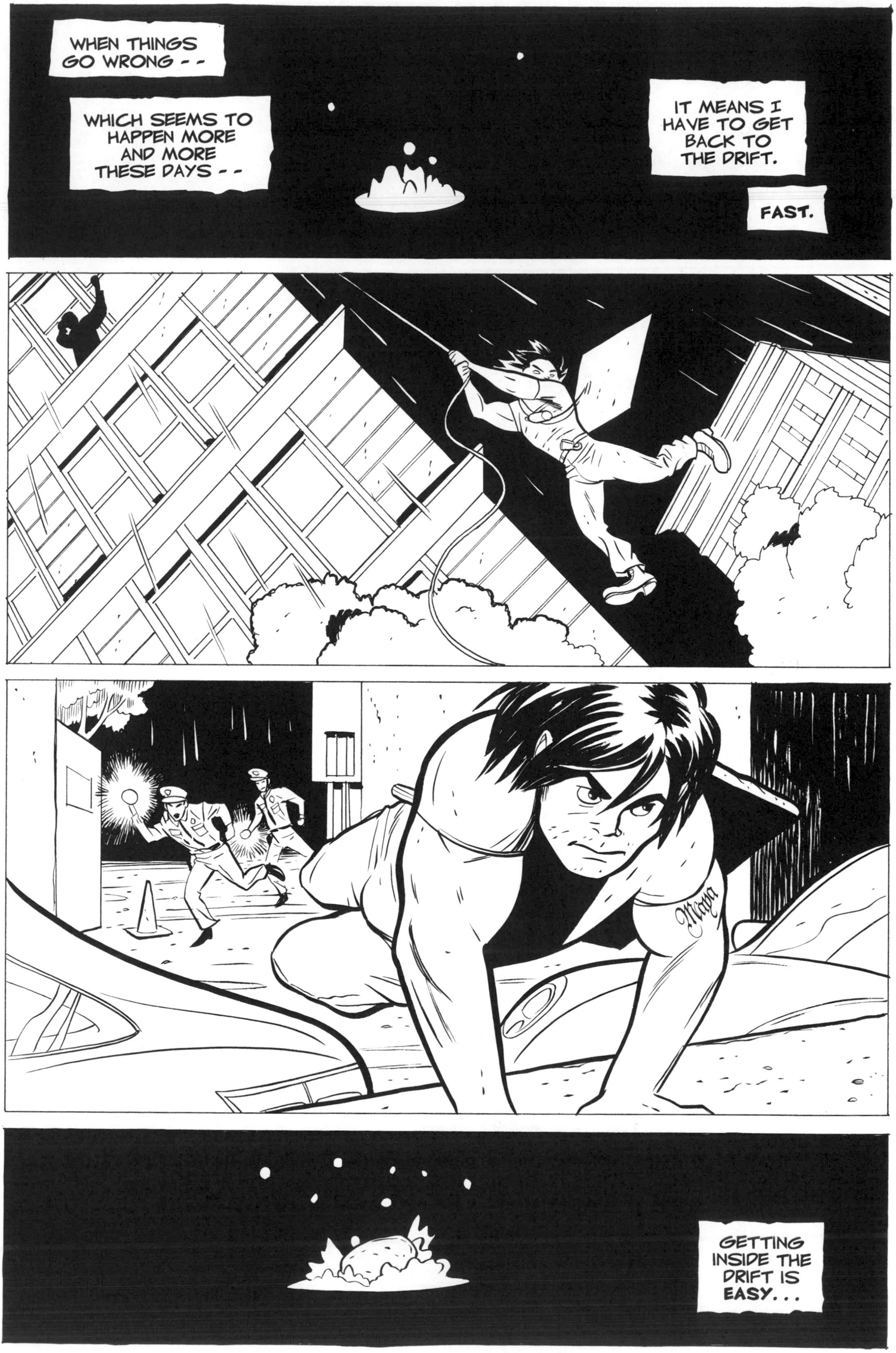
WHEN THINGS GO WRONG - -
WHICH SEEMS TO HAPPEN MORE AND MORE THESE DAYS - -
IT MEANS I HAVE TO GET BACK TO THE DRIFT.
FAST.
GETTING INSIDE THE DRIFT IS EASY. . .

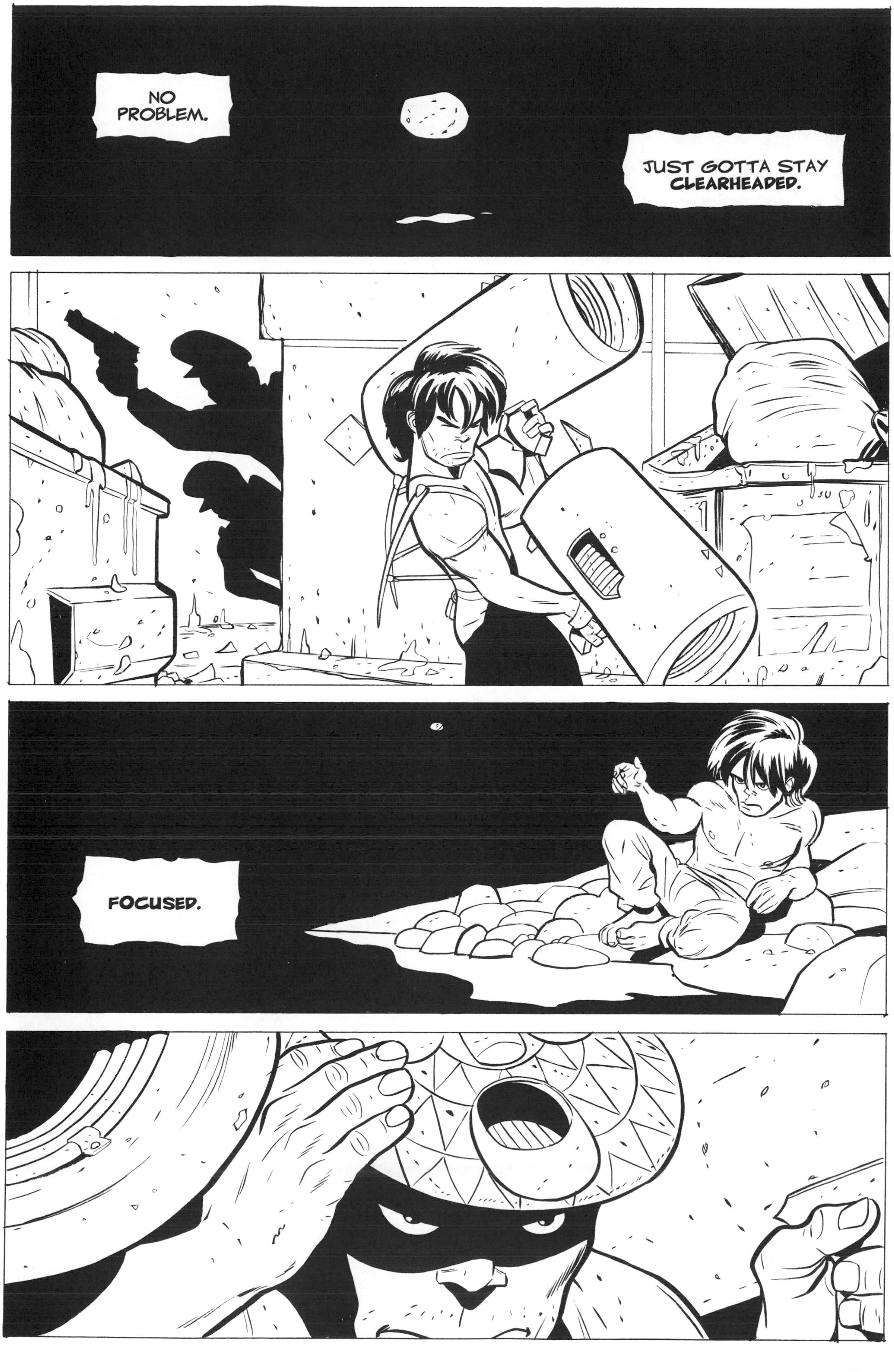
NO PROBLEM.
JUST GOTTA STAY CLEARHEADED.
FOCUSED.

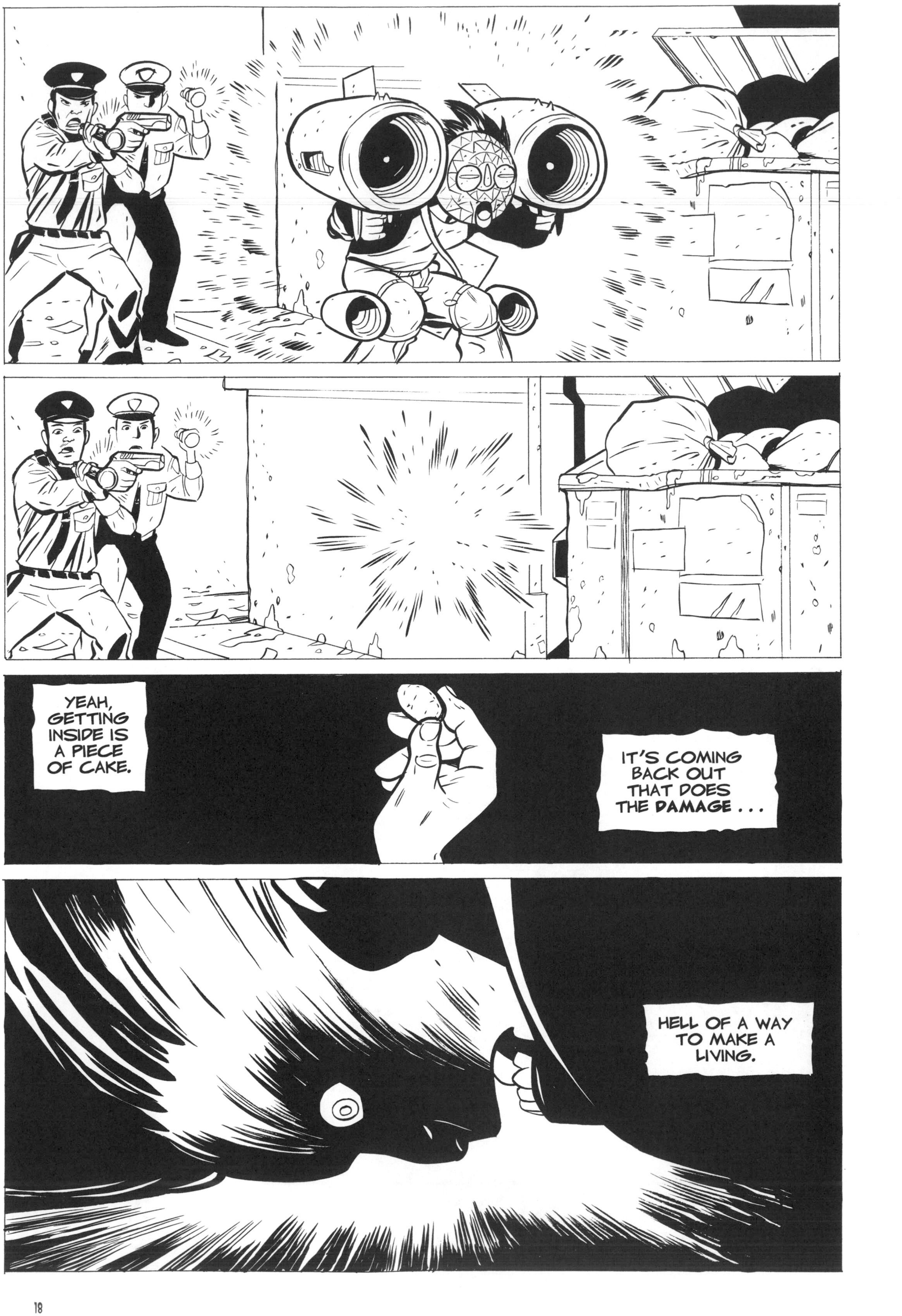
YEAH, GETTING INSIDE IS A PIECE OF CAKE.
IT'S COMING BACK OUT THAT DOES THE DAMAGE . . .
HELL OF A WAY TO MAKE A LIVING.

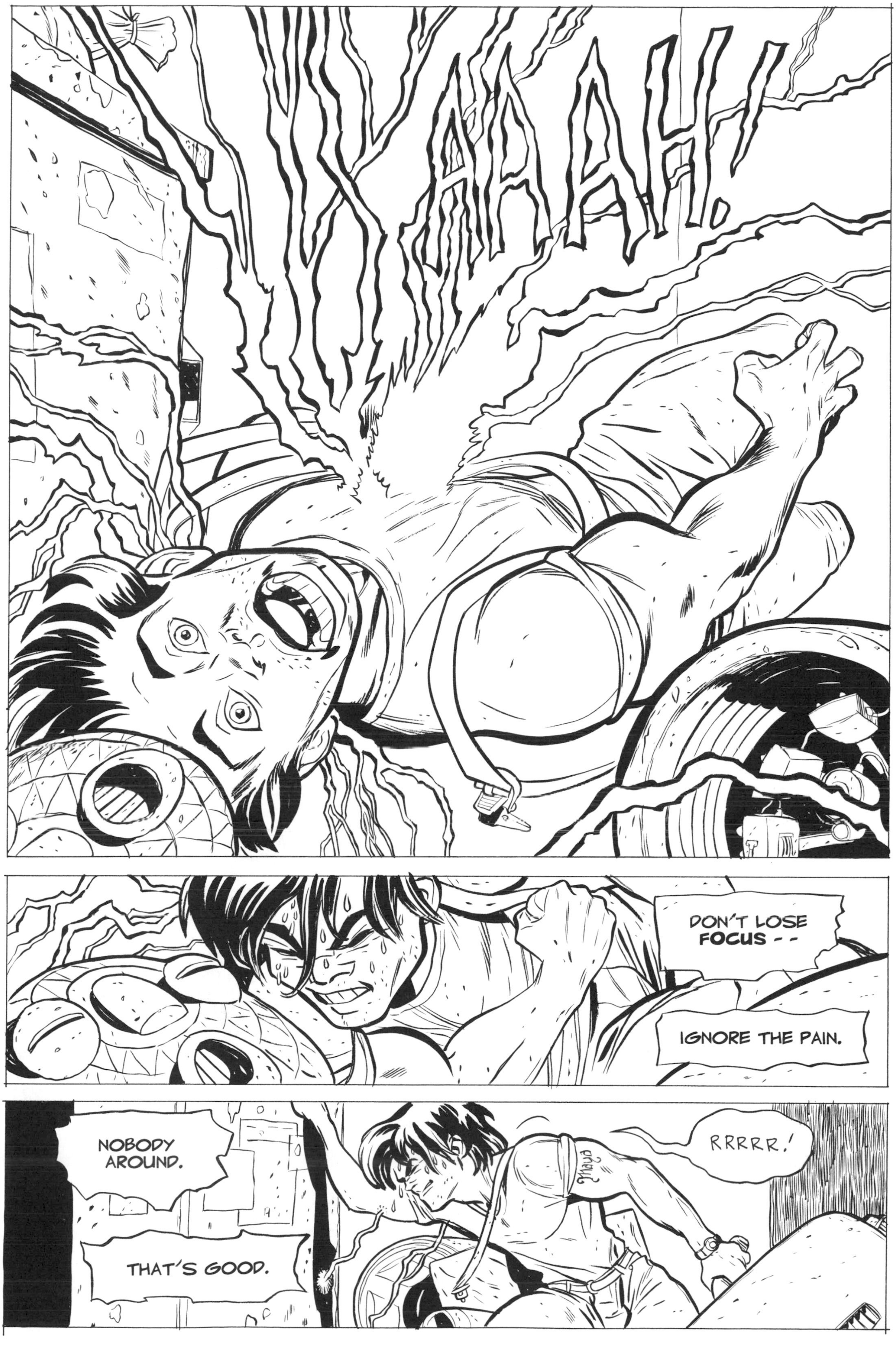
YYAAAH!
DON'T LOSE FOCUS --
IGNORE THE PAIN.
NOBODY AROUND.
THAT'S GOOD.
RRRRR!

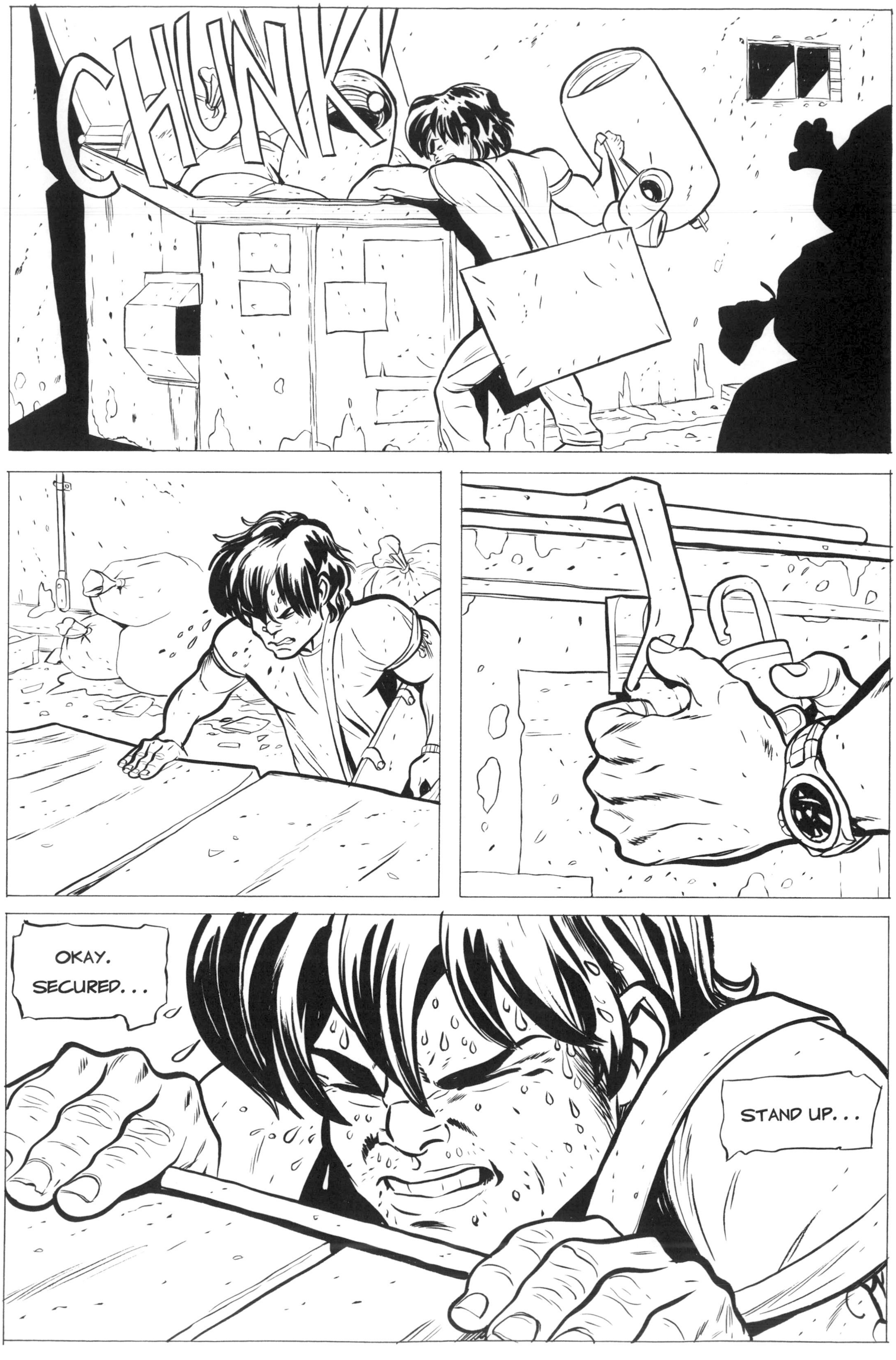
CHUNK!
OKAY. SECURED...
STAND UP...

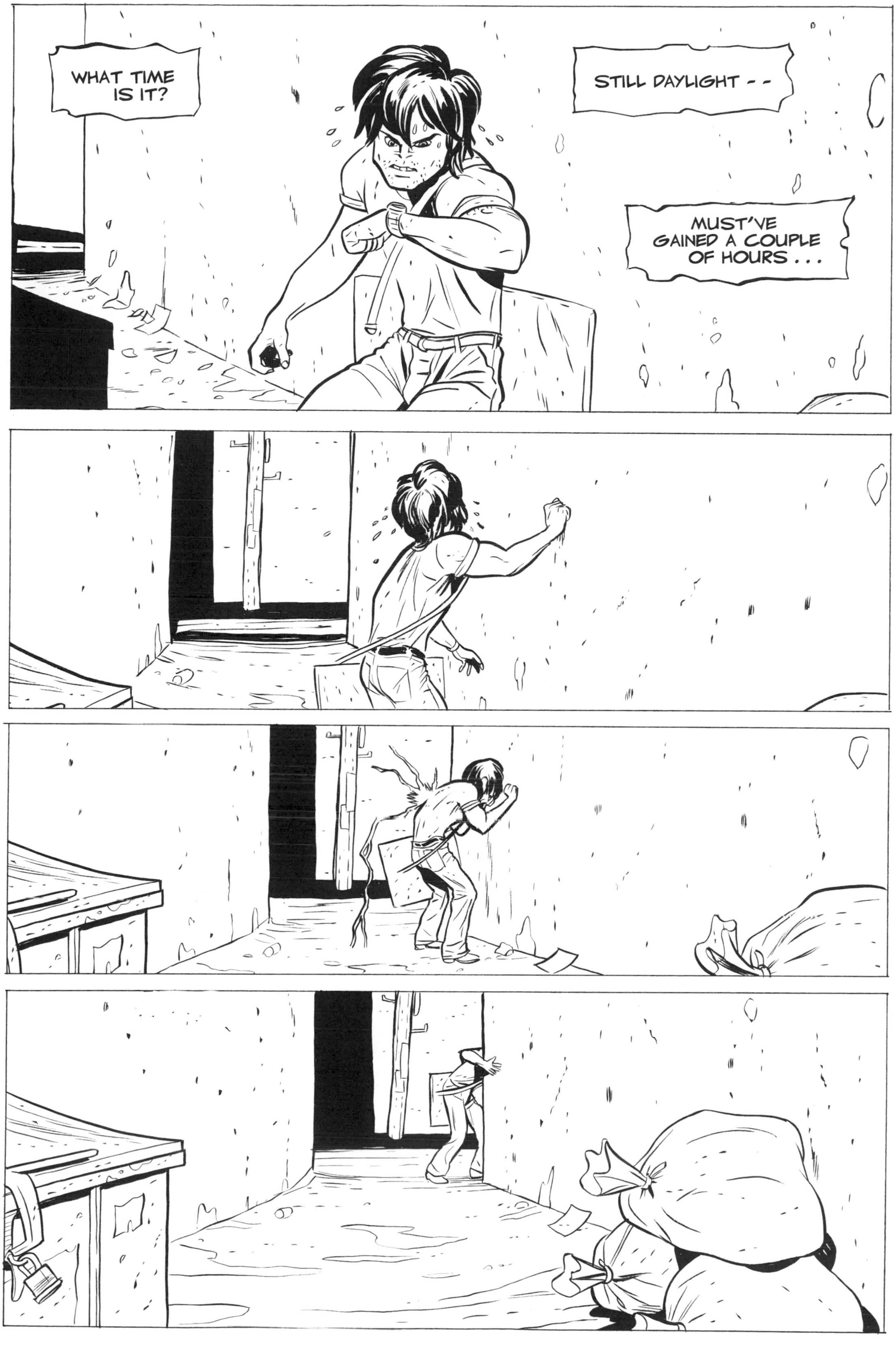
WHAT TIME IS IT?
STILL DAYLIGHT - -
MUST'VE GAINED A COUPLE OF HOURS . . .

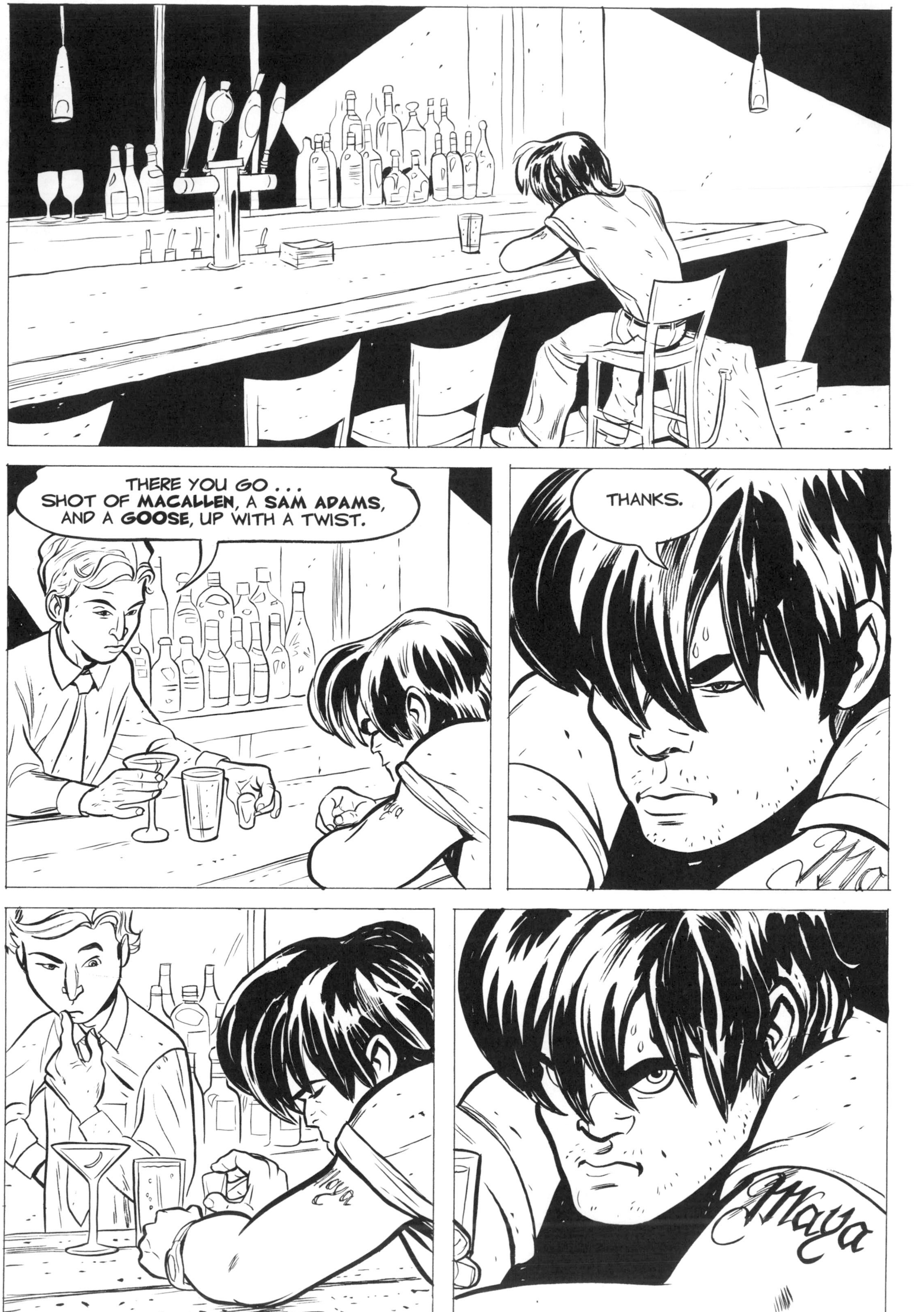
THERE YOU GO . . . SHOT OF MACALLEN, A SAM ADAMS, AND A GOOSE, UP WITH A TWIST.
THANKS.
Maya

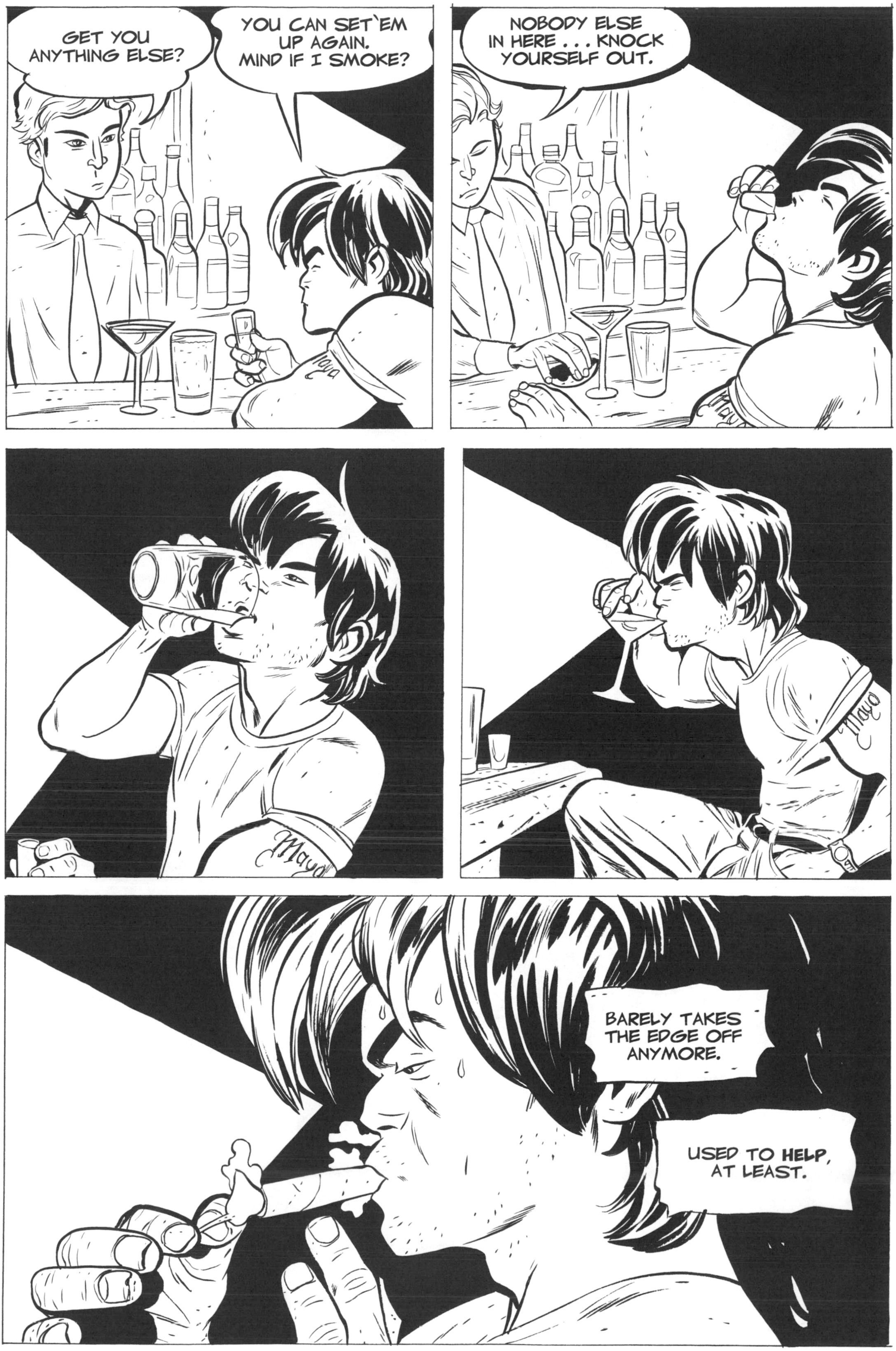

GET YOU ANYTHING ELSE?
YOU CAN SET`EM UP AGAIN. MIND IF I SMOKE?
NOBODY ELSE IN HERE . . . KNOCK YOURSELF OUT.
Maya
Maya
Maya
BARELY TAKES THE EDGE OFF ANYMORE.
USED TO **HELP**, AT LEAST.

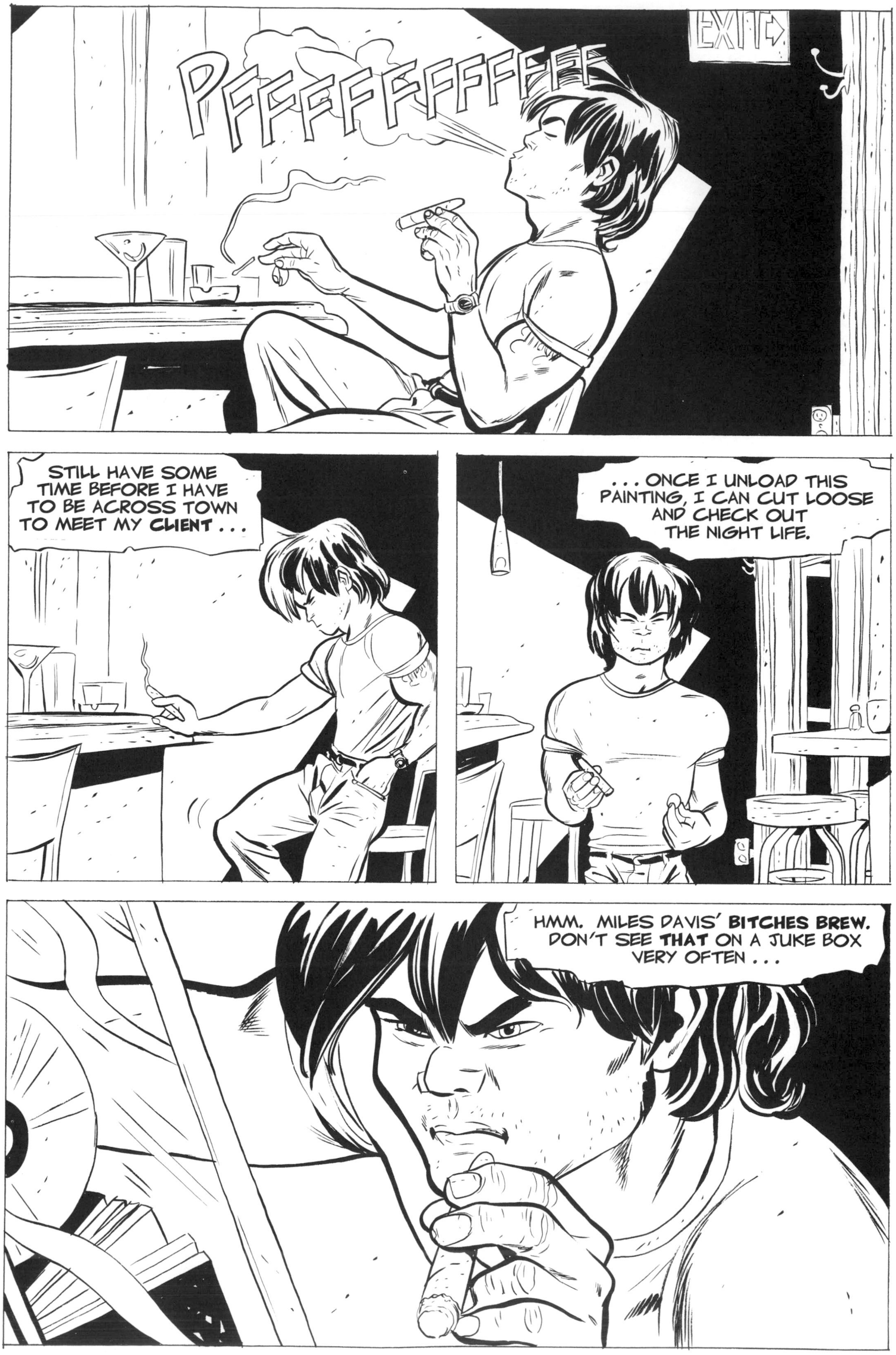
PFFFFFFFFFFFF
EXIT
STILL HAVE SOME TIME BEFORE I HAVE TO BE ACROSS TOWN TO MEET MY **CLIENT** . . .
. . . ONCE I UNLOAD THIS PAINTING, I CAN CUT LOOSE AND CHECK OUT THE NIGHT LIFE.
HMM. MILES DAVIS' **BITCHES BREW.** DON'T SEE **THAT** ON A JUKE BOX VERY OFTEN . . .

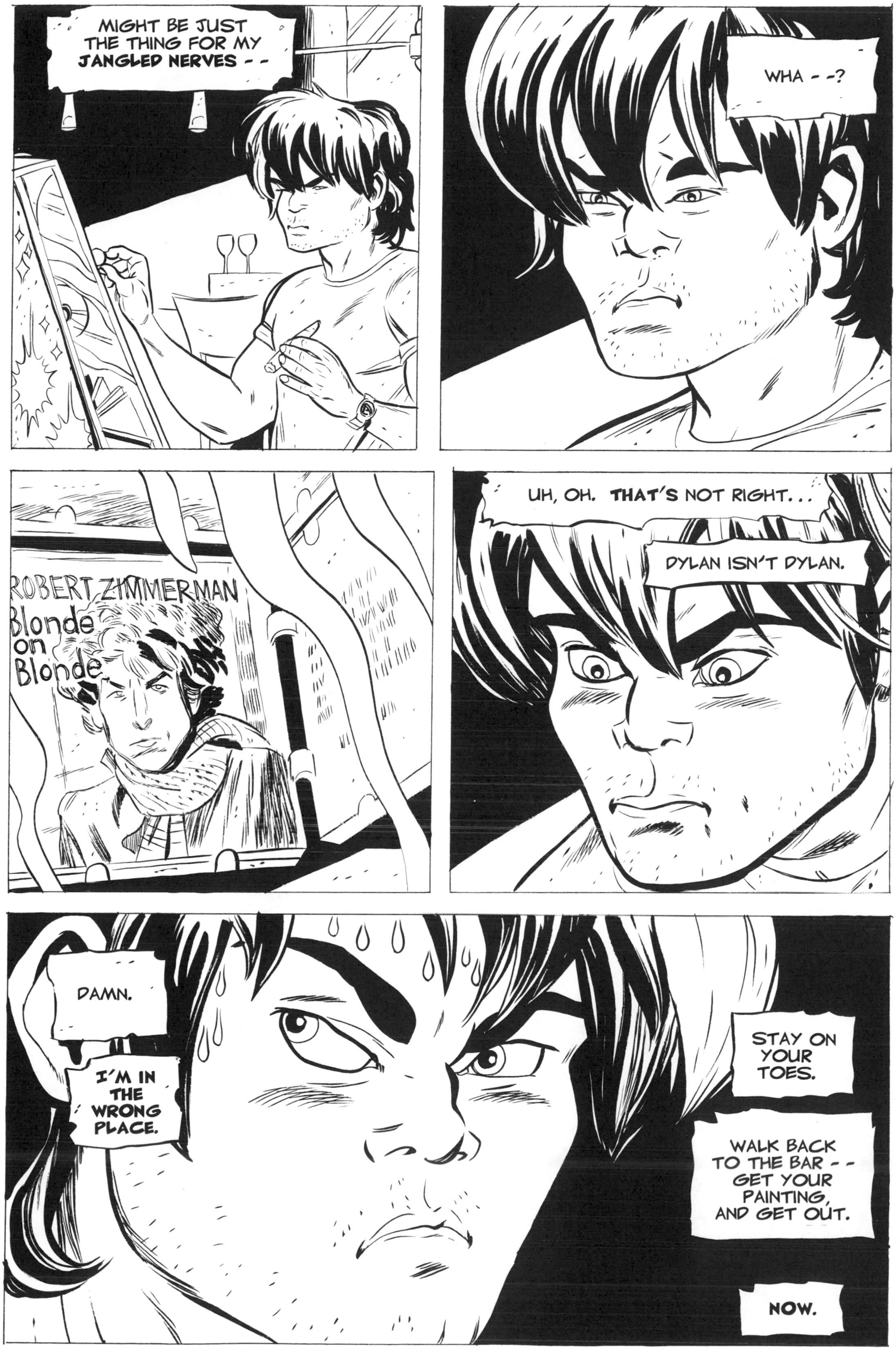

MIGHT BE JUST THE THING FOR MY JANGLED NERVES - -
WHA - -?
ROBERT ZIMMERMAN
Blonde on Blonde
UH, OH. THAT'S NOT RIGHT...
DYLAN ISN'T DYLAN.
DAMN.
I'M IN THE WRONG PLACE.
STAY ON YOUR TOES.
WALK BACK TO THE BAR - - GET YOUR PAINTING, AND GET OUT.
NOW.

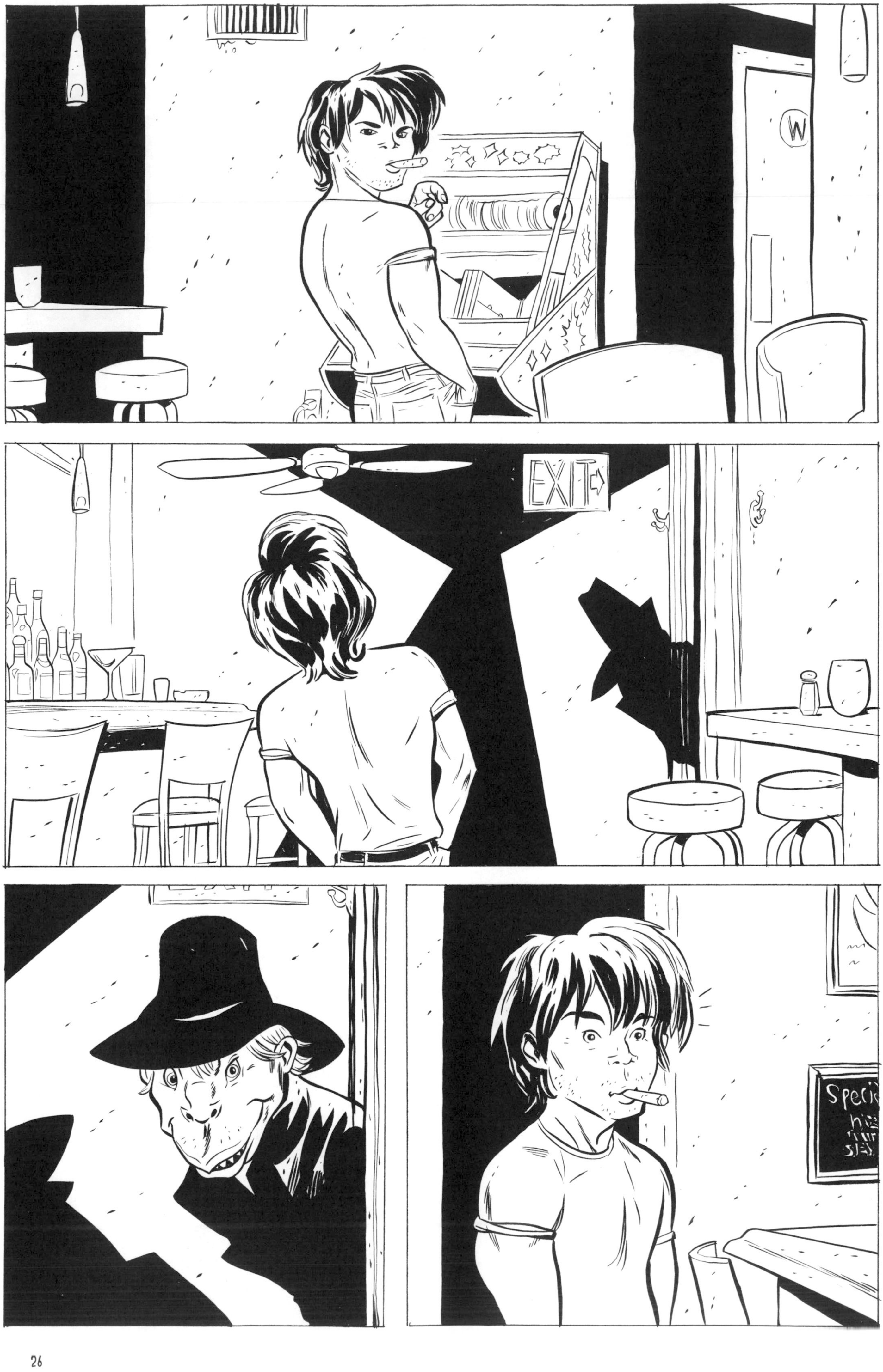
W
EXIT

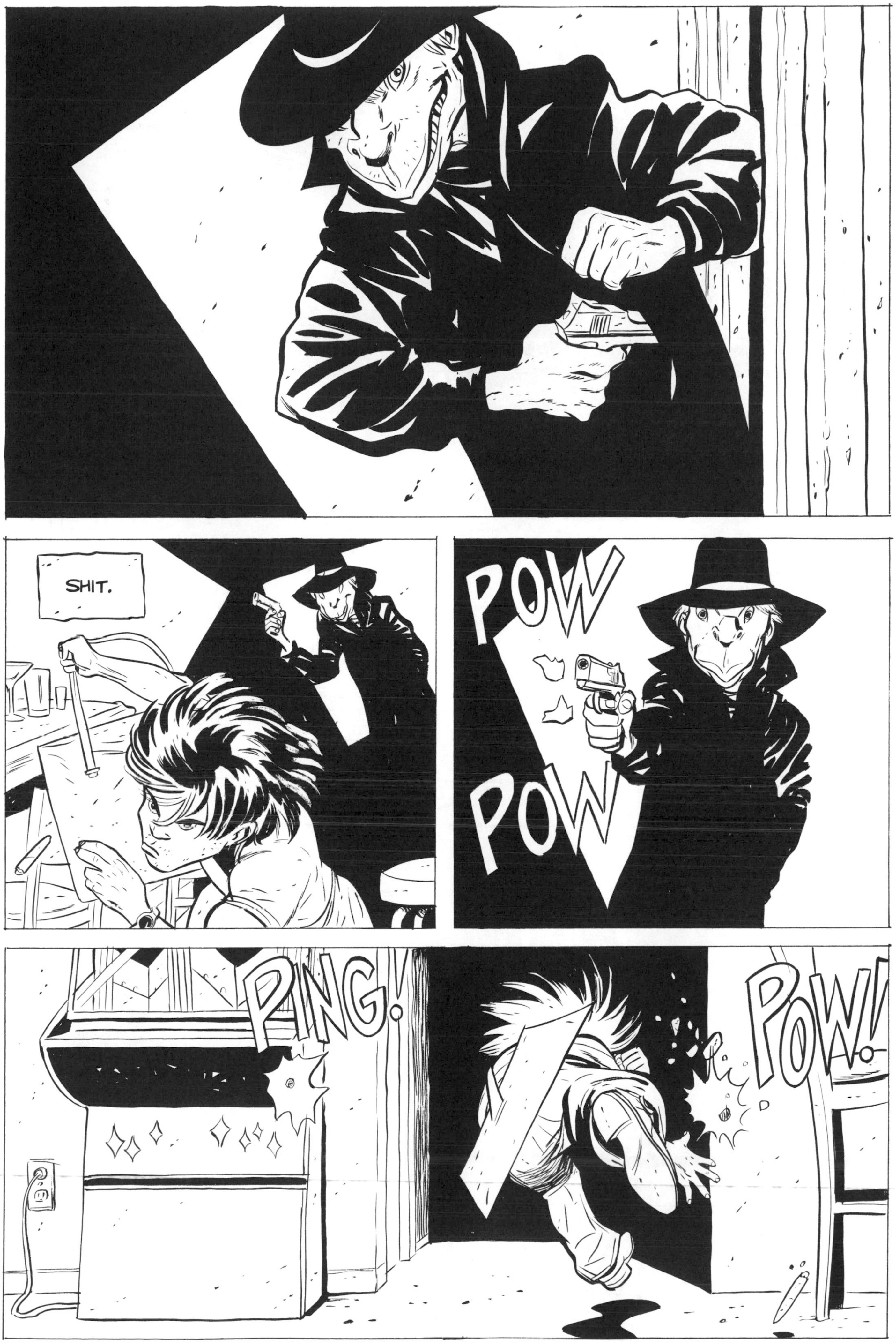
SHIT.
POW
POW
PING!
POW!

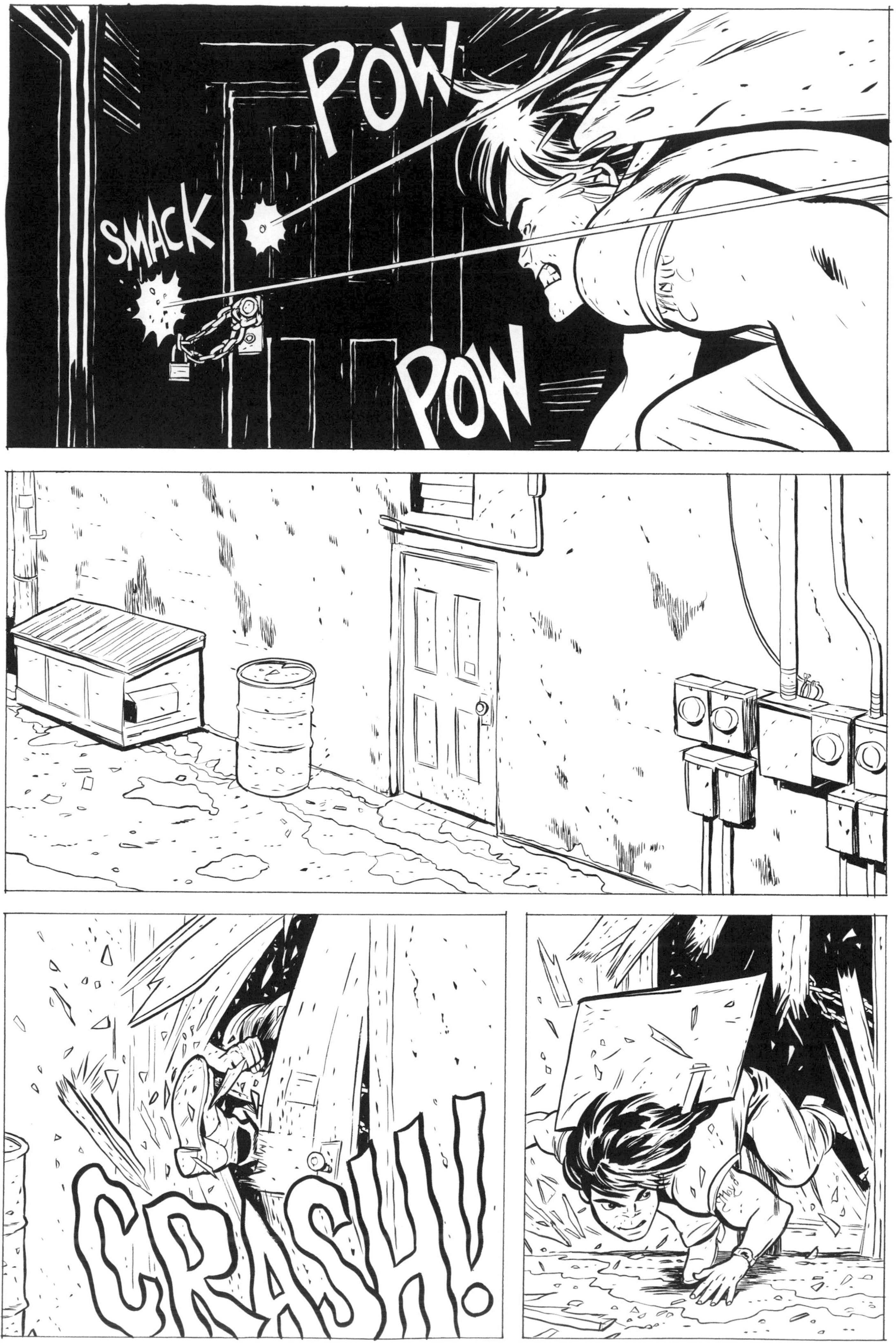
POW
SMACK
POW
CRASH!

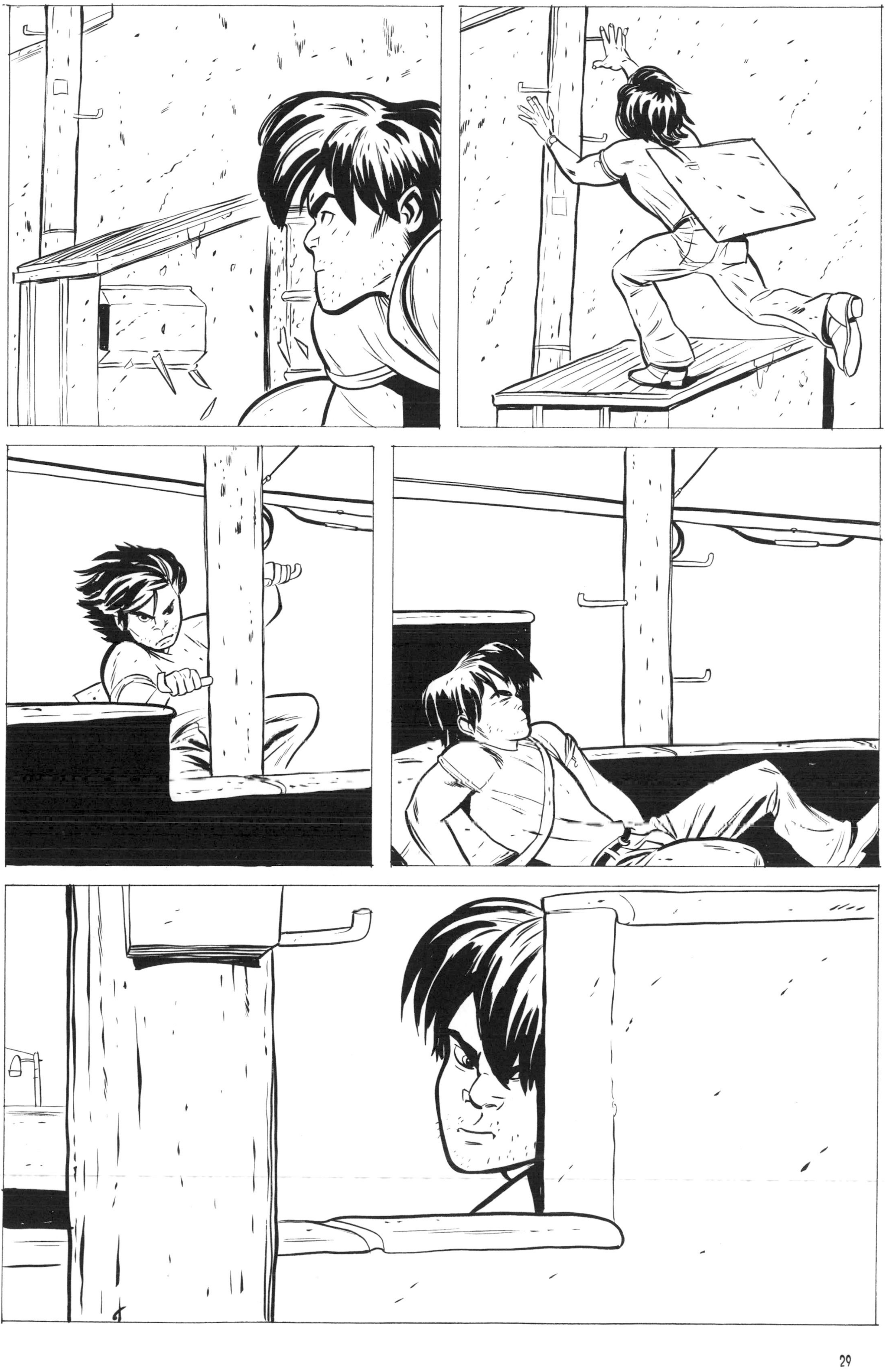

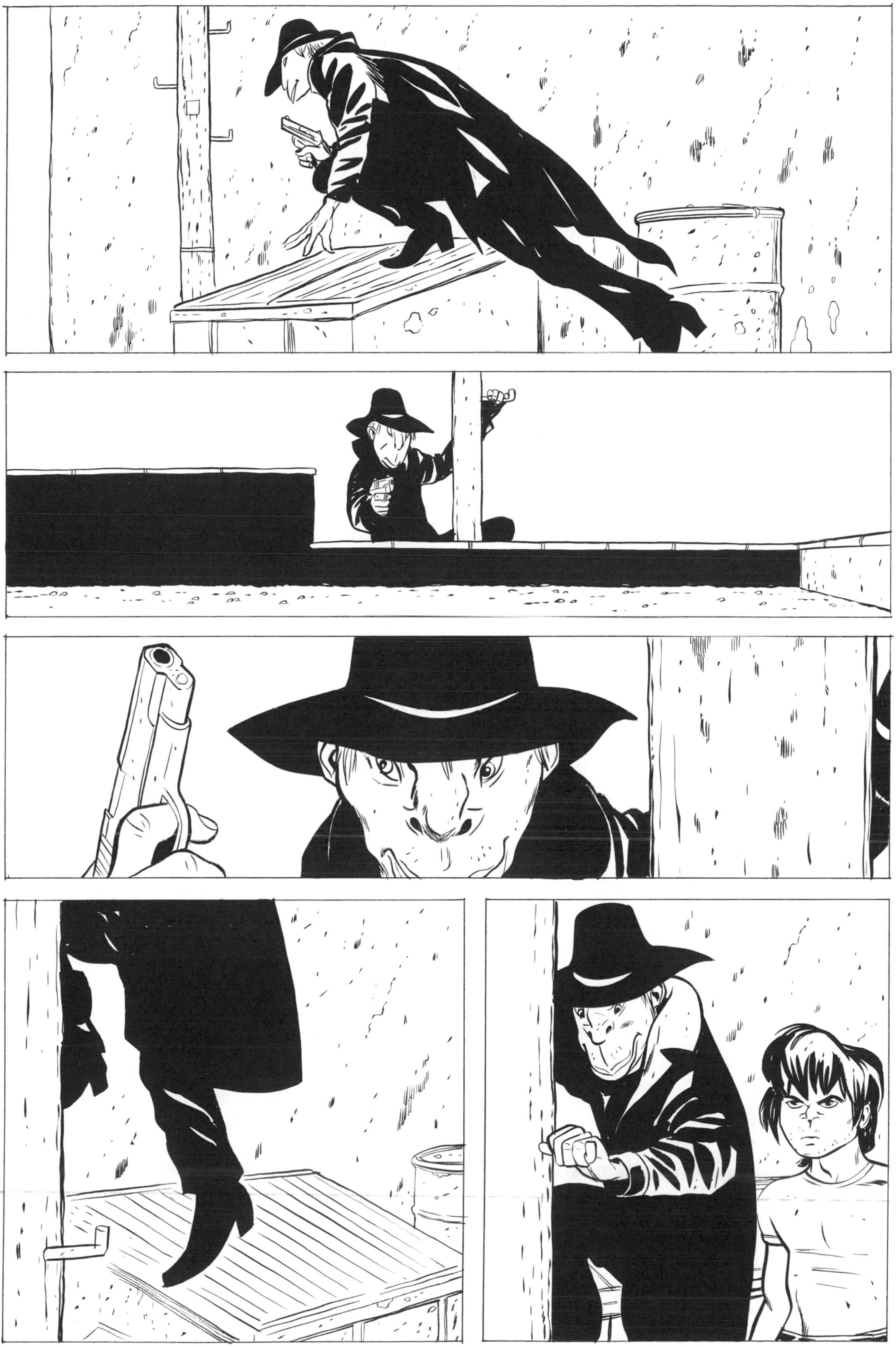

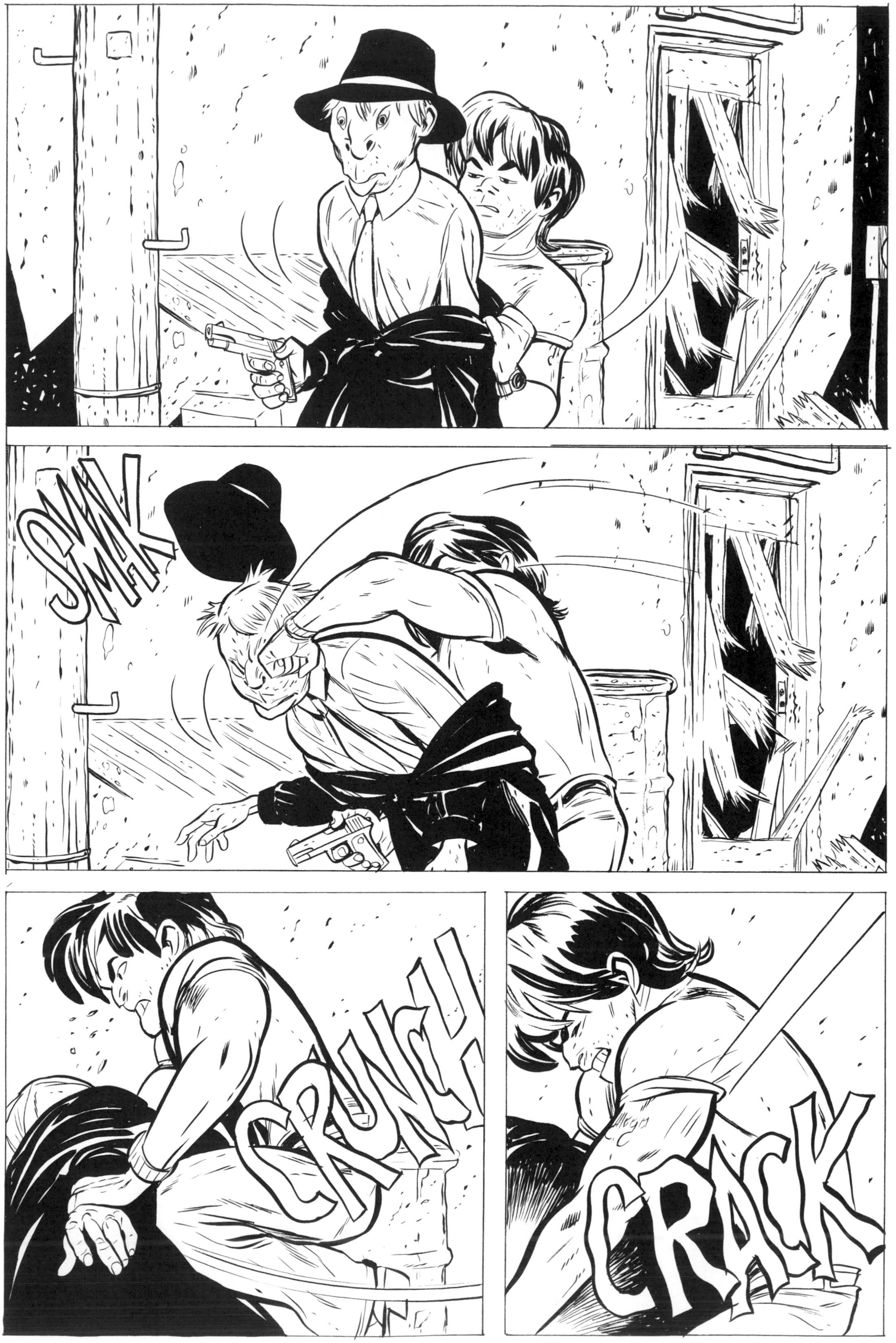
SMAK
CRUNCH
CRACK

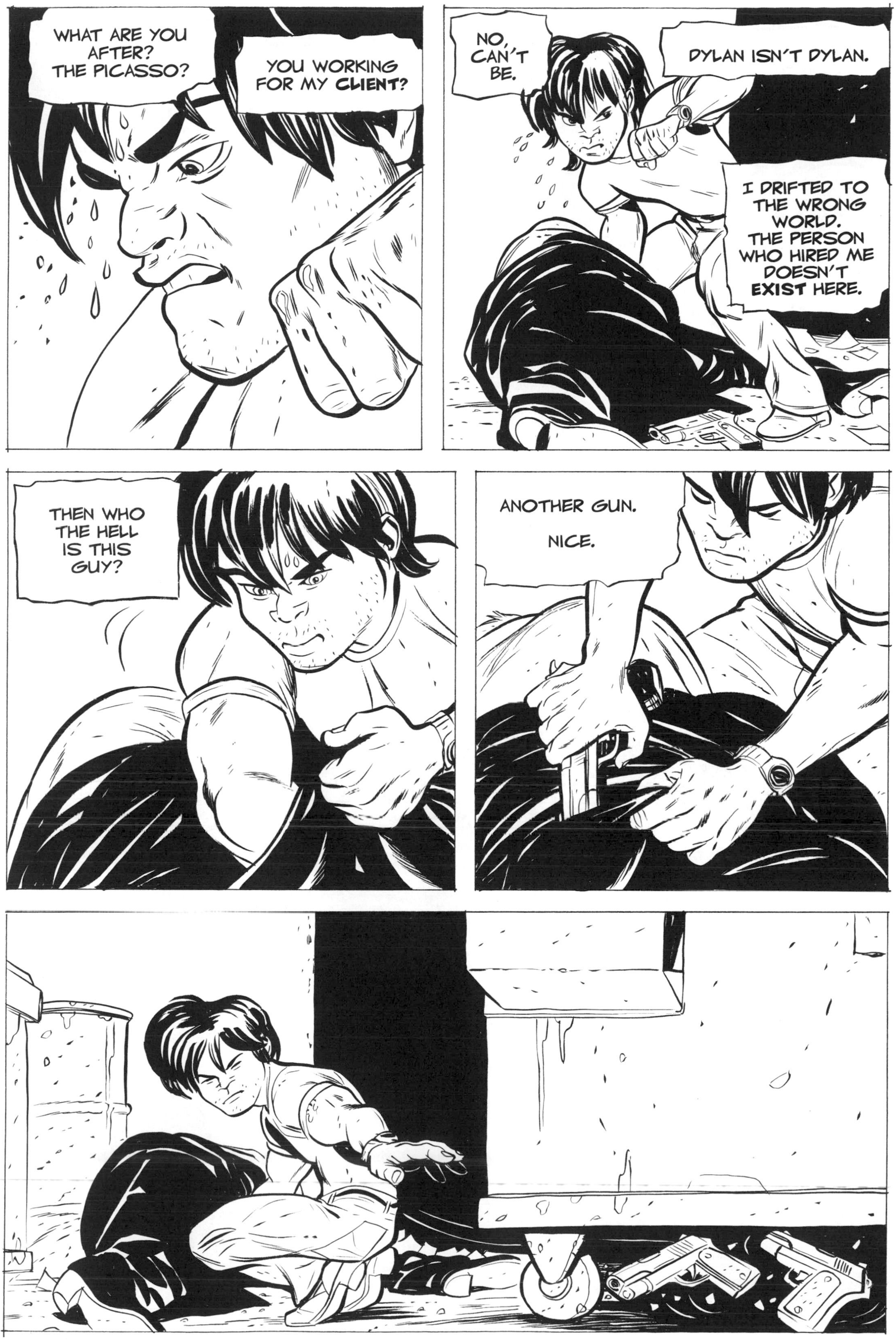
WHAT ARE YOU AFTER? THE PICASSO?
YOU WORKING FOR MY **CLIENT**?
NO, CAN'T BE.
DYLAN ISN'T DYLAN.
I DRIFTED TO THE WRONG WORLD. THE PERSON WHO HIRED ME DOESN'T **EXIST** HERE.
THEN WHO THE HELL IS THIS GUY?
ANOTHER GUN.
NICE.

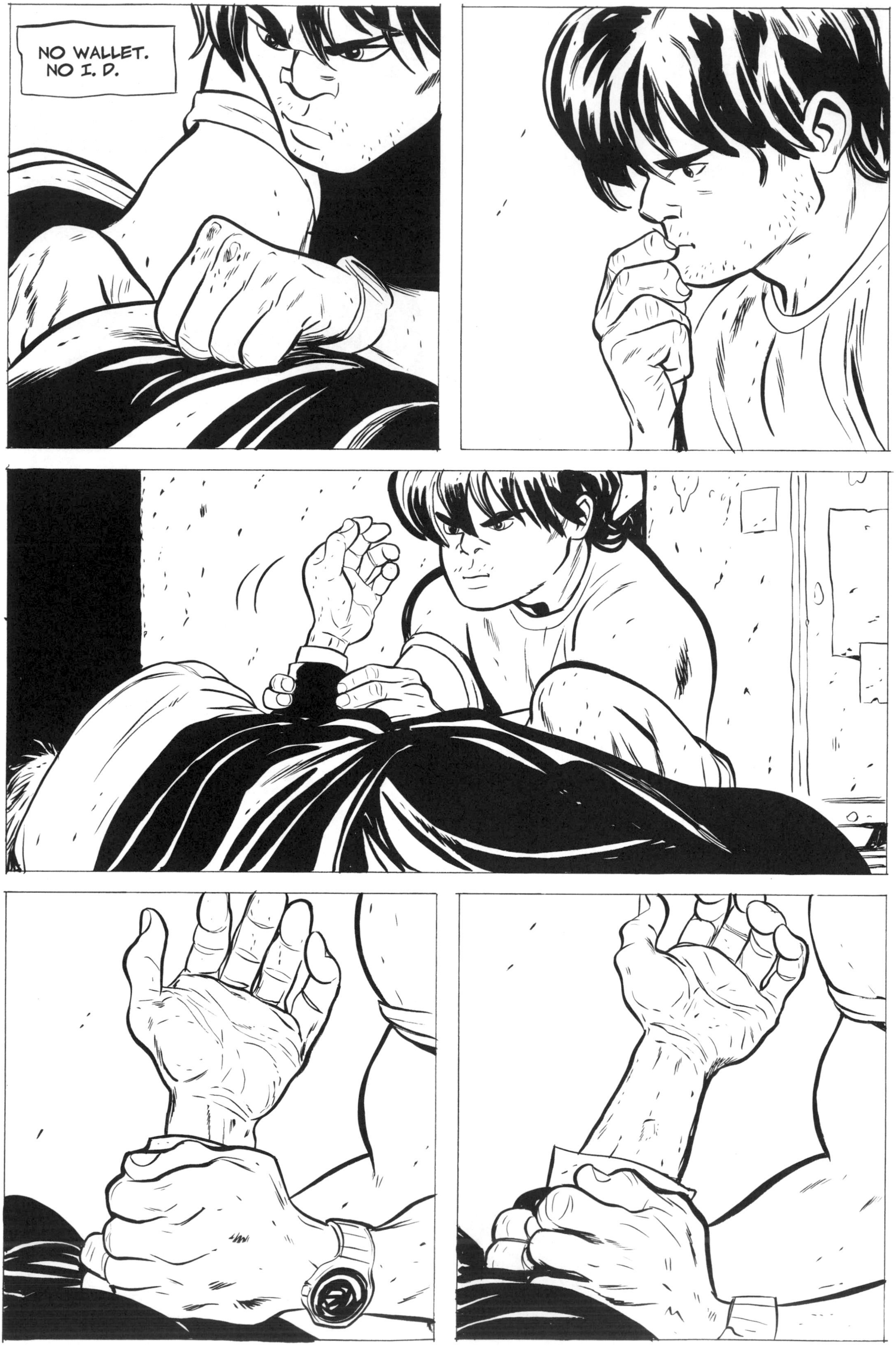
NO WALLET.
NO I. D.

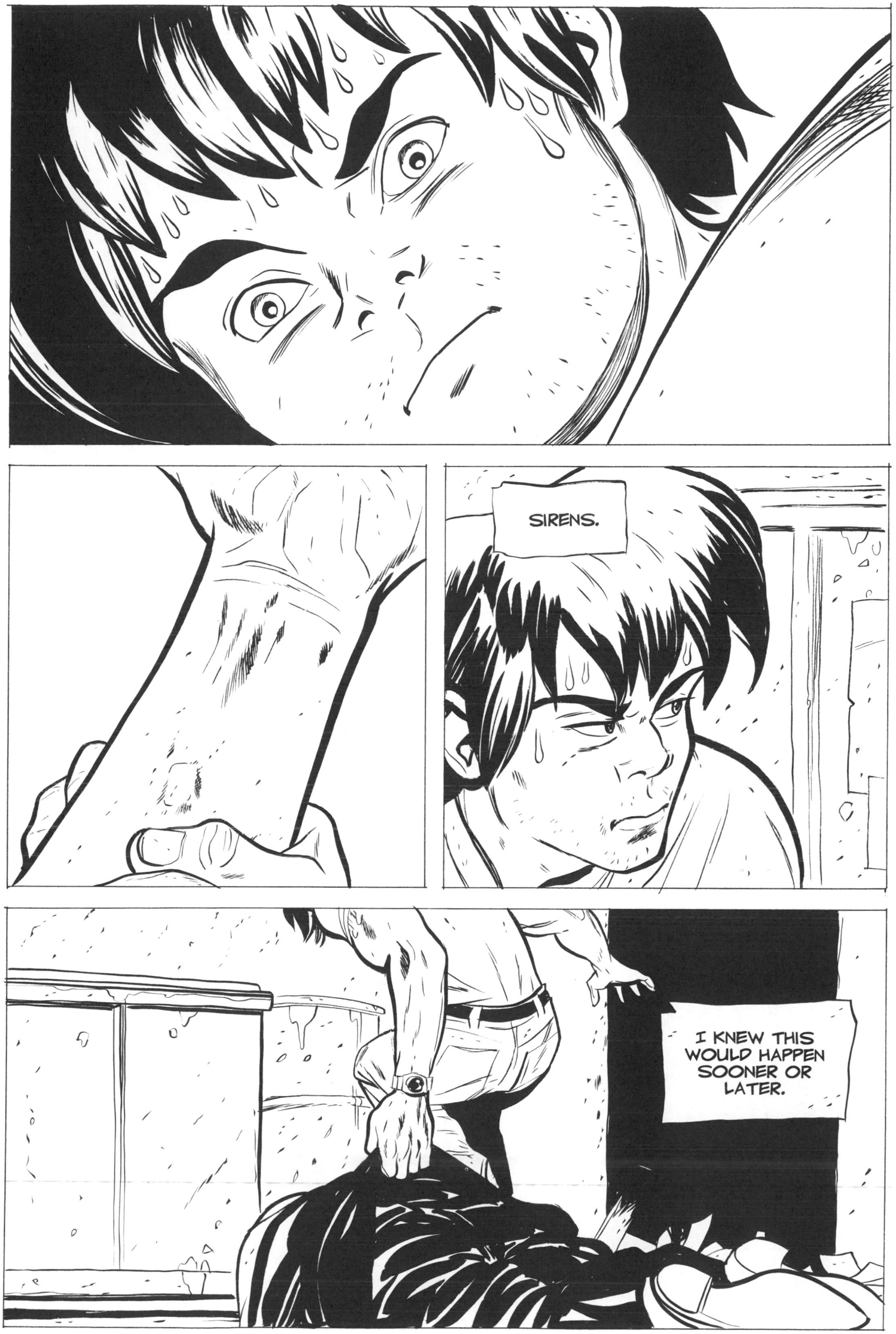
SIRENS.
I KNEW THIS WOULD HAPPEN SOONER OR LATER.

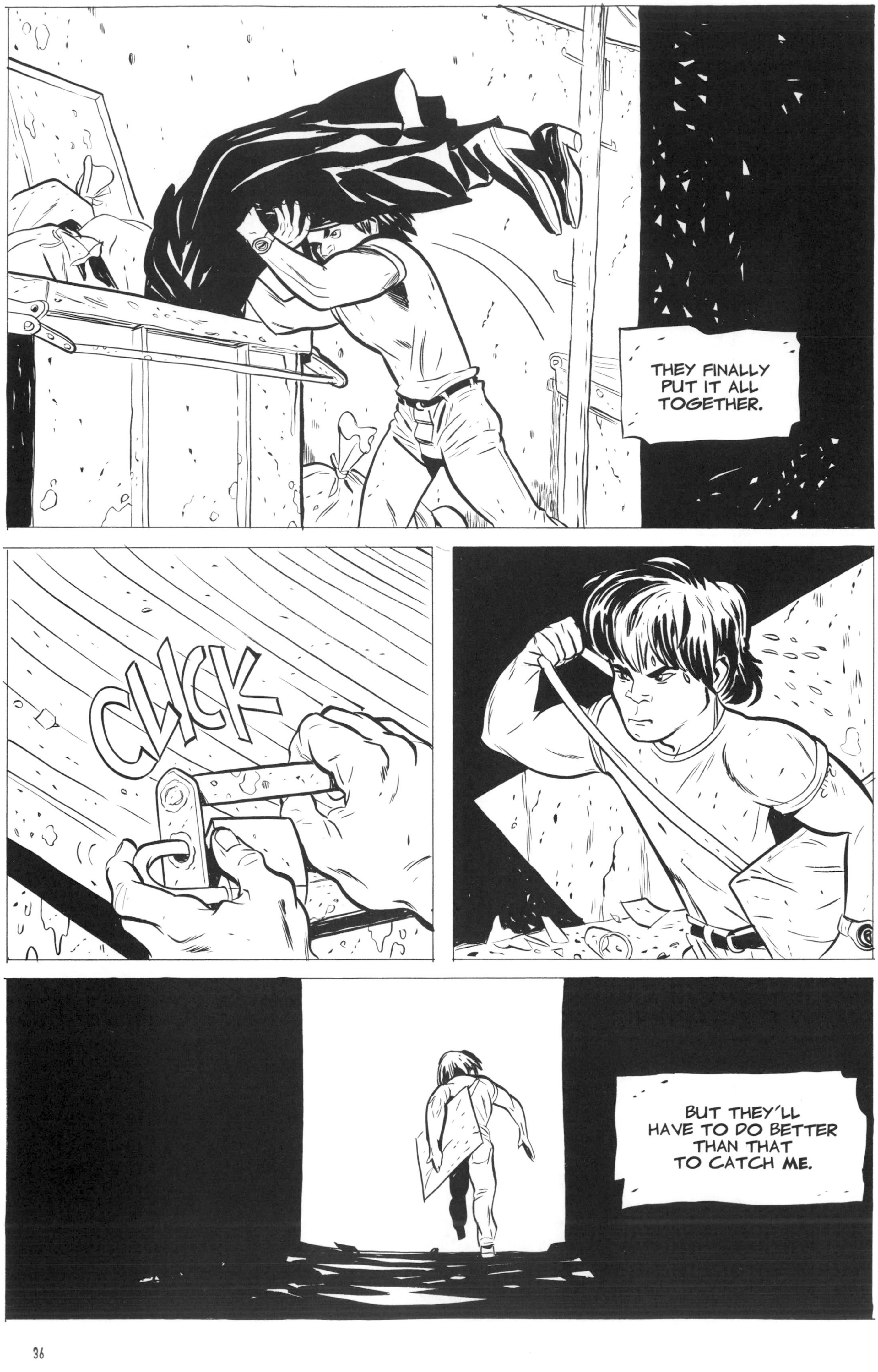
THEY FINALLY PUT IT ALL TOGETHER.
CLICK
BUT THEY'LL HAVE TO DO BETTER THAN THAT TO CATCH ME.

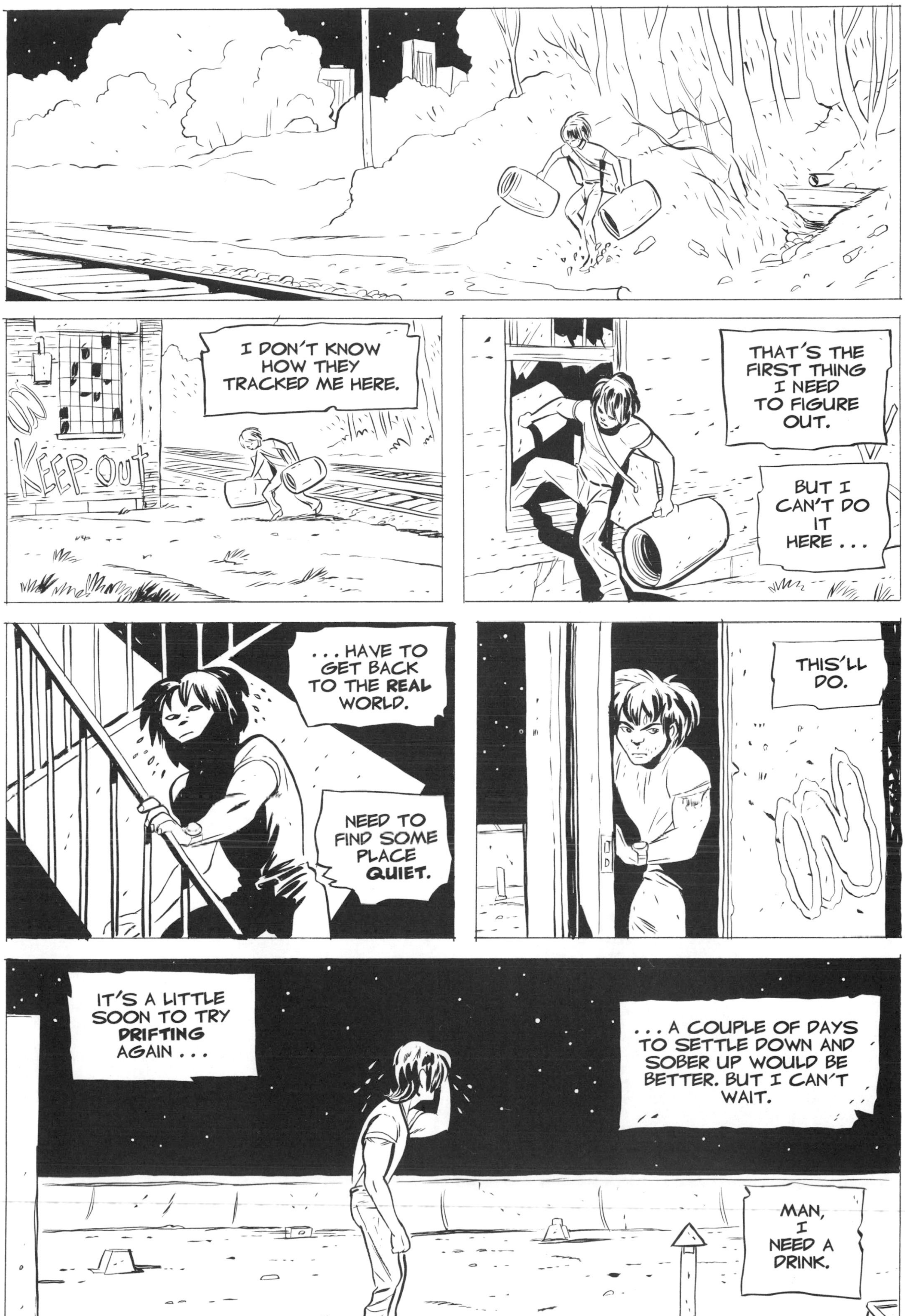
I DON'T KNOW HOW THEY TRACKED ME HERE.
KEEP OUT
THAT'S THE FIRST THING I NEED TO FIGURE OUT.
BUT I CAN'T DO IT HERE . . .
. . . HAVE TO GET BACK TO THE REAL WORLD.
NEED TO FIND SOME PLACE QUIET.
THIS'LL DO.
IT'S A LITTLE SOON TO TRY DRIFTING AGAIN . . .
. . . A COUPLE OF DAYS TO SETTLE DOWN AND SOBER UP WOULD BE BETTER. BUT I CAN'T WAIT.
MAN, I NEED A DRINK.

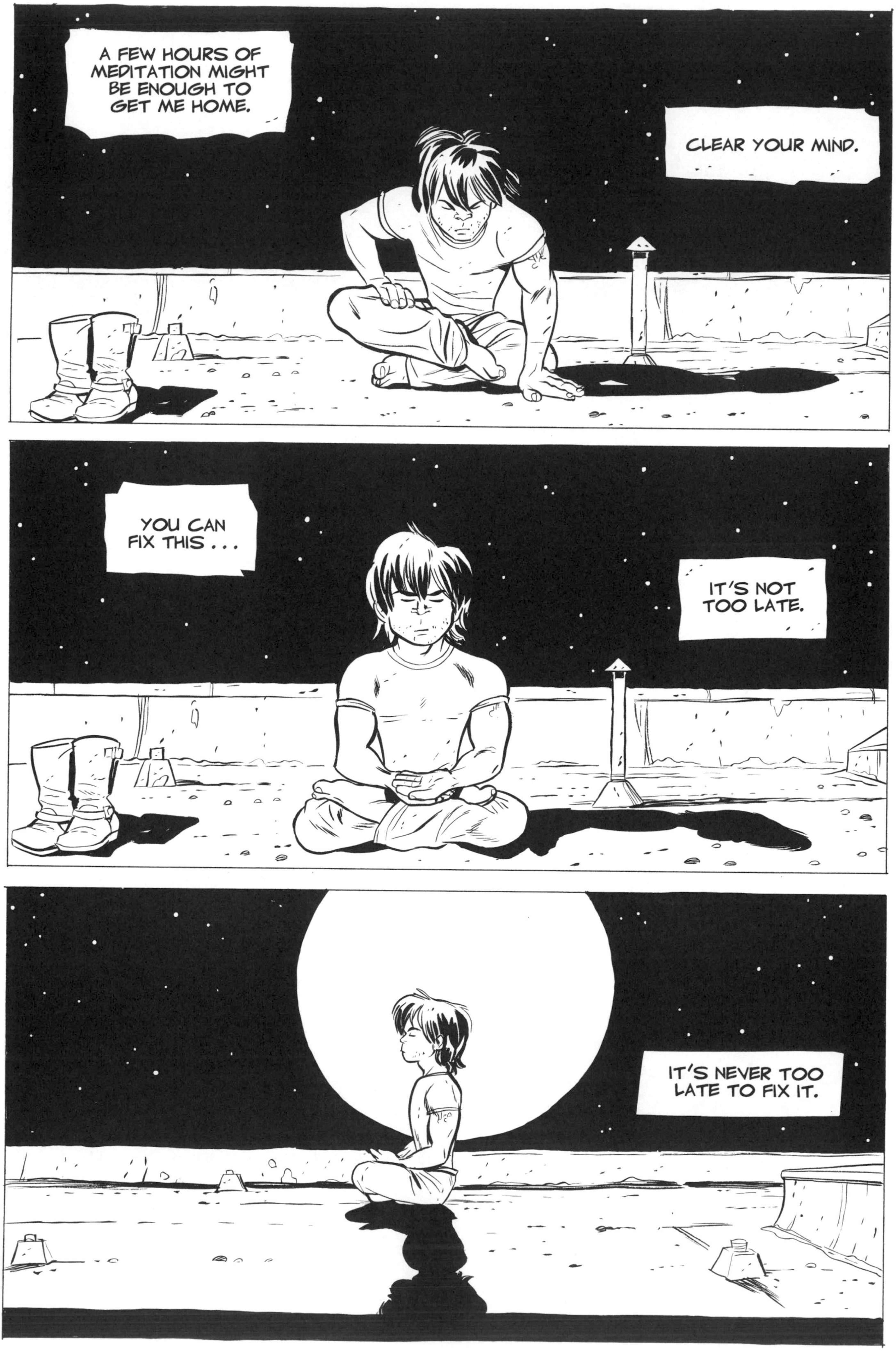
A FEW HOURS OF MEDITATION MIGHT BE ENOUGH TO GET ME HOME.
CLEAR YOUR MIND.
YOU CAN FIX THIS . . .
IT'S NOT TOO LATE.
IT'S NEVER TOO LATE TO FIX IT.

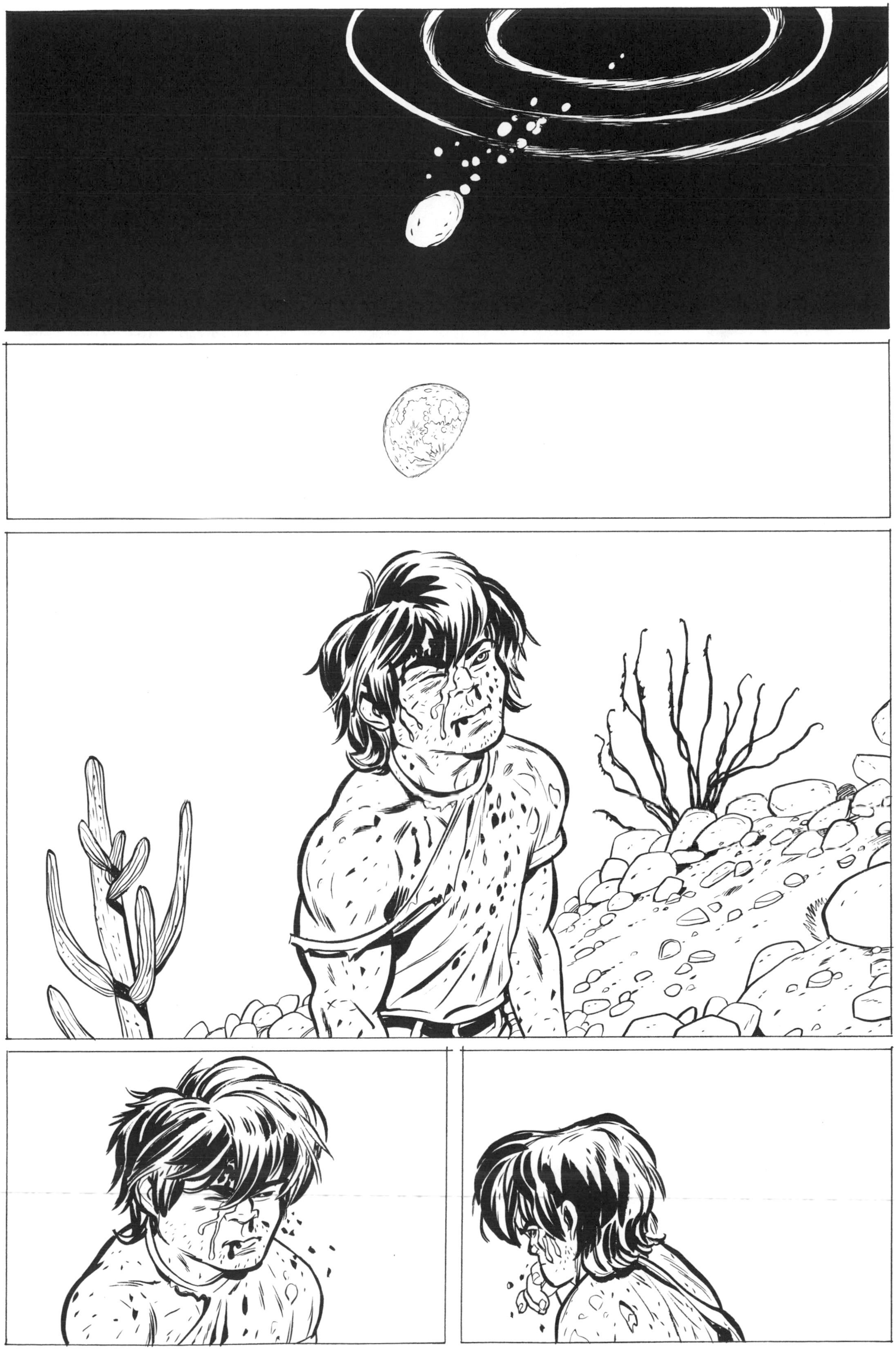

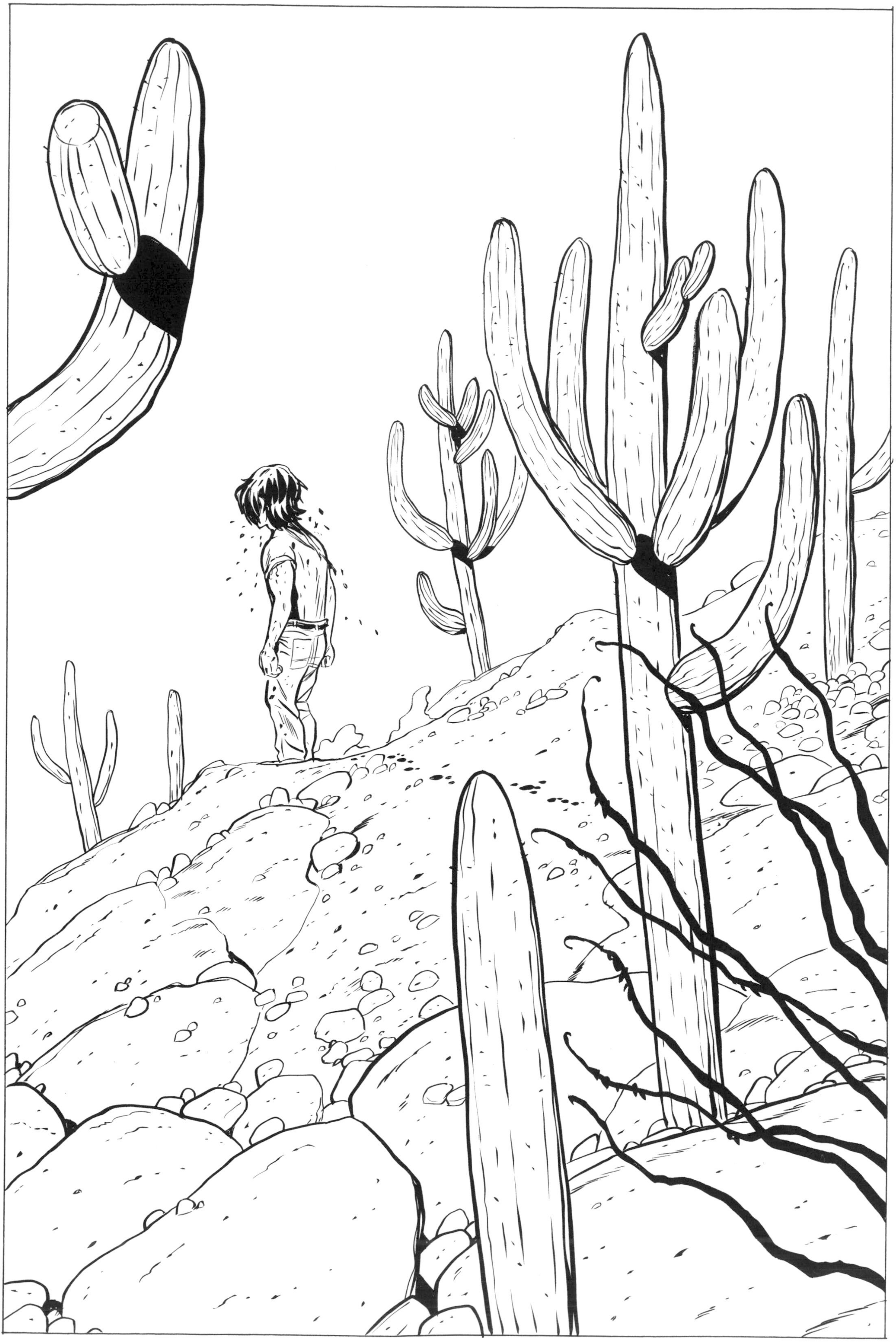

2.
ANNIE

$\nabla \cdot B = 0$
$\nabla \cdot E = \frac{\rho}{\epsilon_0}$
$\nabla \times E = -\frac{\partial B}{\partial t}$
$\nabla \times B = \mu_0 J + \mu_0 \epsilon_0 \frac{\partial E}{\partial t}$

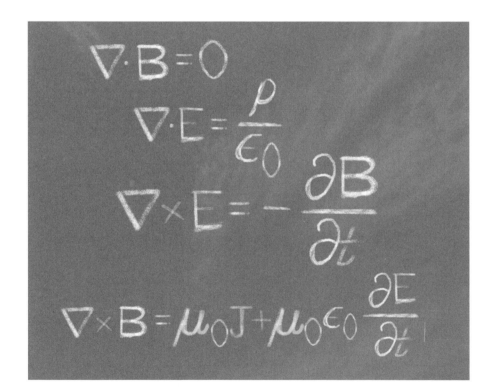

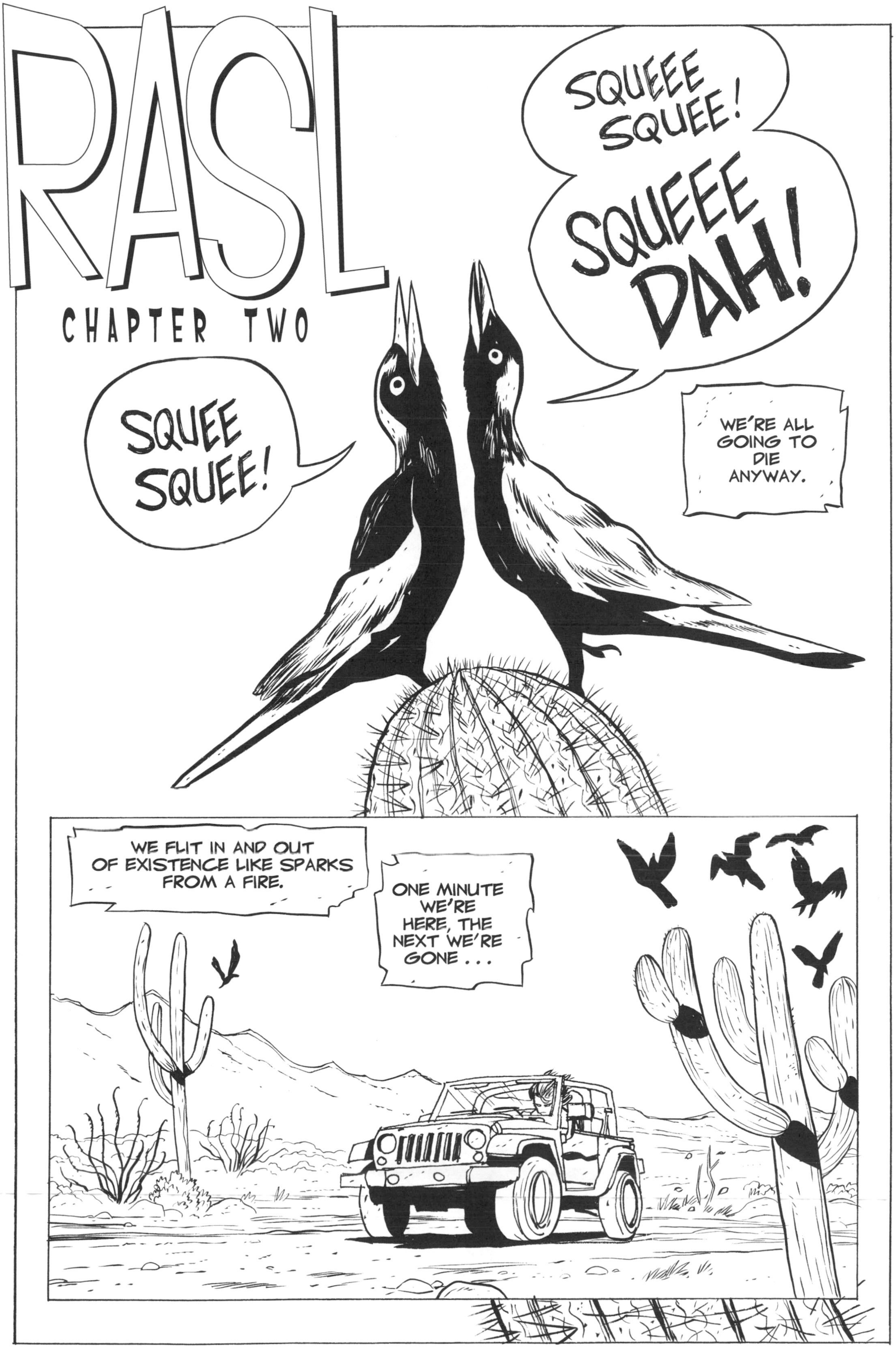
RASL
CHAPTER TWO
SQUEE SQUEE!
SQUEEE SQUEE!
SQUEEE SQUEEE DAH!
WE'RE ALL GOING TO DIE ANYWAY.
WE FLIT IN AND OUT OF EXISTENCE LIKE SPARKS FROM A FIRE.
ONE MINUTE WE'RE HERE, THE NEXT WE'RE GONE . . .

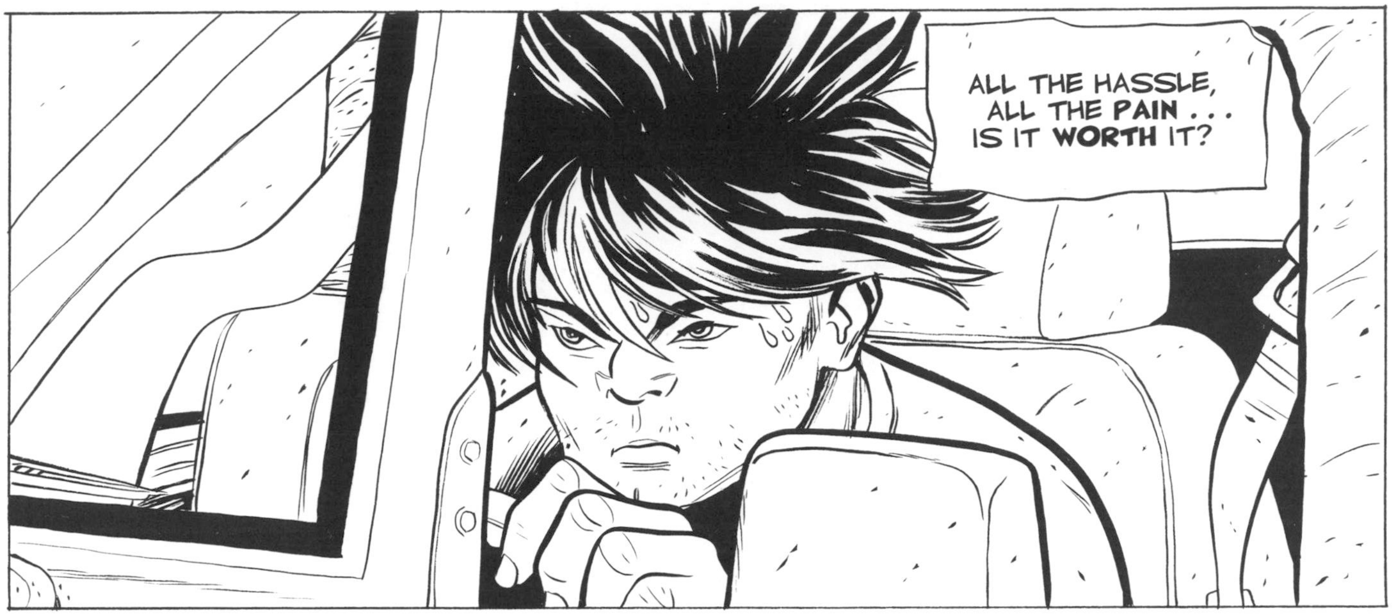
ALL THE HASSLE, ALL THE PAIN . . . IS IT WORTH IT?

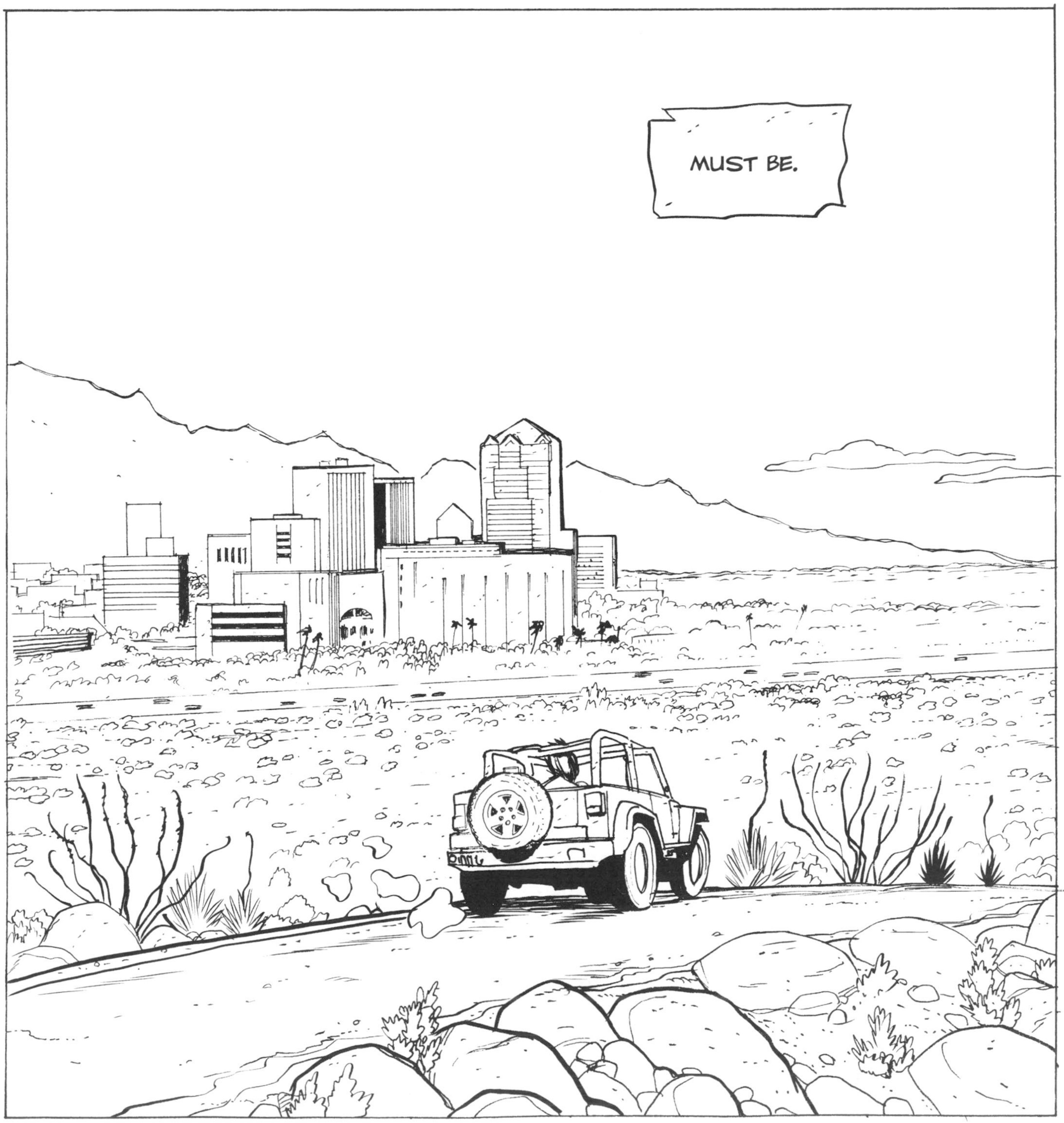
MUST BE.

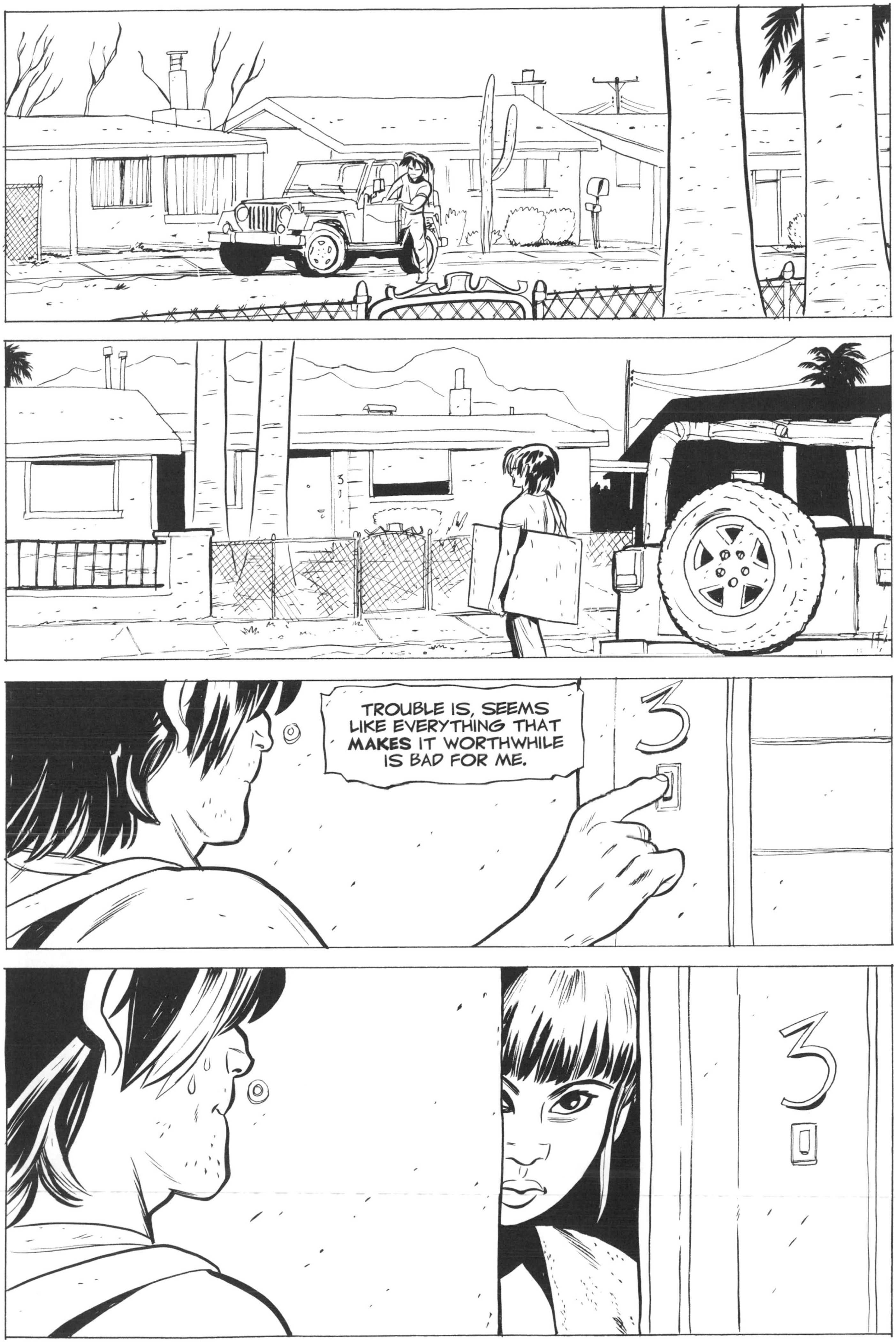
TROUBLE IS, SEEMS LIKE EVERYTHING THAT MAKES IT WORTHWHILE IS BAD FOR ME.

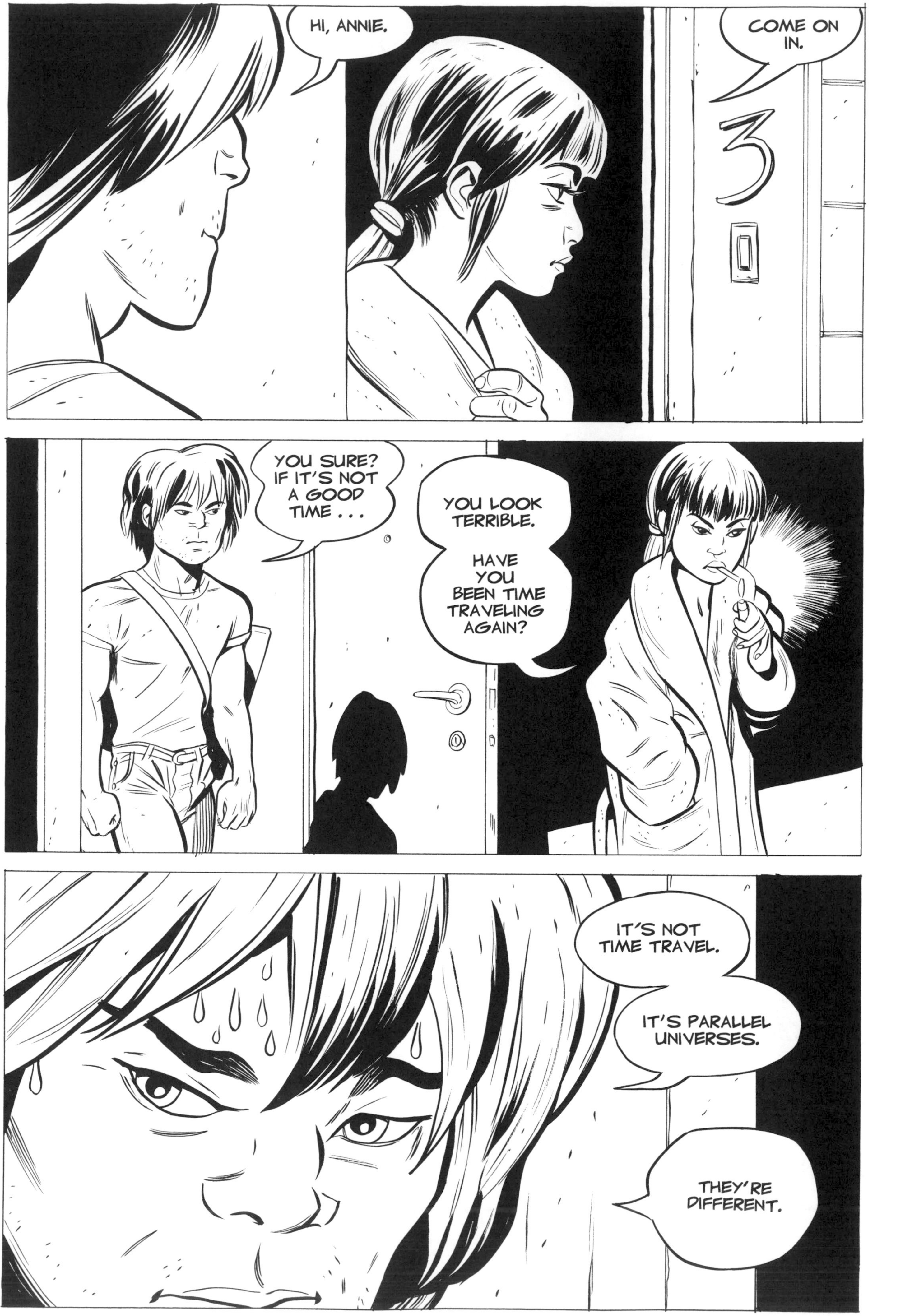
HI, ANNIE.
COME ON IN.
YOU SURE? IF IT'S NOT A GOOD TIME . . .
YOU LOOK TERRIBLE.
HAVE YOU BEEN TIME TRAVELING AGAIN?
IT'S NOT TIME TRAVEL.
IT'S PARALLEL UNIVERSES.
THEY'RE DIFFERENT.

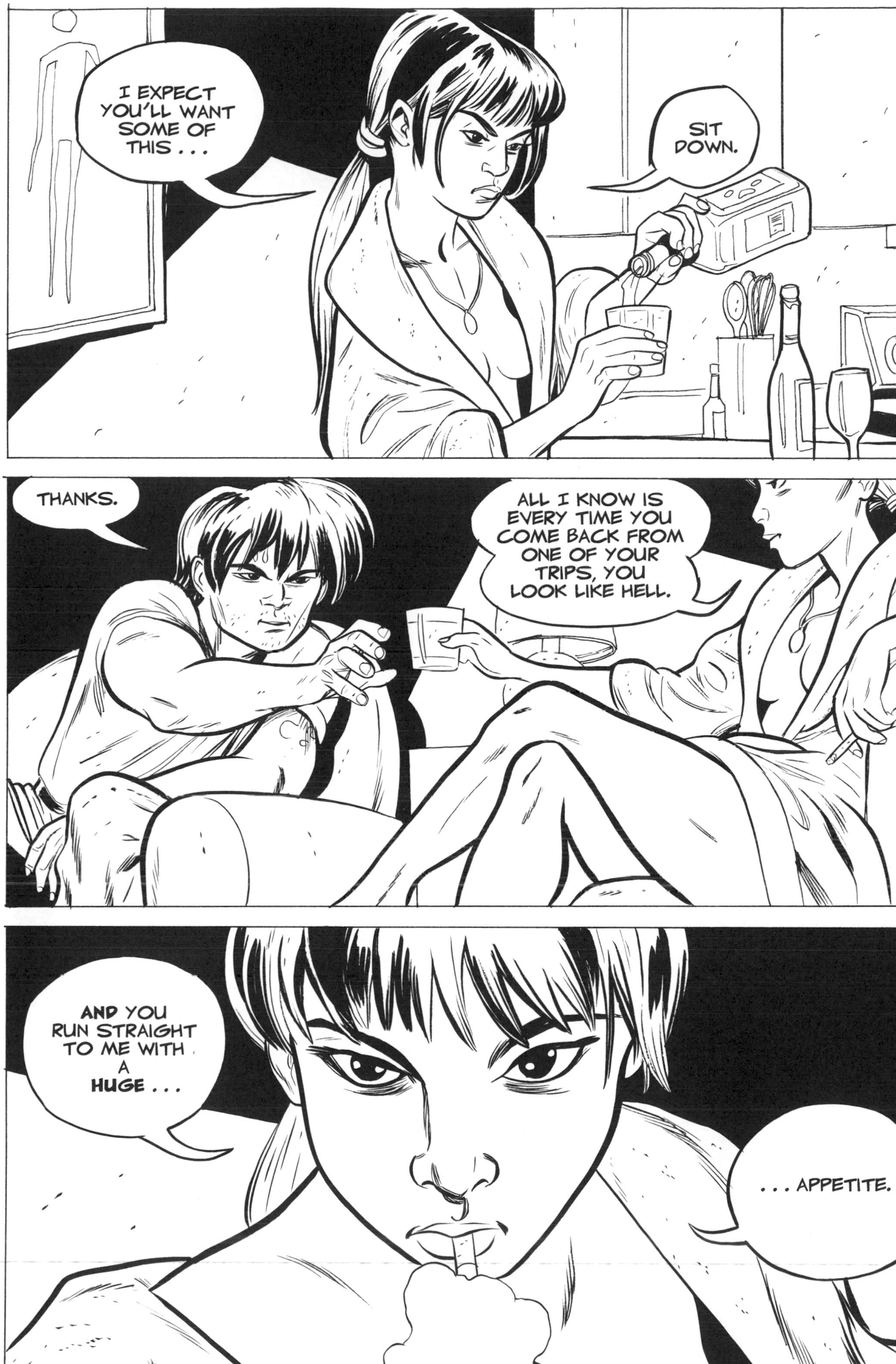
I EXPECT YOU'LL WANT SOME OF THIS . . .
SIT DOWN.
THANKS.
ALL I KNOW IS EVERY TIME YOU COME BACK FROM ONE OF YOUR TRIPS, YOU LOOK LIKE HELL.
AND YOU RUN STRAIGHT TO ME WITH A HUGE . . .
. . . APPETITE.

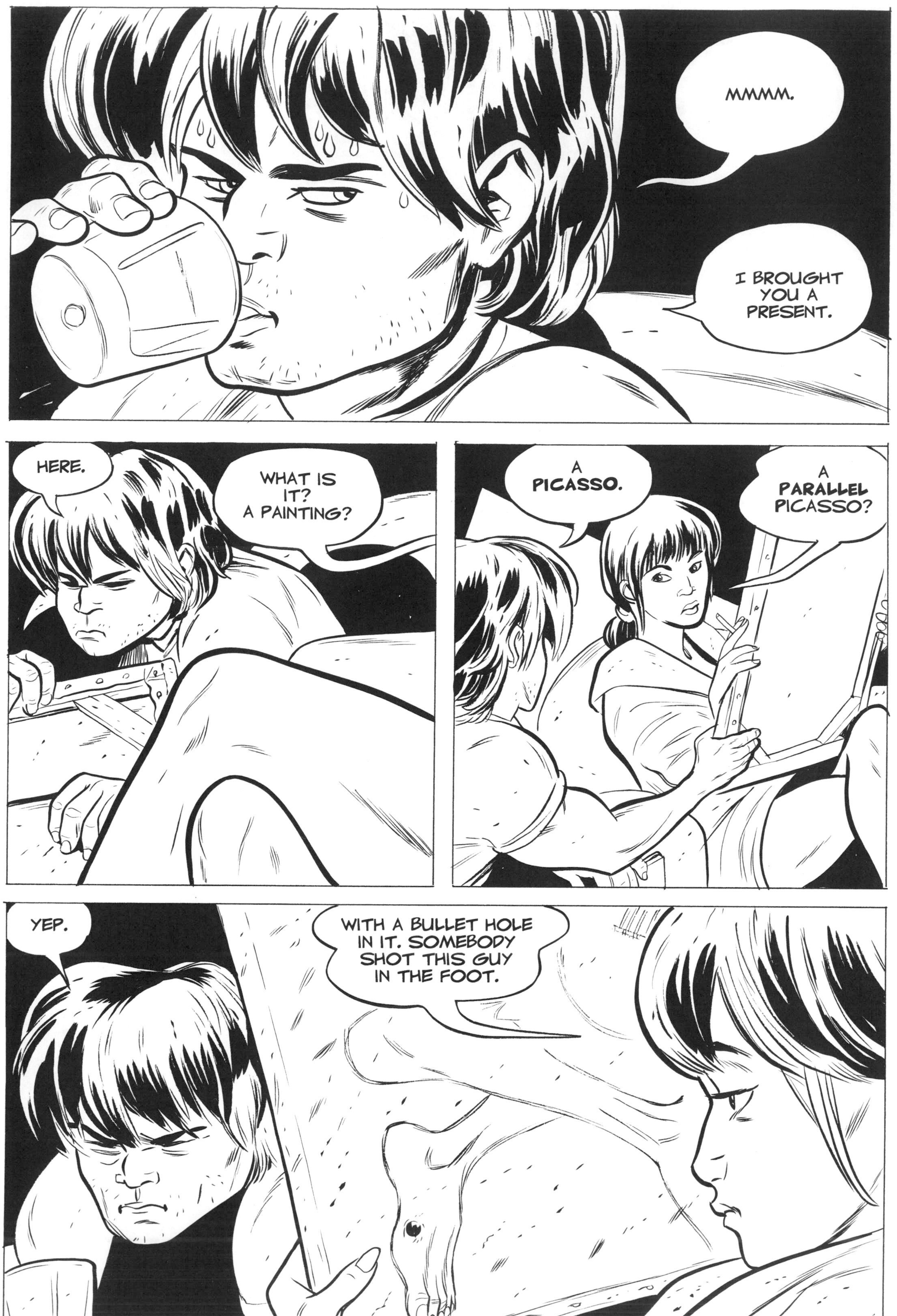
MMMM.
I BROUGHT YOU A PRESENT.
HERE.
WHAT IS IT? A PAINTING?
A PICASSO.
A PARALLEL PICASSO?
YEP.
WITH A BULLET HOLE IN IT. SOMEBODY SHOT THIS GUY IN THE FOOT.

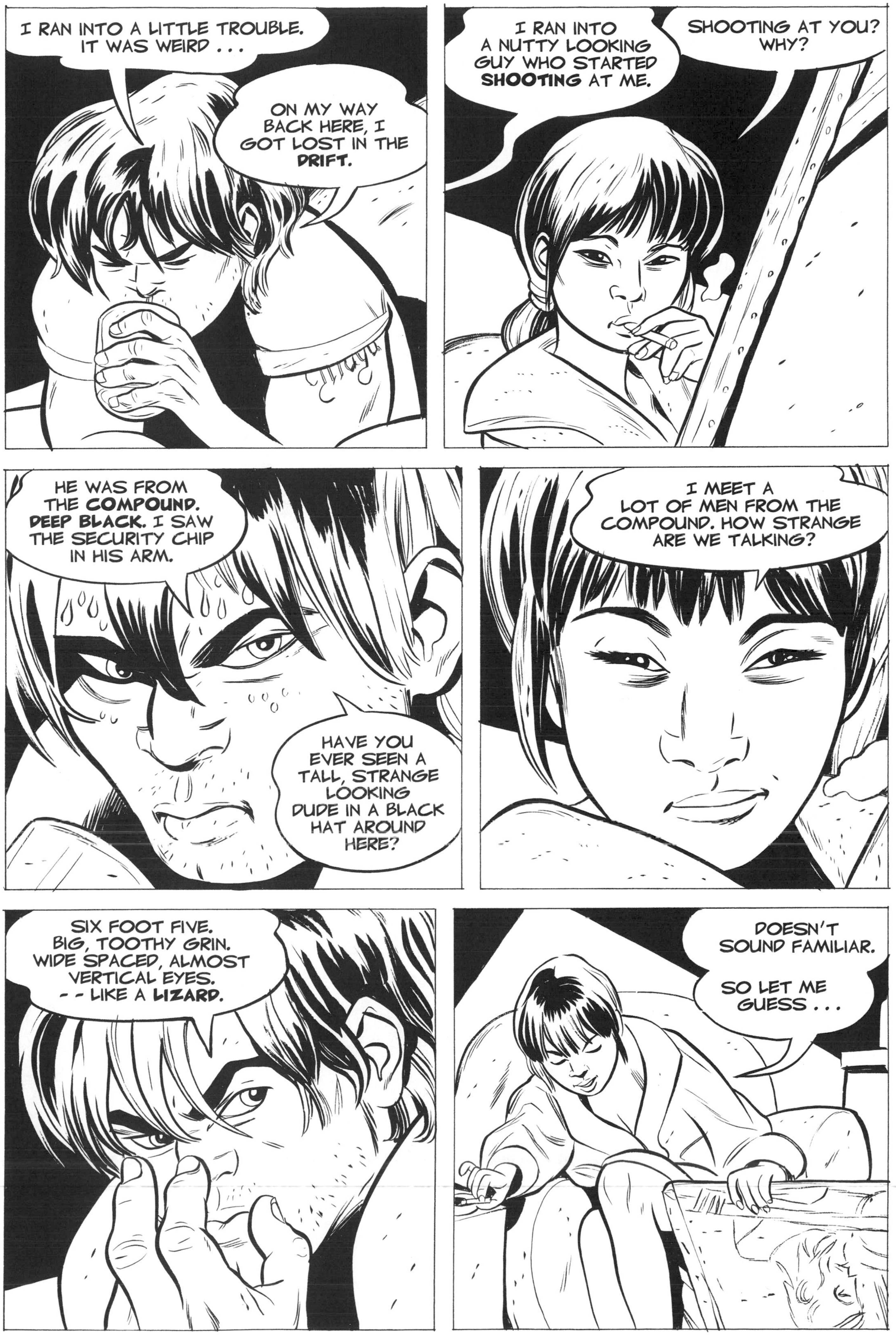
I RAN INTO A LITTLE TROUBLE. IT WAS WEIRD . . .
ON MY WAY BACK HERE, I GOT LOST IN THE **DRIFT.**
I RAN INTO A NUTTY LOOKING GUY WHO STARTED **SHOOTING** AT ME.
SHOOTING AT YOU? WHY?
HE WAS FROM THE **COMPOUND. DEEP BLACK.** I SAW THE SECURITY CHIP IN HIS ARM.
HAVE YOU EVER SEEN A TALL, STRANGE LOOKING DUDE IN A BLACK HAT AROUND HERE?
I MEET A LOT OF MEN FROM THE COMPOUND. HOW STRANGE ARE WE TALKING?
SIX FOOT FIVE. BIG, TOOTHY GRIN. WIDE SPACED, ALMOST VERTICAL EYES. - - LIKE A **LIZARD.**
DOESN'T SOUND FAMILIAR.
SO LET ME GUESS . . .

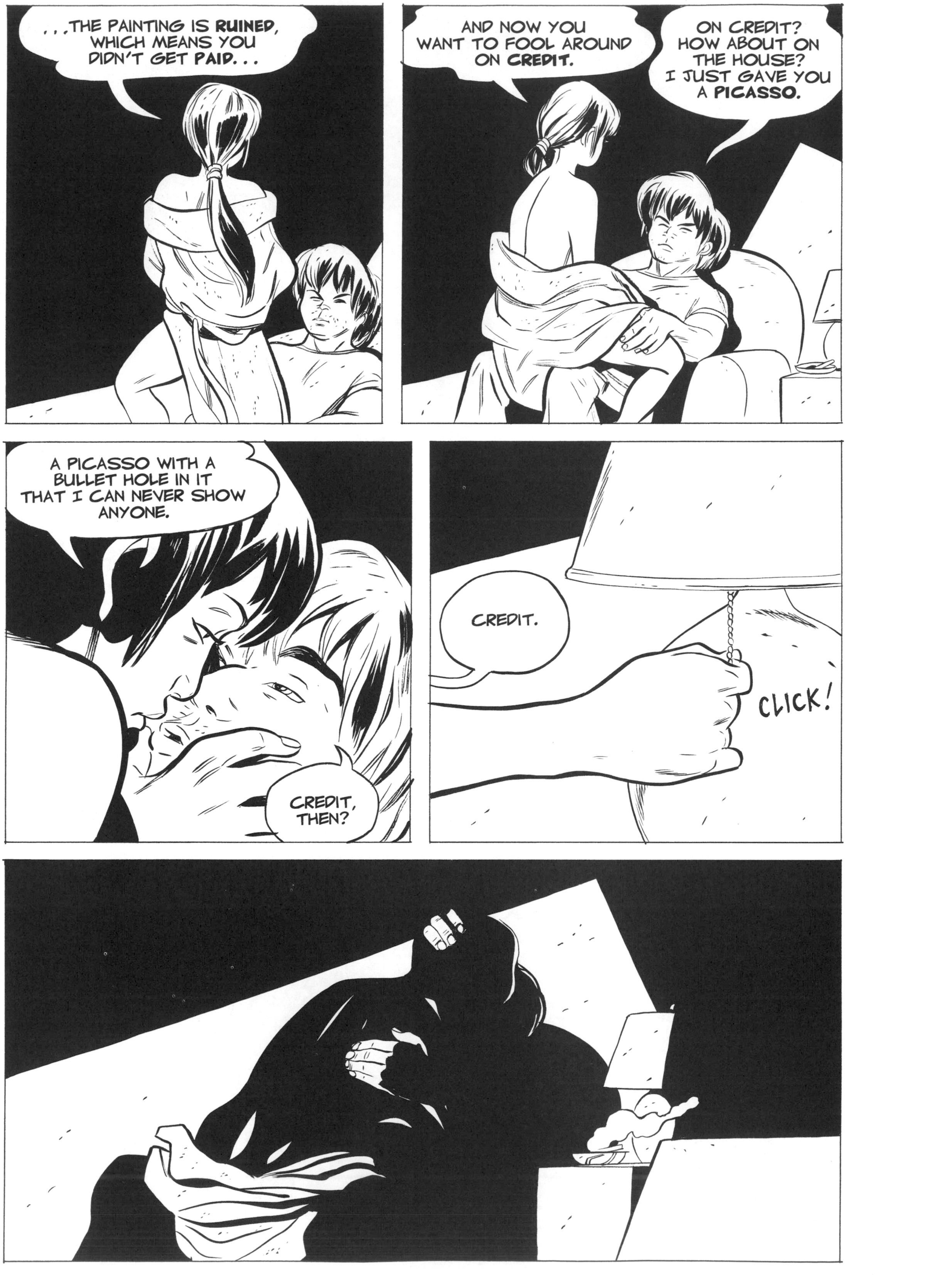
. . .THE PAINTING IS RUINED, WHICH MEANS YOU DIDN'T GET PAID. . .
AND NOW YOU WANT TO FOOL AROUND ON CREDIT.
ON CREDIT? HOW ABOUT ON THE HOUSE? I JUST GAVE YOU A PICASSO.
A PICASSO WITH A BULLET HOLE IN IT THAT I CAN NEVER SHOW ANYONE.
CREDIT, THEN?
CREDIT.
CLICK!

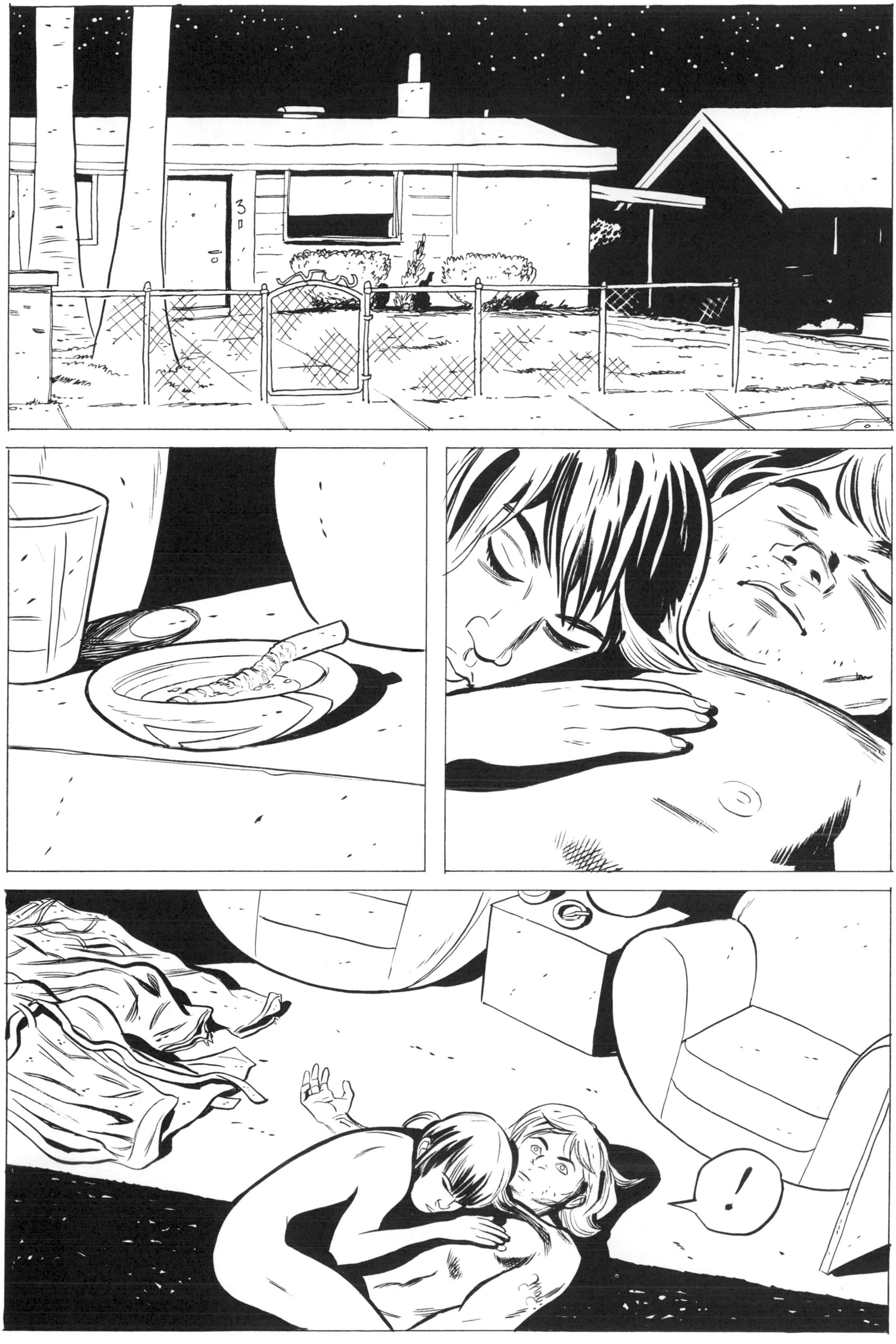
!

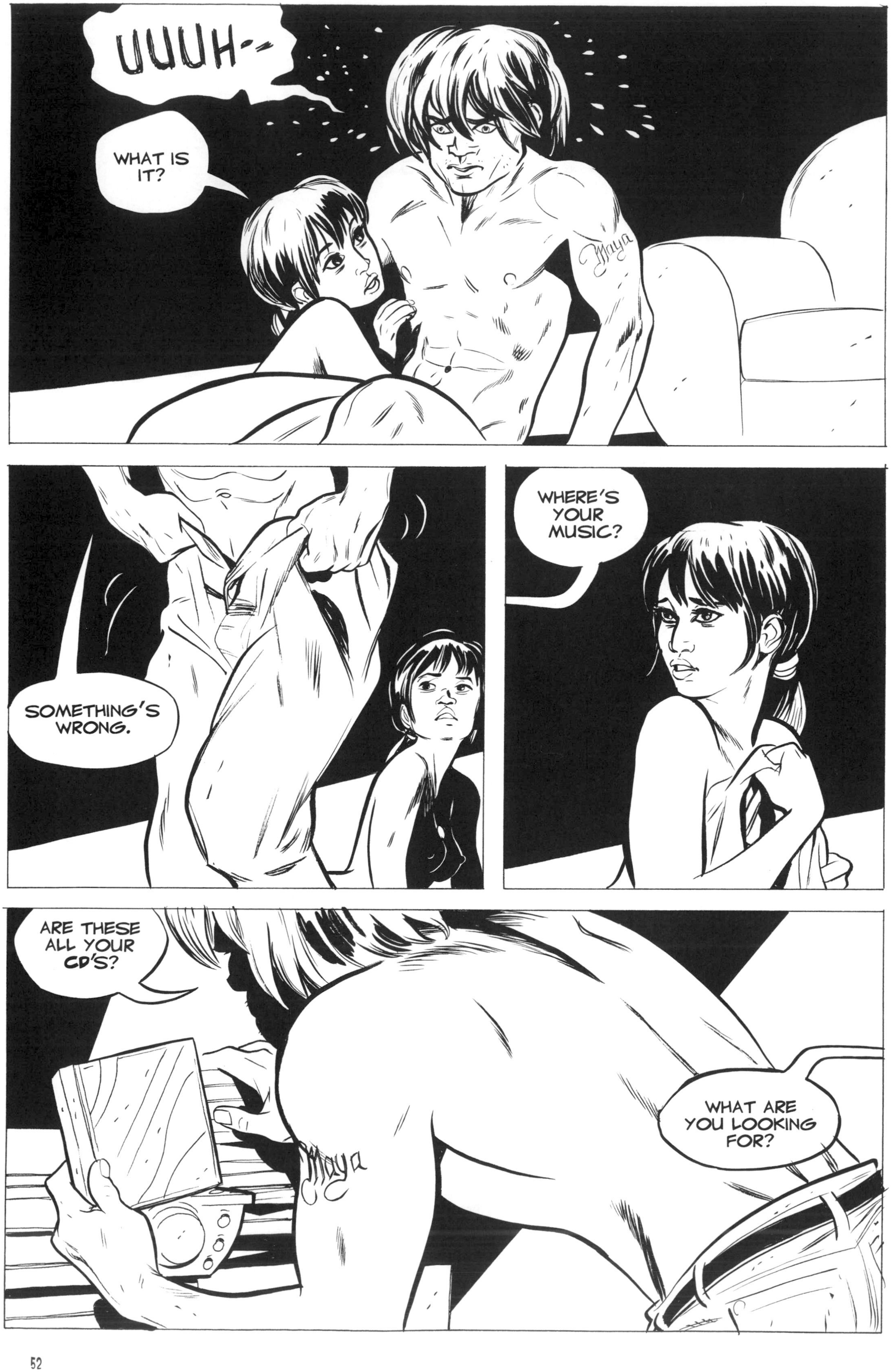
UUUH--
WHAT IS IT?
SOMETHING'S WRONG.
WHERE'S YOUR MUSIC?
ARE THESE ALL YOUR CD'S?
WHAT ARE YOU LOOKING FOR?
Maya
Maya

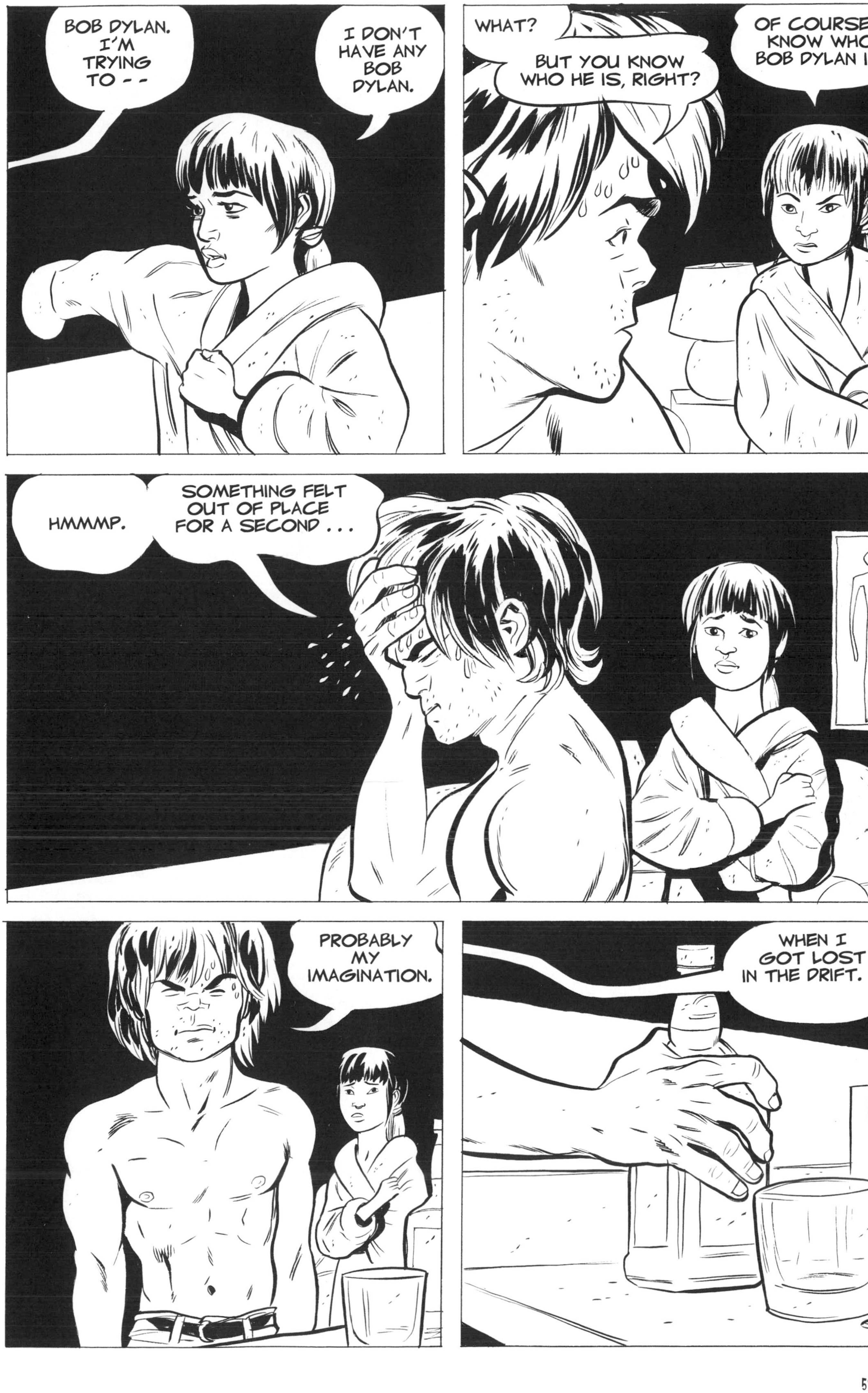
BOB DYLAN. I'M TRYING TO - -
I DON'T HAVE ANY BOB DYLAN.
WHAT?
BUT YOU KNOW WHO HE IS, RIGHT?
OF COURSE I KNOW WHO BOB DYLAN IS.
HMMMP.
SOMETHING FELT OUT OF PLACE FOR A SECOND . . .
PROBABLY MY IMAGINATION.
WHEN I GOT LOST IN THE DRIFT. . .

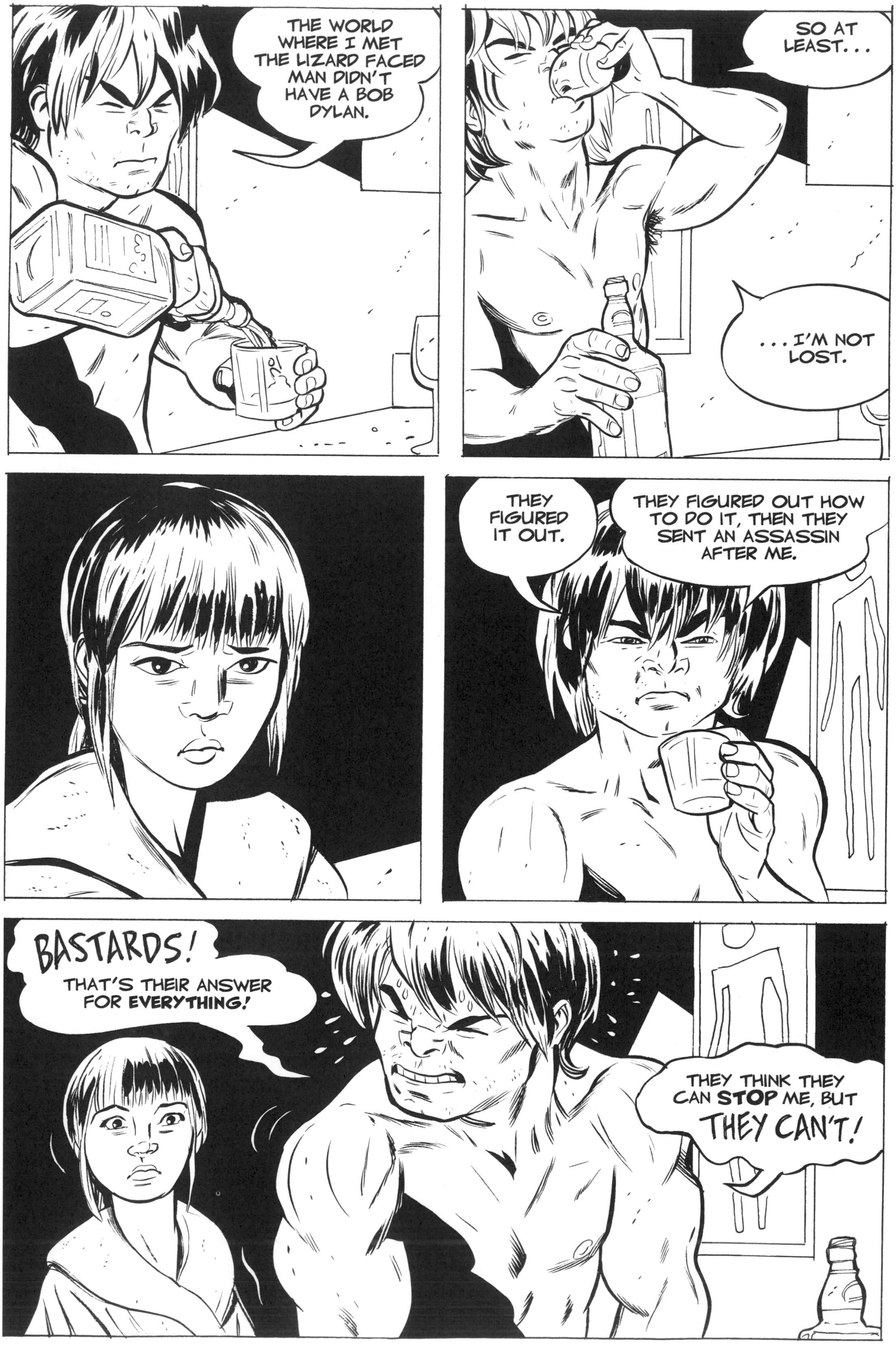
THE WORLD WHERE I MET THE LIZARD FACED MAN DIDN'T HAVE A BOB DYLAN.
SO AT LEAST...
...I'M NOT LOST.
THEY FIGURED IT OUT.
THEY FIGURED OUT HOW TO DO IT, THEN THEY SENT AN ASSASSIN AFTER ME.
BASTARDS!
THAT'S THEIR ANSWER FOR EVERYTHING!
THEY THINK THEY CAN STOP ME, BUT THEY CAN'T!

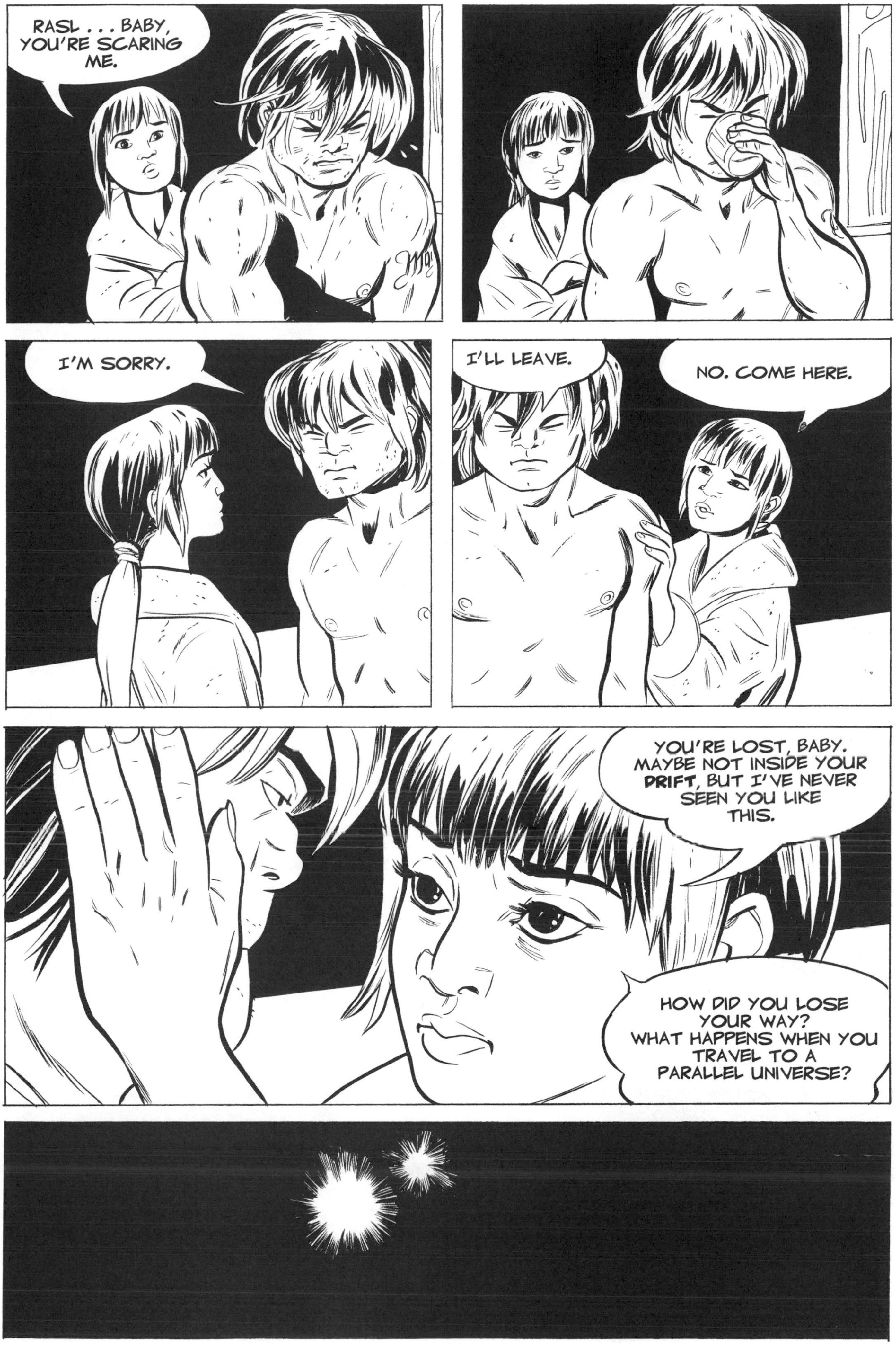
RASL . . . BABY, YOU'RE SCARING ME.
I'M SORRY.
I'LL LEAVE.
NO. COME HERE.
YOU'RE LOST, BABY. MAYBE NOT INSIDE YOUR **DRIFT**, BUT I'VE NEVER SEEN YOU LIKE THIS.
HOW DID YOU LOSE YOUR WAY? WHAT HAPPENS WHEN YOU TRAVEL TO A PARALLEL UNIVERSE?

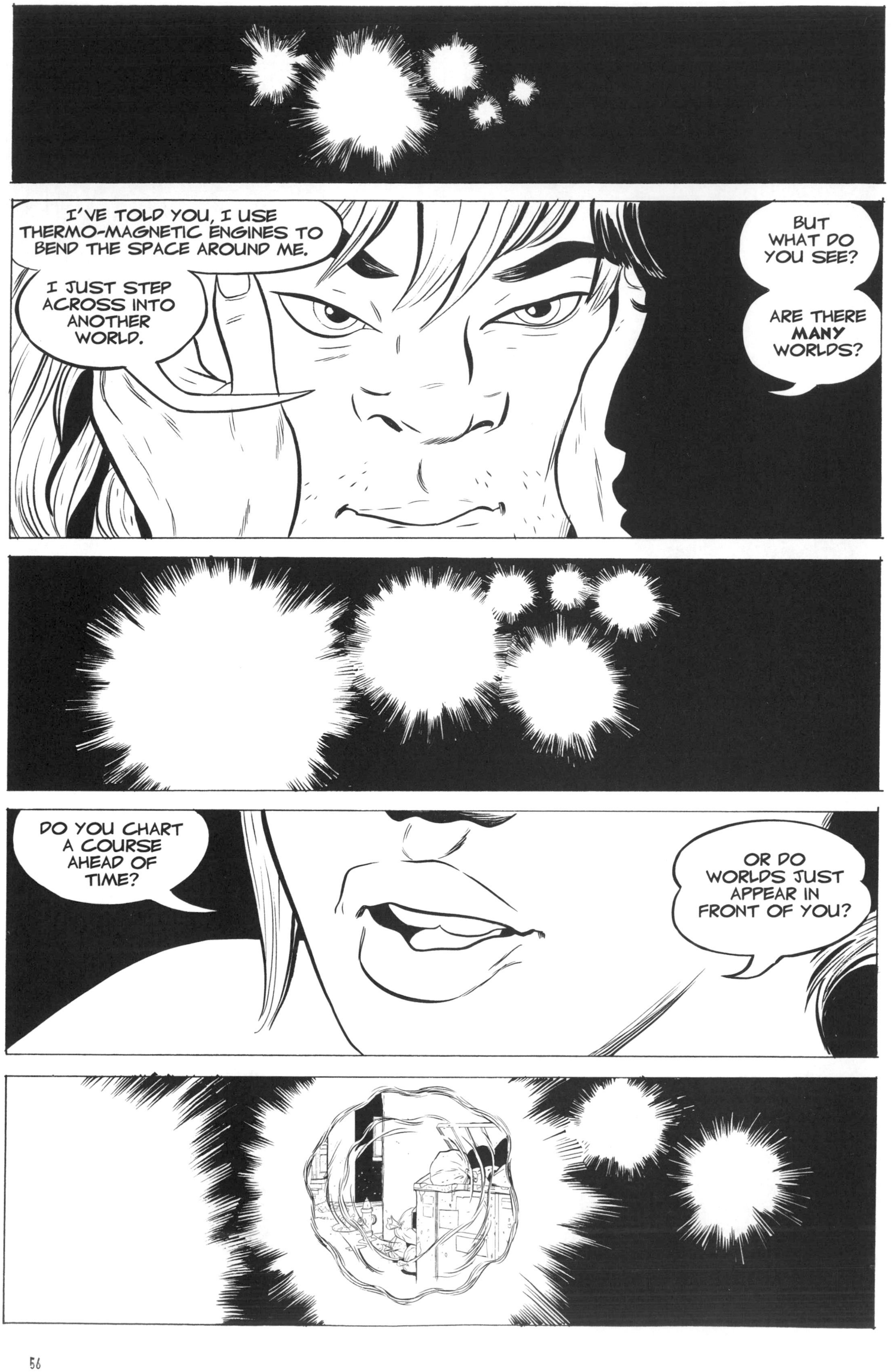
I'VE TOLD YOU, I USE THERMO-MAGNETIC ENGINES TO BEND THE SPACE AROUND ME.
I JUST STEP ACROSS INTO ANOTHER WORLD.
BUT WHAT DO YOU SEE?
ARE THERE MANY WORLDS?
DO YOU CHART A COURSE AHEAD OF TIME?
OR DO WORLDS JUST APPEAR IN FRONT OF YOU?

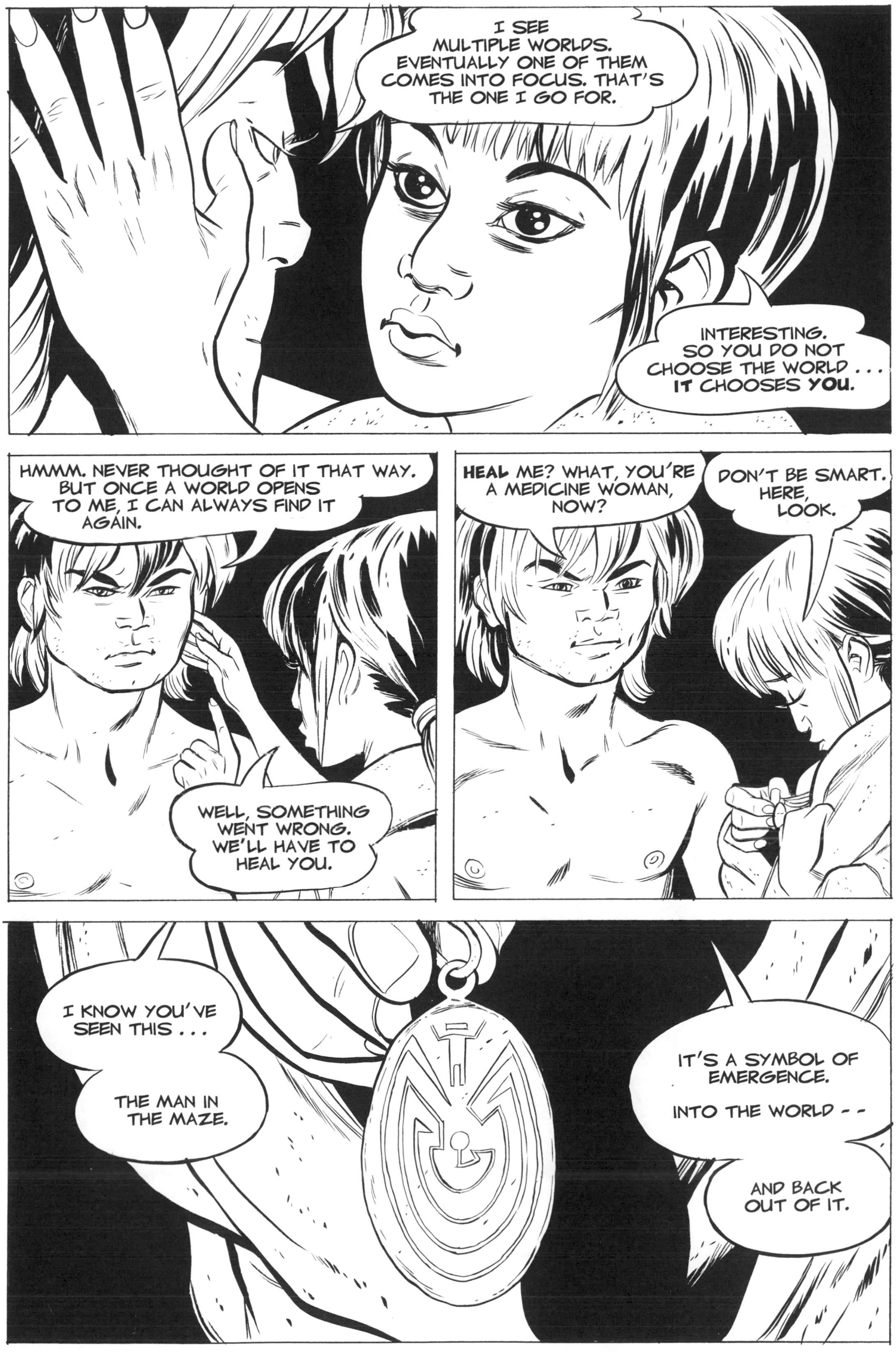
I SEE MULTIPLE WORLDS. EVENTUALLY ONE OF THEM COMES INTO FOCUS. THAT'S THE ONE I GO FOR.
INTERESTING. SO YOU DO NOT CHOOSE THE WORLD . . . IT CHOOSES YOU.
HMMM. NEVER THOUGHT OF IT THAT WAY. BUT ONCE A WORLD OPENS TO ME, I CAN ALWAYS FIND IT AGAIN.
WELL, SOMETHING WENT WRONG. WE'LL HAVE TO HEAL YOU.
HEAL ME? WHAT, YOU'RE A MEDICINE WOMAN, NOW?
DON'T BE SMART. HERE, LOOK.
I KNOW YOU'VE SEEN THIS . . .
THE MAN IN THE MAZE.
IT'S A SYMBOL OF EMERGENCE.
INTO THE WORLD - -
AND BACK OUT OF IT.

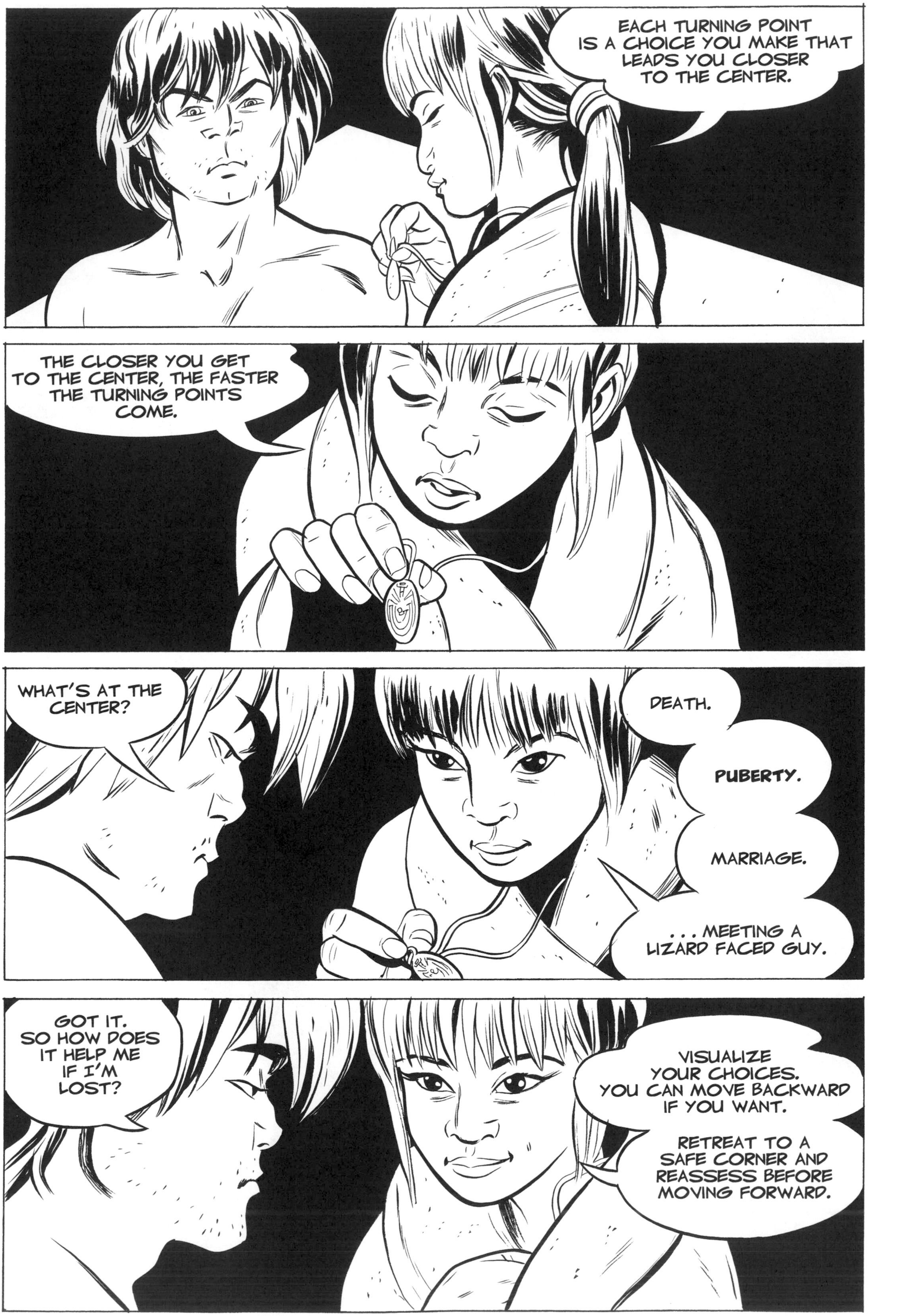
EACH TURNING POINT IS A CHOICE YOU MAKE THAT LEADS YOU CLOSER TO THE CENTER.
THE CLOSER YOU GET TO THE CENTER, THE FASTER THE TURNING POINTS COME.
WHAT'S AT THE CENTER?
DEATH.
PUBERTY.
MARRIAGE.
. . . MEETING A LIZARD FACED GUY.
GOT IT. SO HOW DOES IT HELP ME IF I'M LOST?
VISUALIZE YOUR CHOICES. YOU CAN MOVE BACKWARD IF YOU WANT.
RETREAT TO A SAFE CORNER AND REASSESS BEFORE MOVING FORWARD.

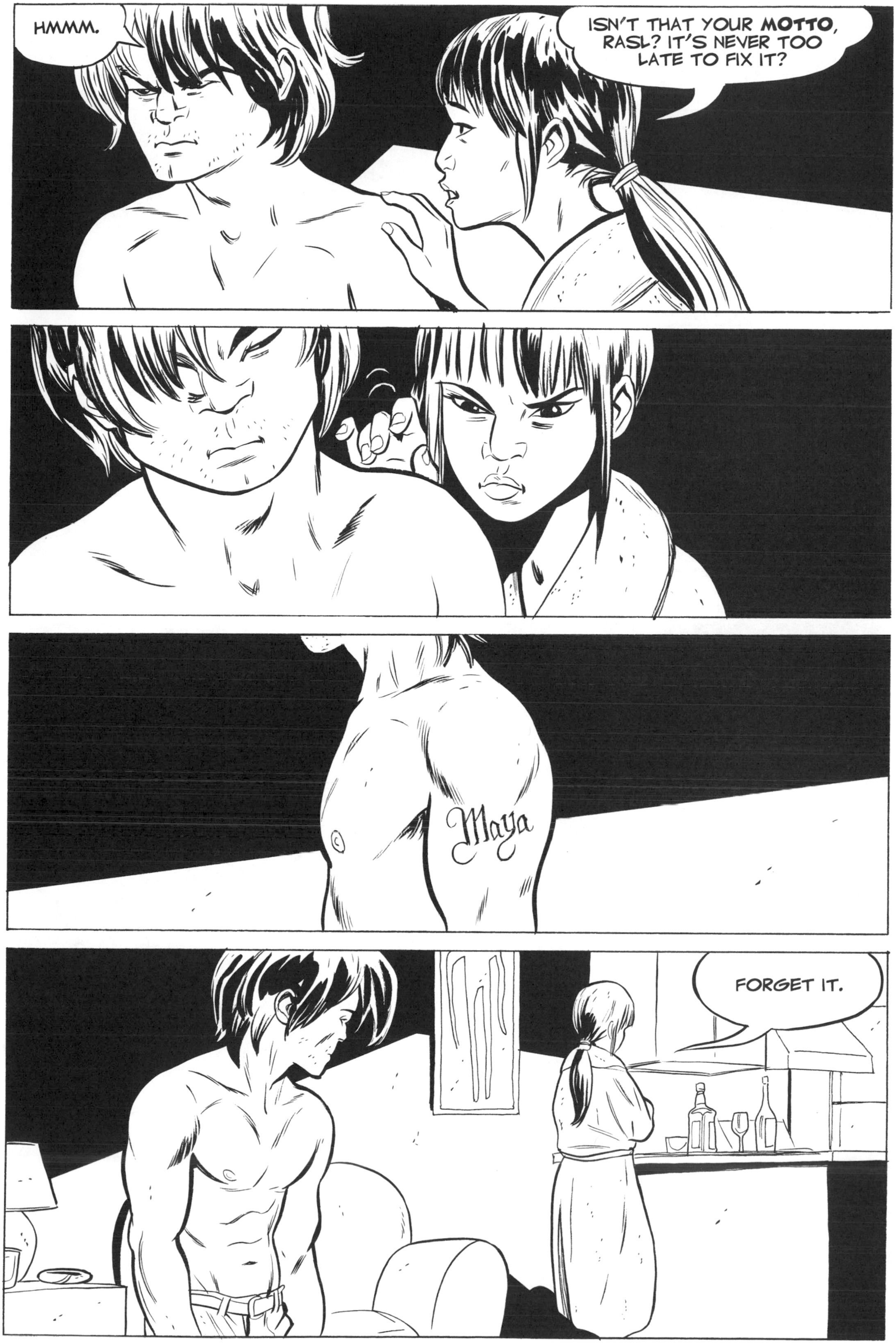
HMMM.
ISN'T THAT YOUR MOTTO, RASL? IT'S NEVER TOO LATE TO FIX IT?
Maya
FORGET IT.

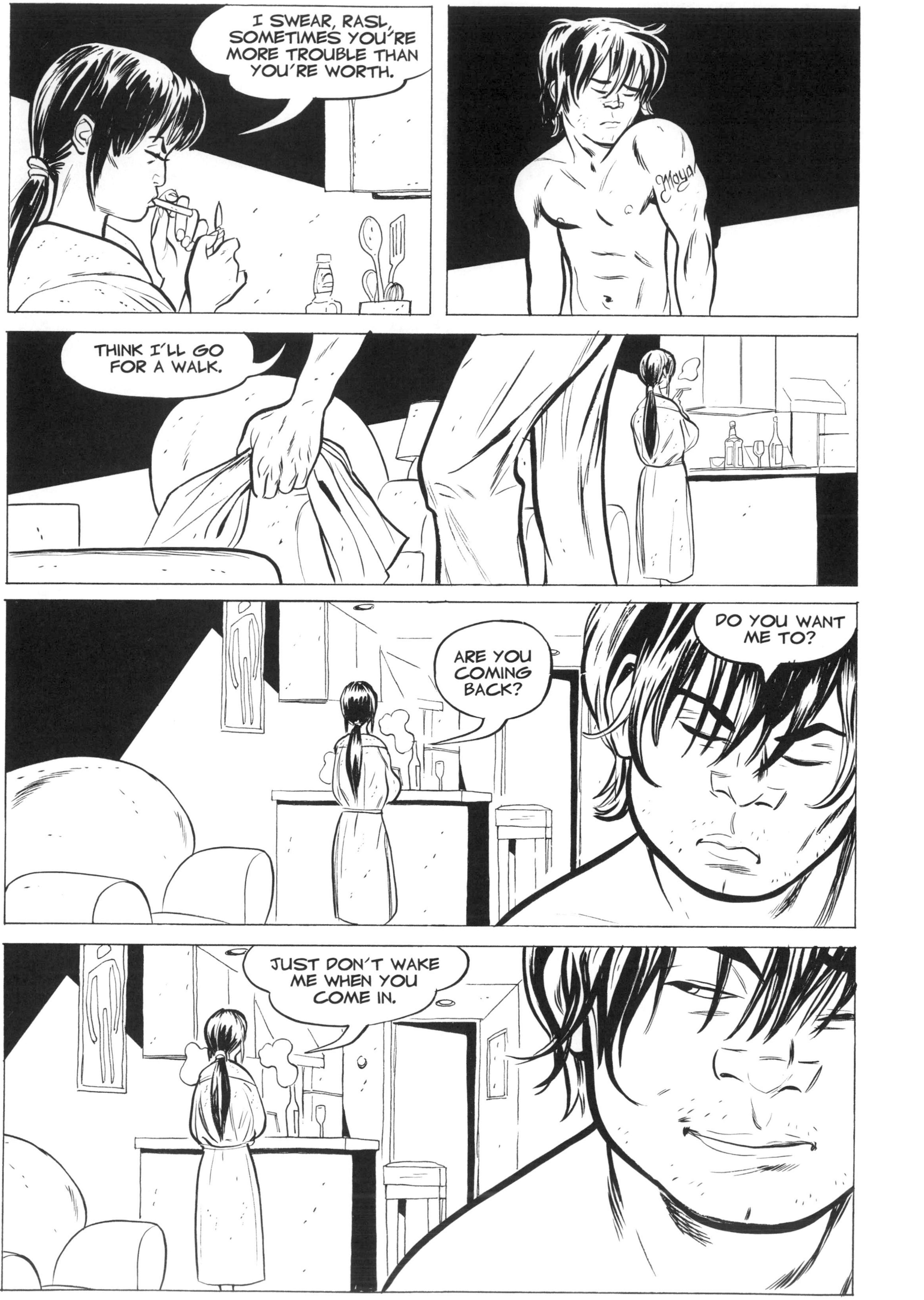
I SWEAR, RASL, SOMETIMES YOU'RE MORE TROUBLE THAN YOU'RE WORTH.
Maya
THINK I'LL GO FOR A WALK.
ARE YOU COMING BACK?
DO YOU WANT ME TO?
JUST DON'T WAKE ME WHEN YOU COME IN.

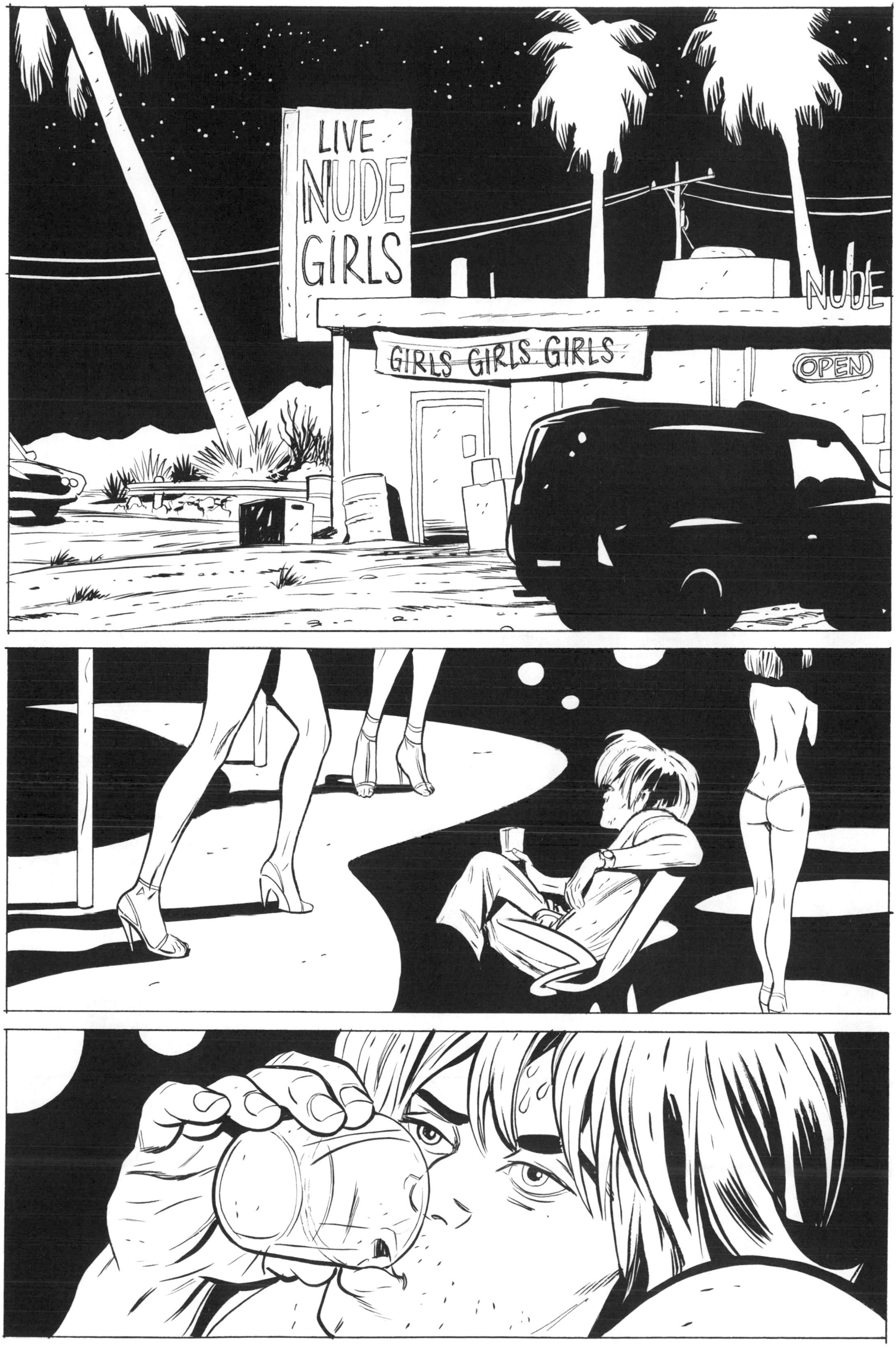
LIVE NUDE GIRLS
NUDE
GIRLS GIRLS GIRLS
OPEN

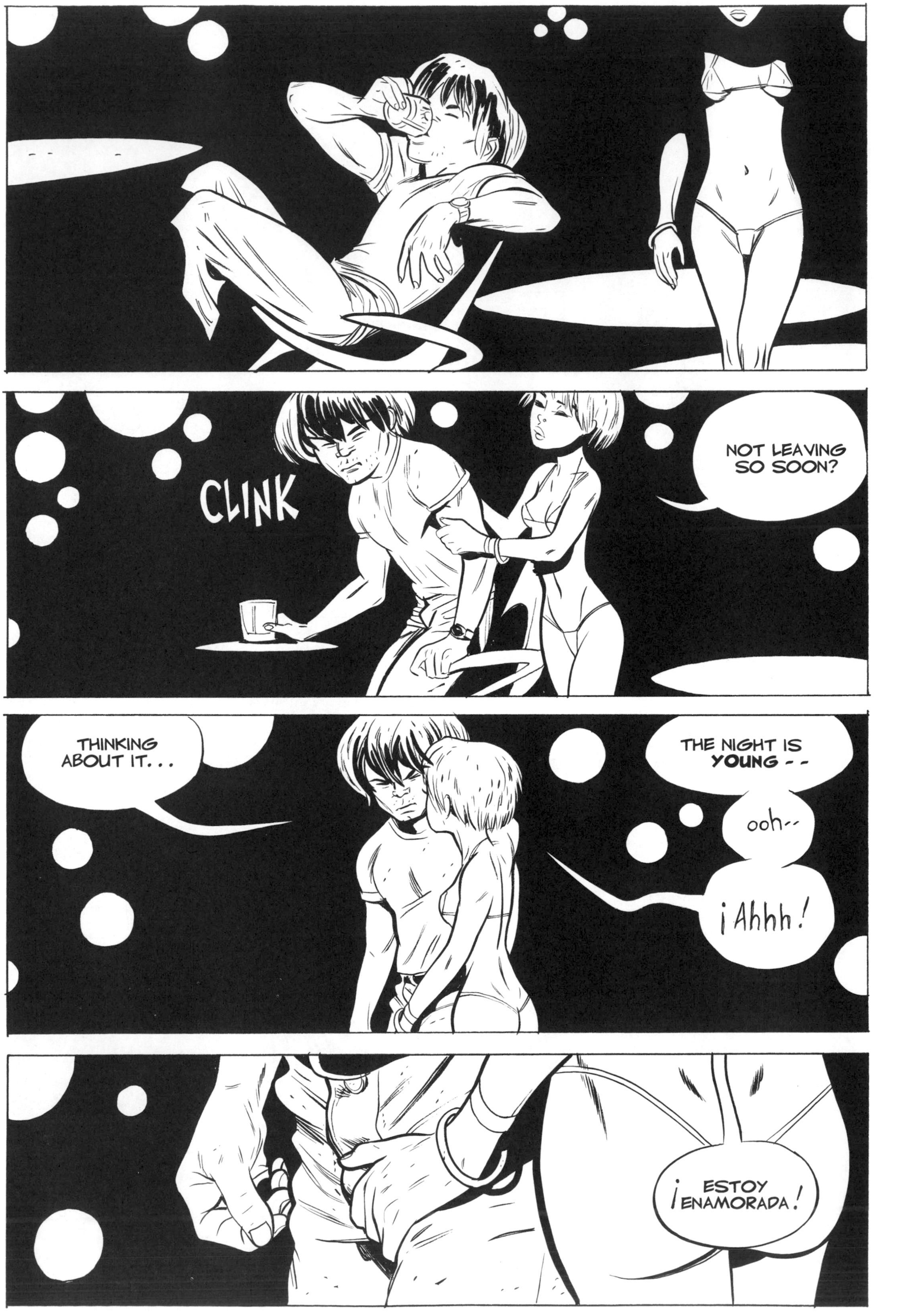
NOT LEAVING SO SOON?
CLINK
THINKING ABOUT IT...
THE NIGHT IS YOUNG --
ooh--
¡Ahhh!
¡ESTOY ENAMORADA!

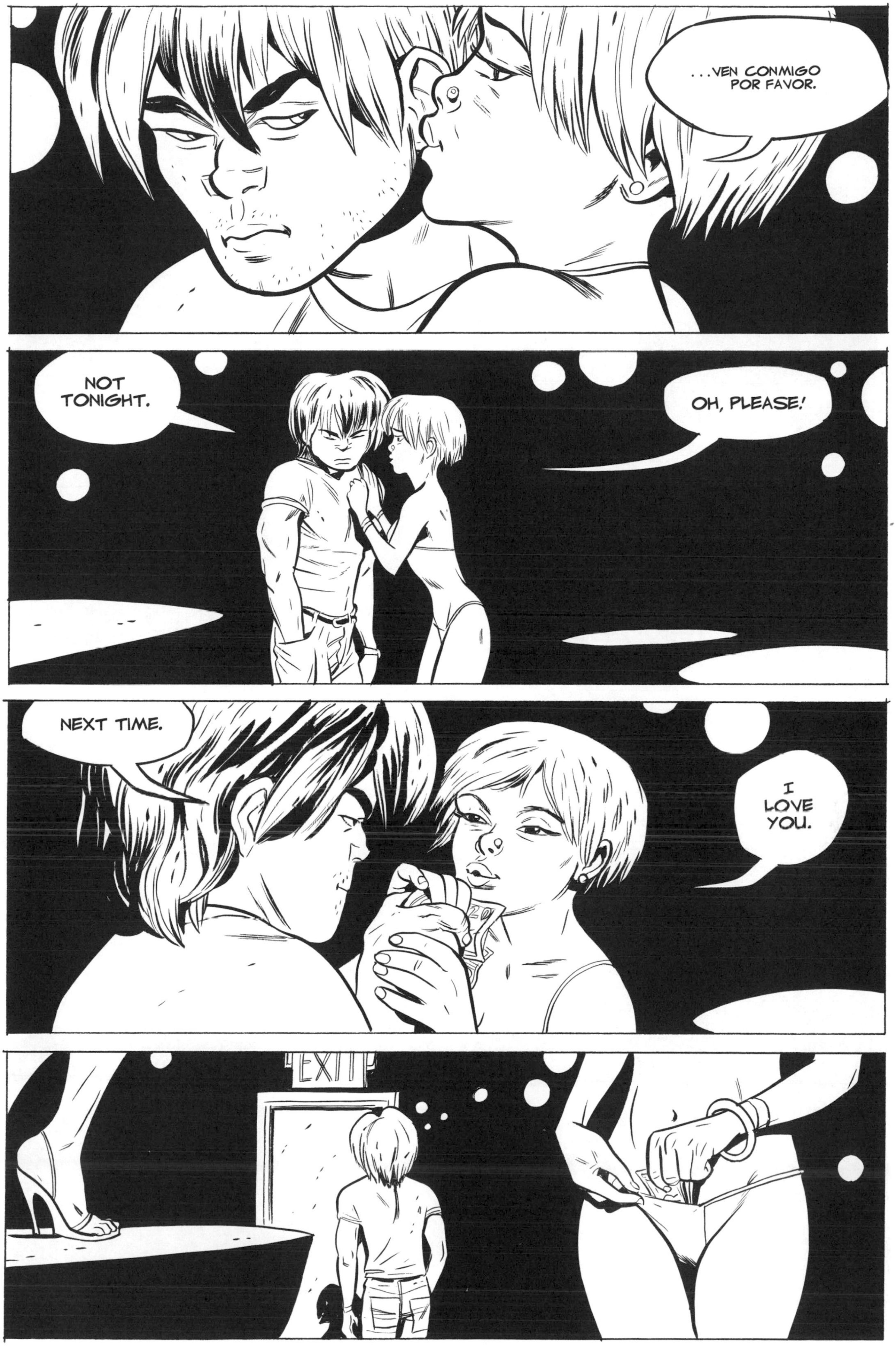
...VEN CONMIGO POR FAVOR.
NOT TONIGHT.
OH, PLEASE!
NEXT TIME.
I LOVE YOU.
EXIT

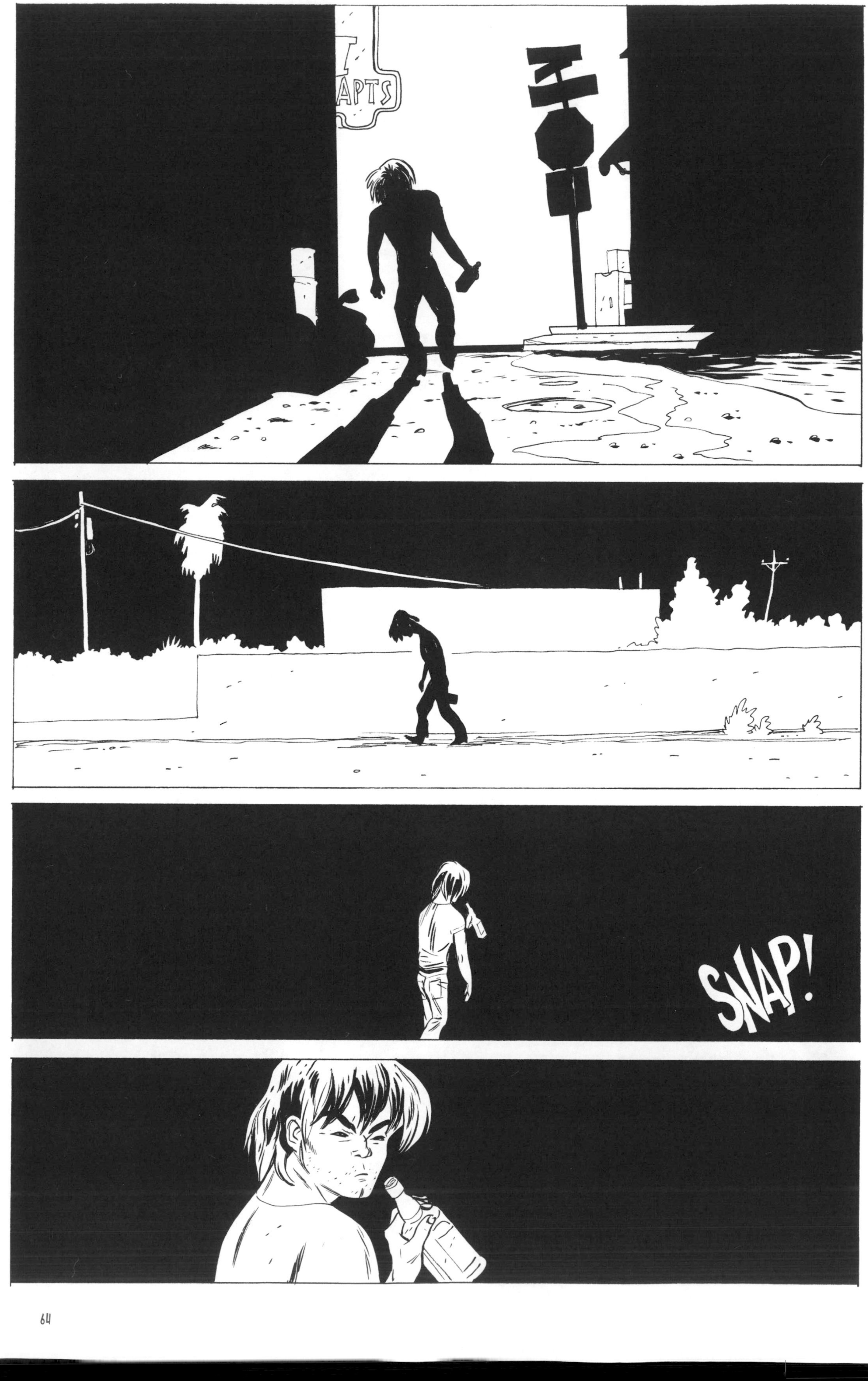
APTS
SNAP!

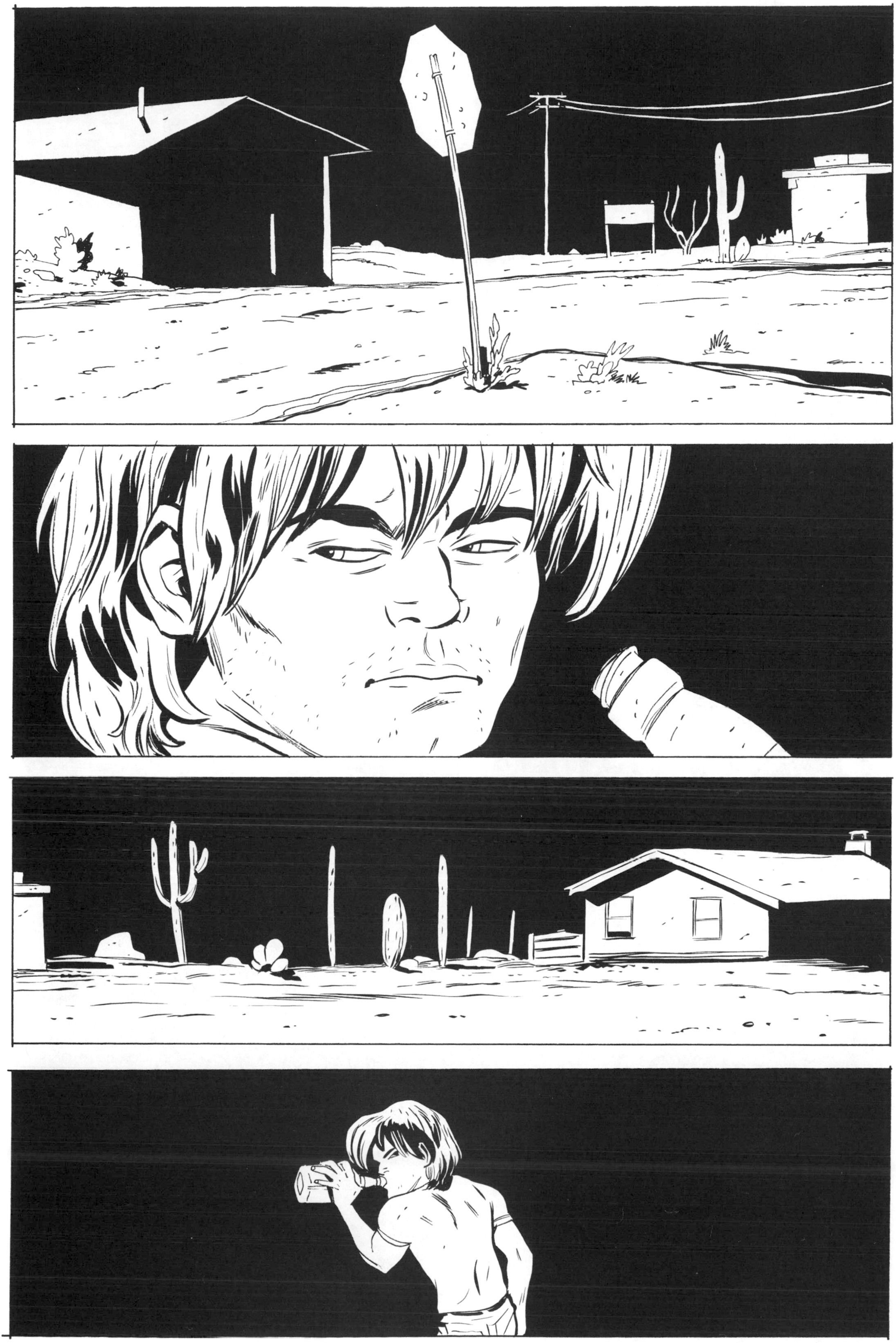

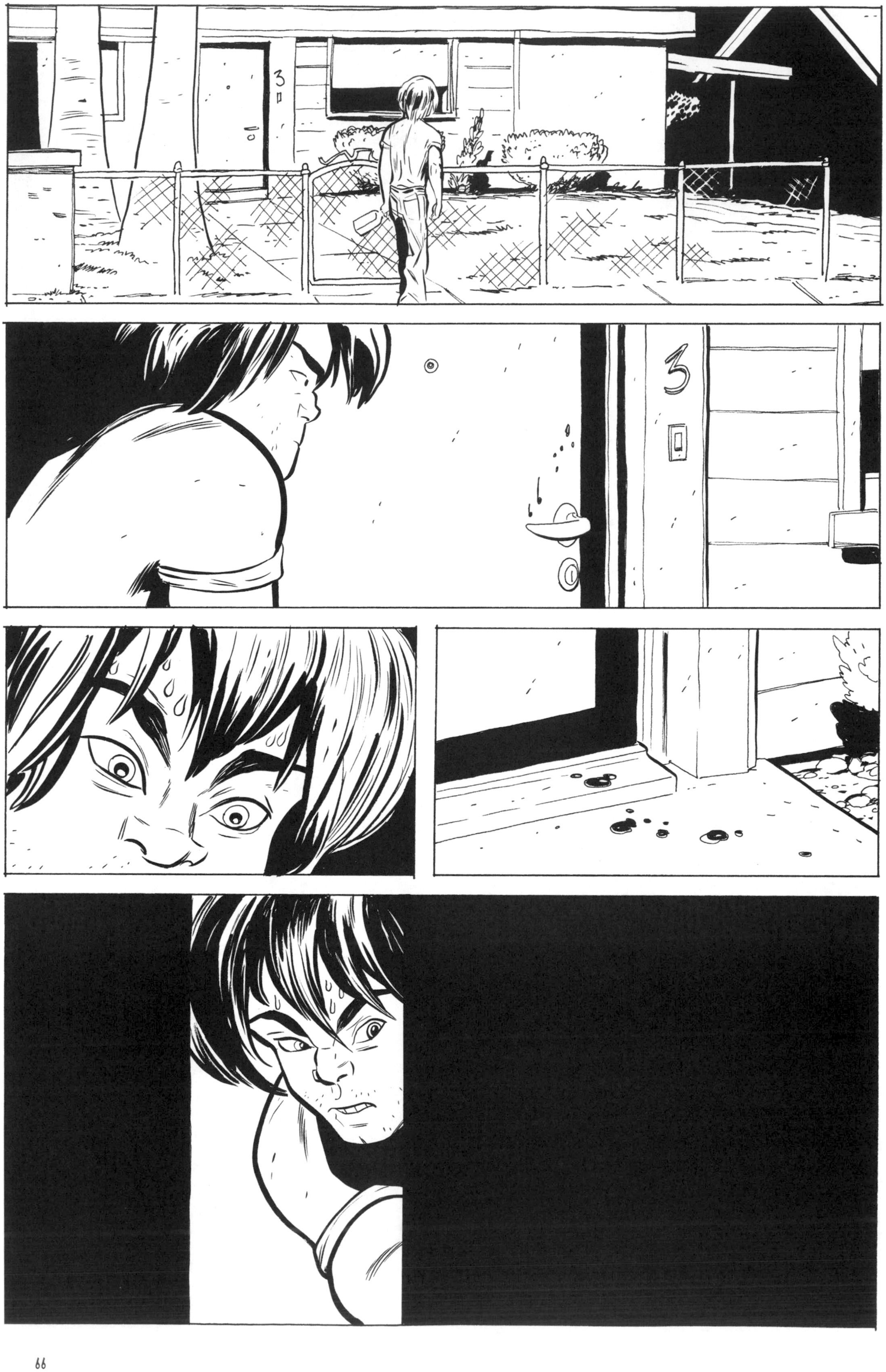

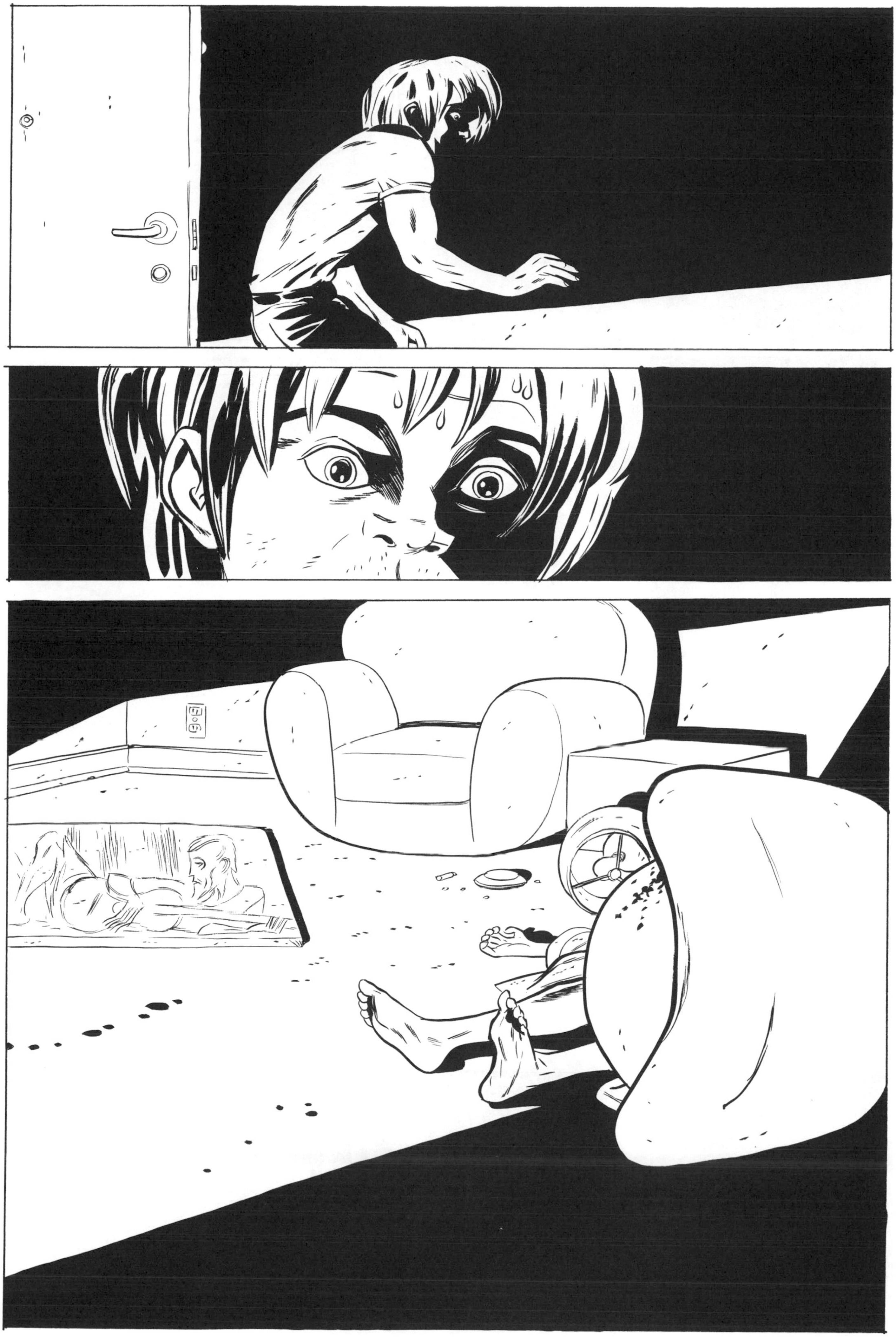

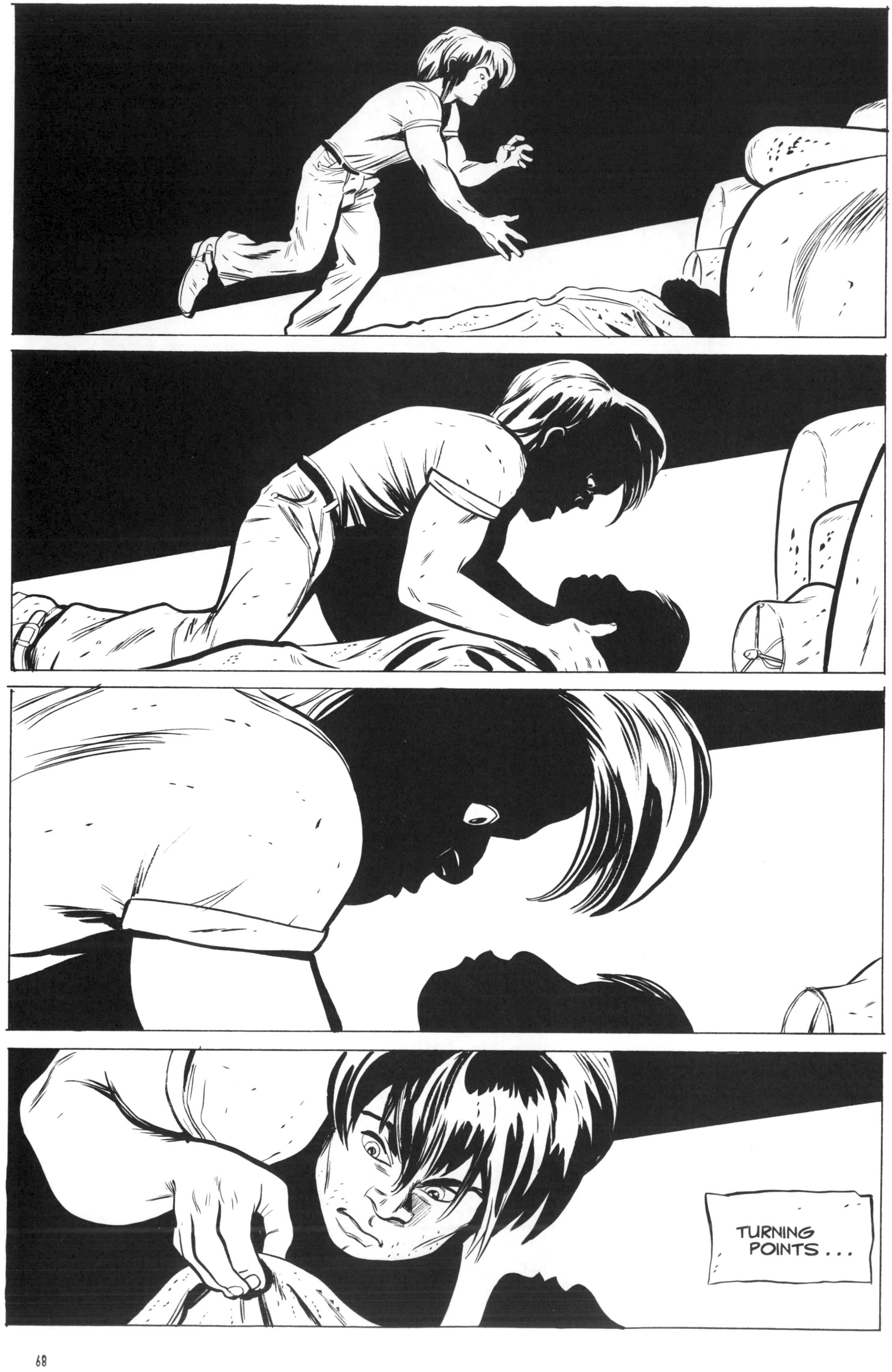
TURNING POINTS . . .

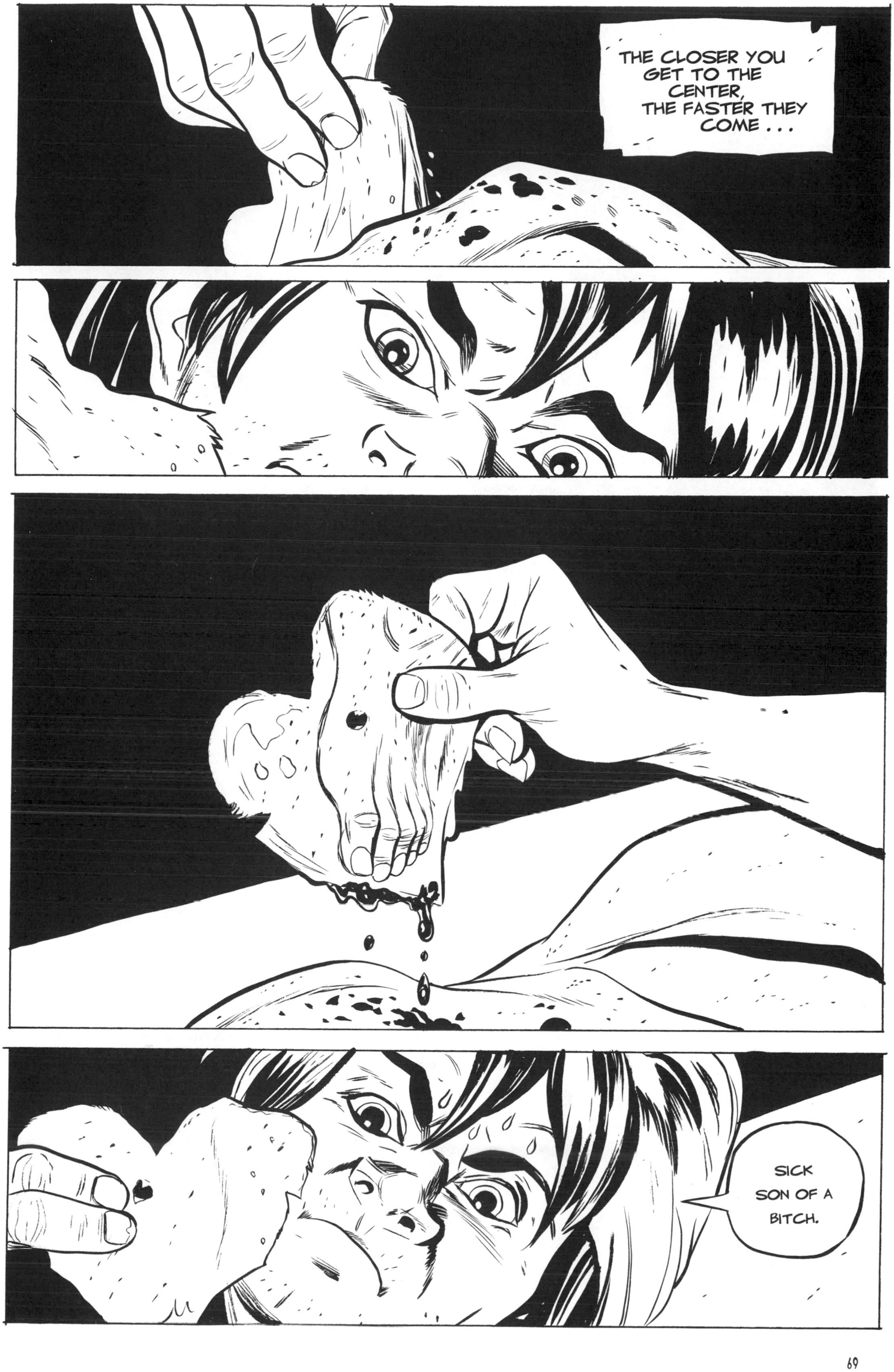
THE CLOSER YOU GET TO THE CENTER, THE FASTER THEY COME . . .
SICK SON OF A BITCH.

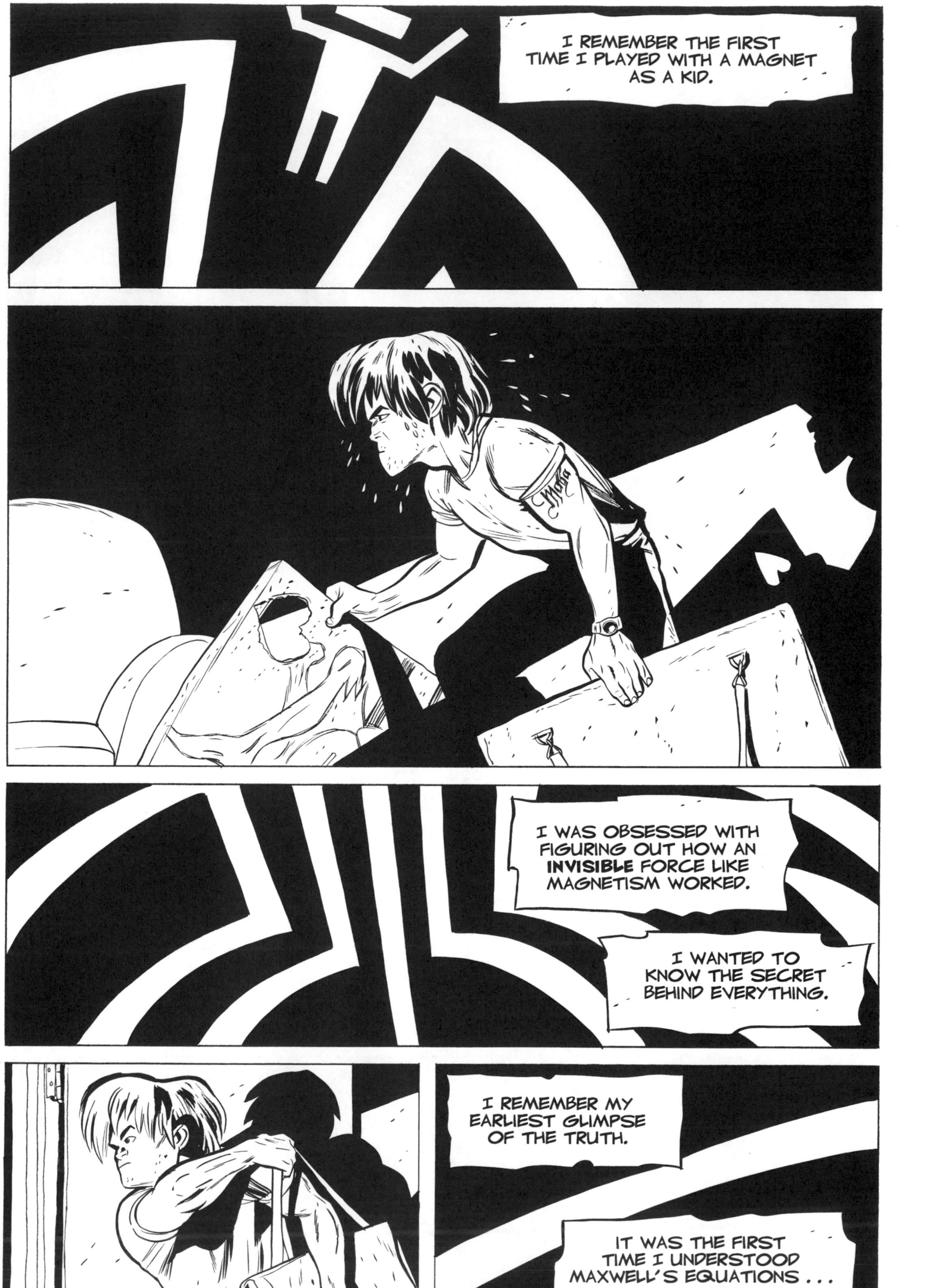
I REMEMBER THE FIRST TIME I PLAYED WITH A MAGNET AS A KID.
I WAS OBSESSED WITH FIGURING OUT HOW AN **INVISIBLE** FORCE LIKE MAGNETISM WORKED.
I WANTED TO KNOW THE SECRET BEHIND EVERYTHING.
I REMEMBER MY EARLIEST GLIMPSE OF THE TRUTH.
IT WAS THE FIRST TIME I UNDERSTOOD MAXWELL'S EQUATIONS . . .

FOUR ELEGANT EQUATIONS, THAT PERFECTLY DESCRIBED ELECTRICITY AND MAGNETISM, UNITING THEM IN A SINGLE FORCE...

THE WORLD WAS **KNOWABLE.**

KEEP OUT

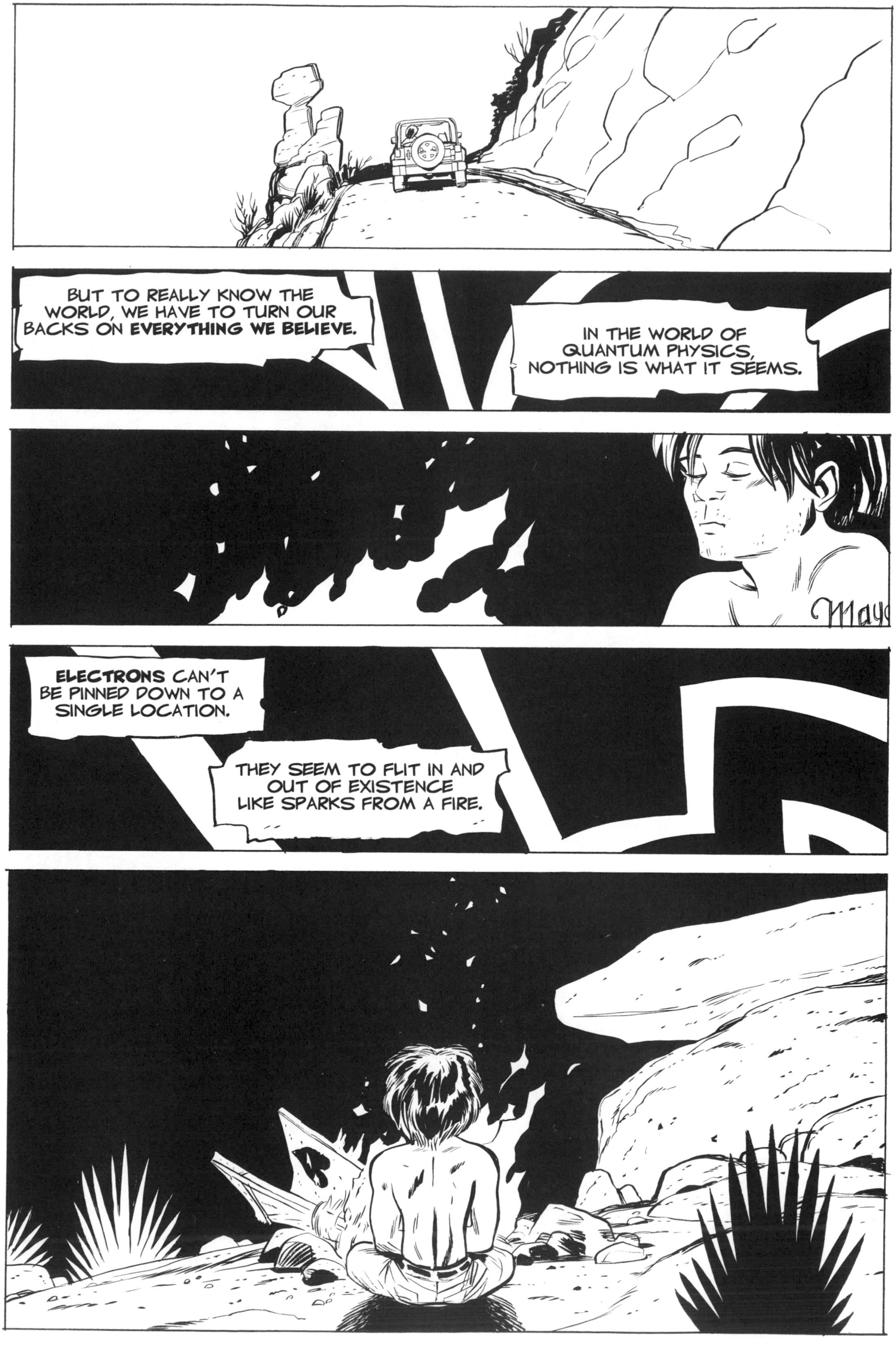
BUT TO REALLY KNOW THE WORLD, WE HAVE TO TURN OUR BACKS ON **EVERYTHING WE BELIEVE.**
IN THE WORLD OF QUANTUM PHYSICS, NOTHING IS WHAT IT SEEMS.
ELECTRONS CAN'T BE PINNED DOWN TO A SINGLE LOCATION.
THEY SEEM TO FLIT IN AND OUT OF EXISTENCE LIKE SPARKS FROM A FIRE.

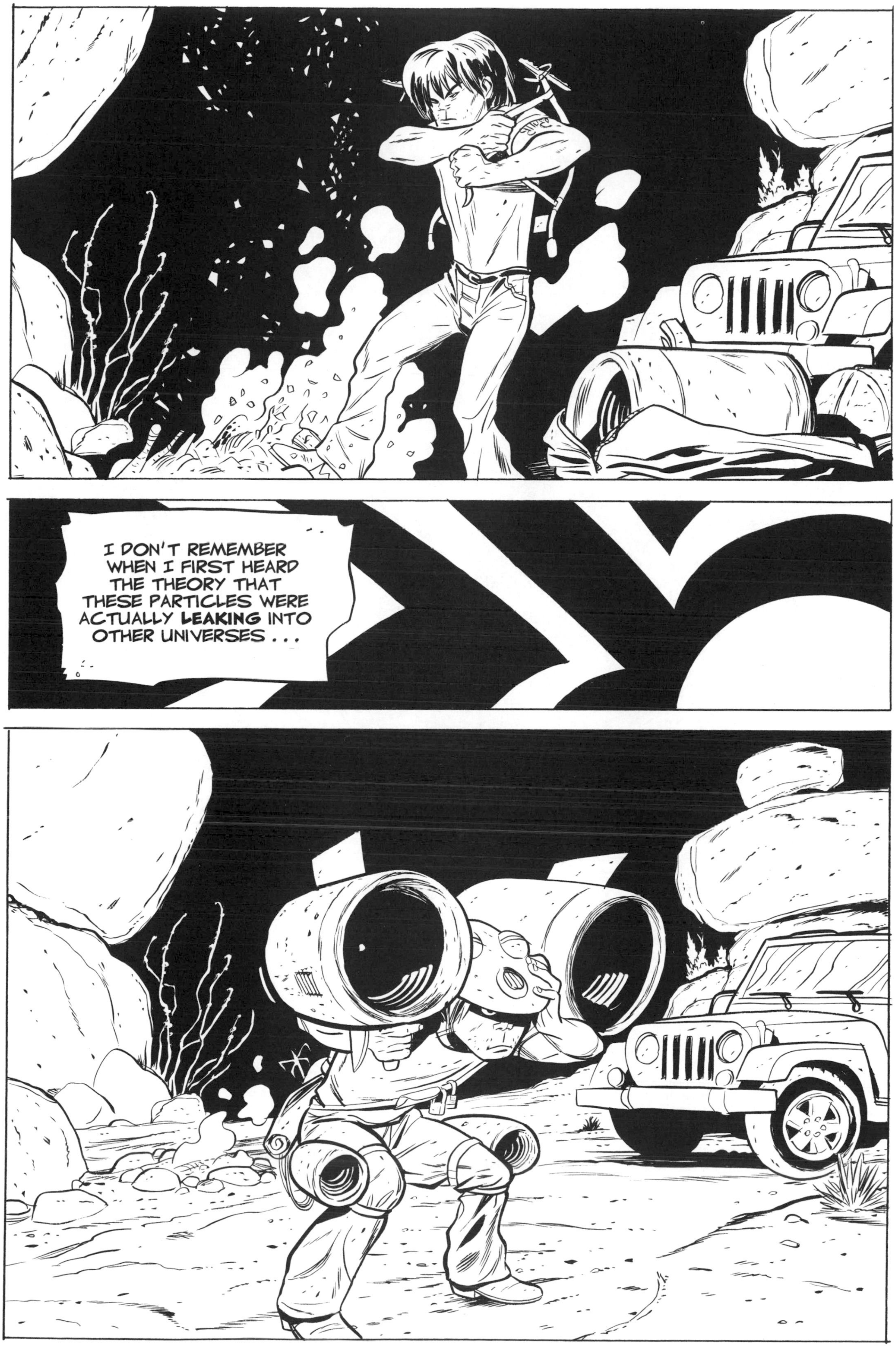
I DON'T REMEMBER
WHEN I FIRST HEARD
THE THEORY THAT
THESE PARTICLES WERE
ACTUALLY **LEAKING** INTO
OTHER UNIVERSES . . .

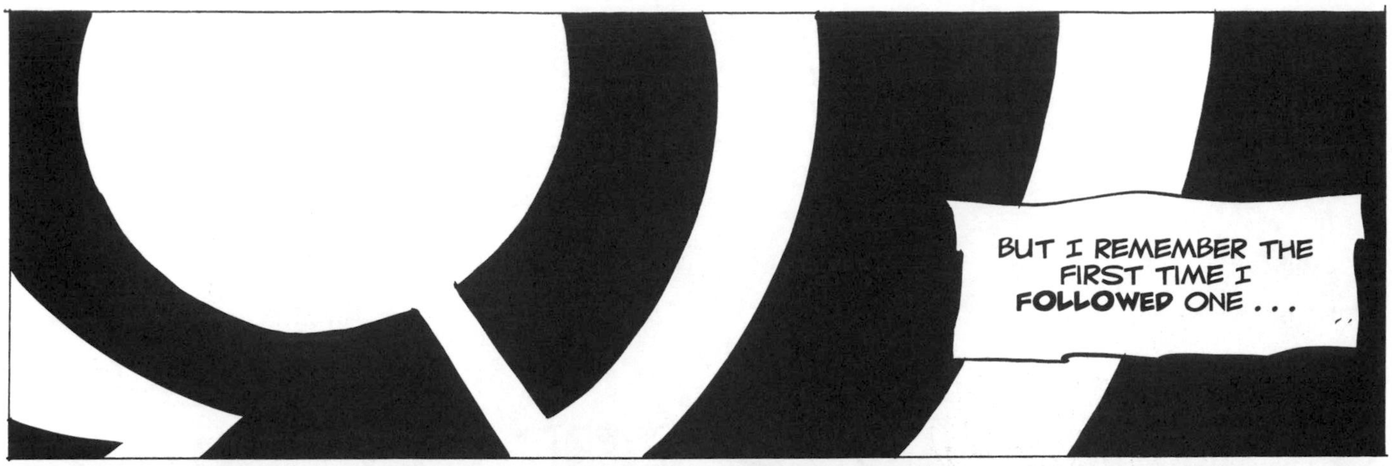
BUT I REMEMBER THE FIRST TIME I **FOLLOWED** ONE . . .

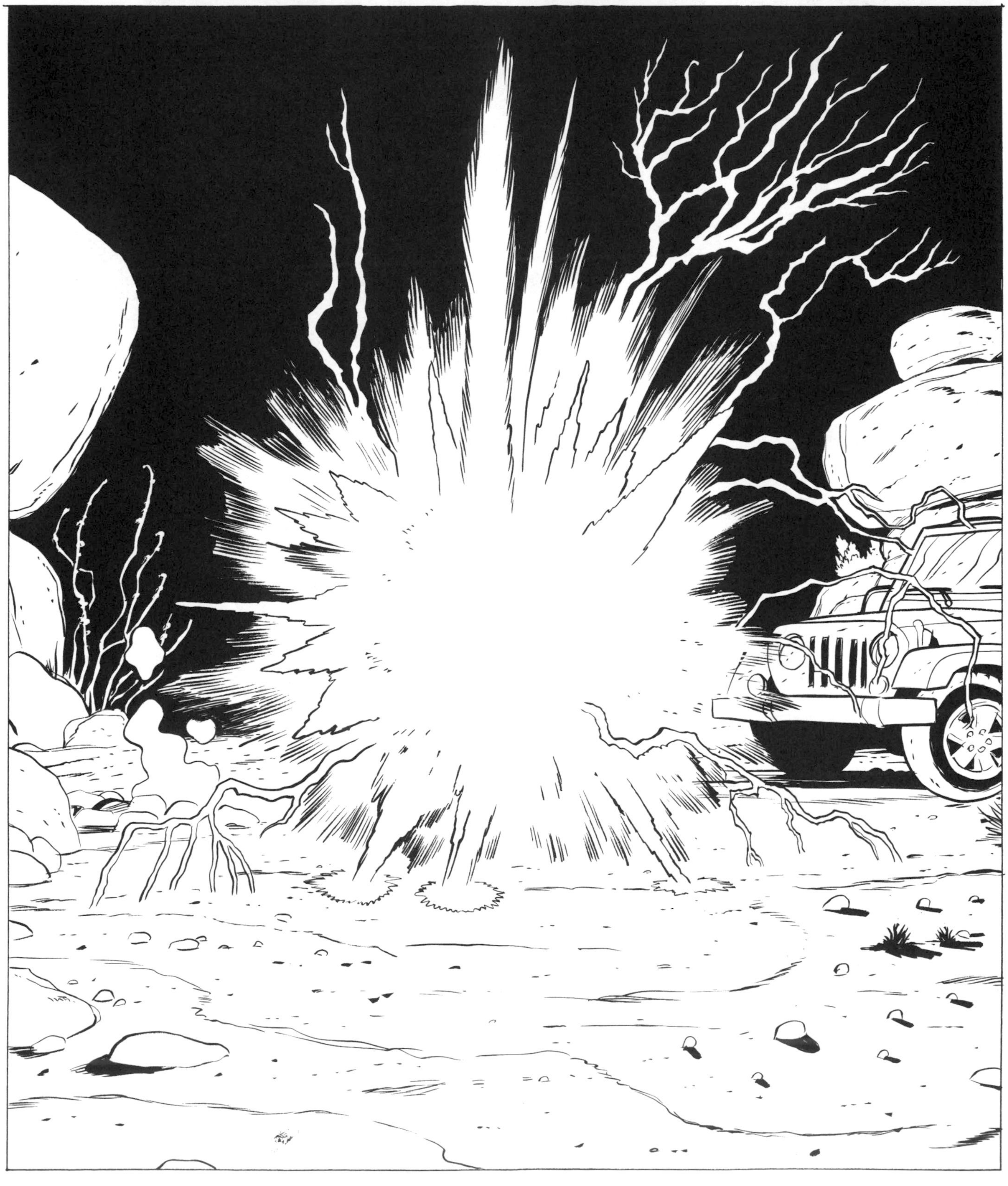

3.
MAYA

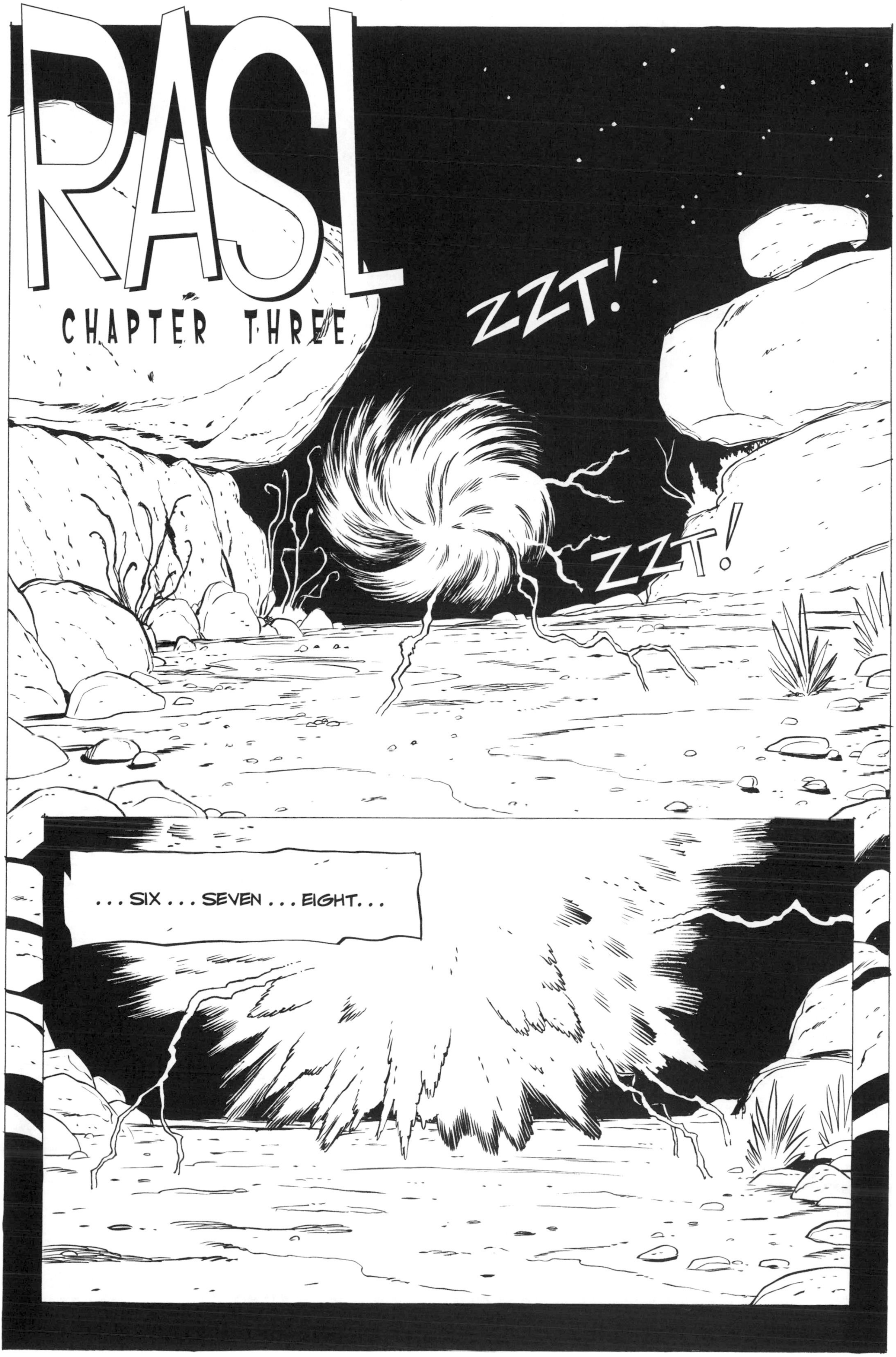
RASL
CHAPTER THREE
ZZT!
ZZT!
. . . SIX . . . SEVEN . . . EIGHT. . .

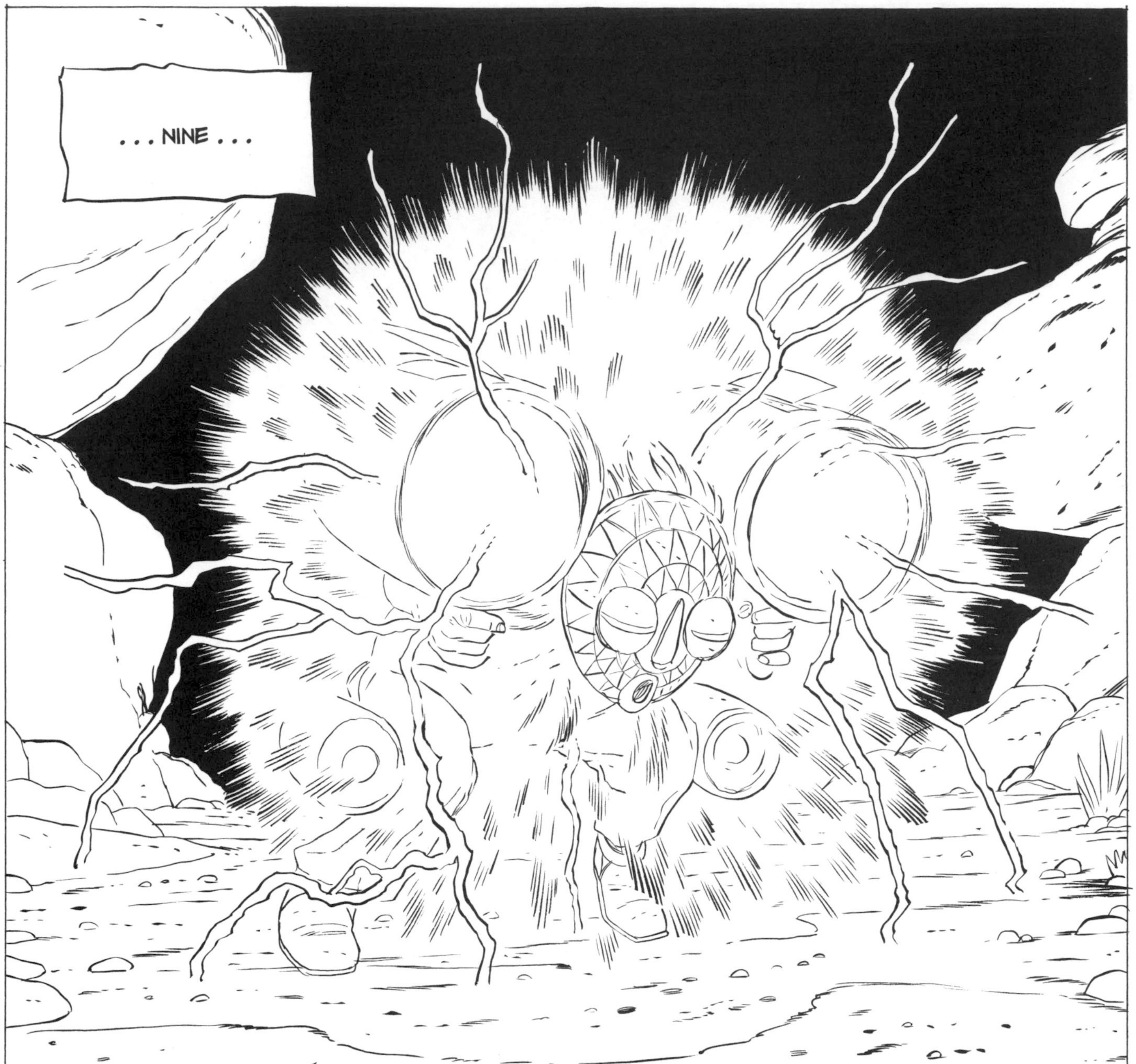
. . . NINE . . .

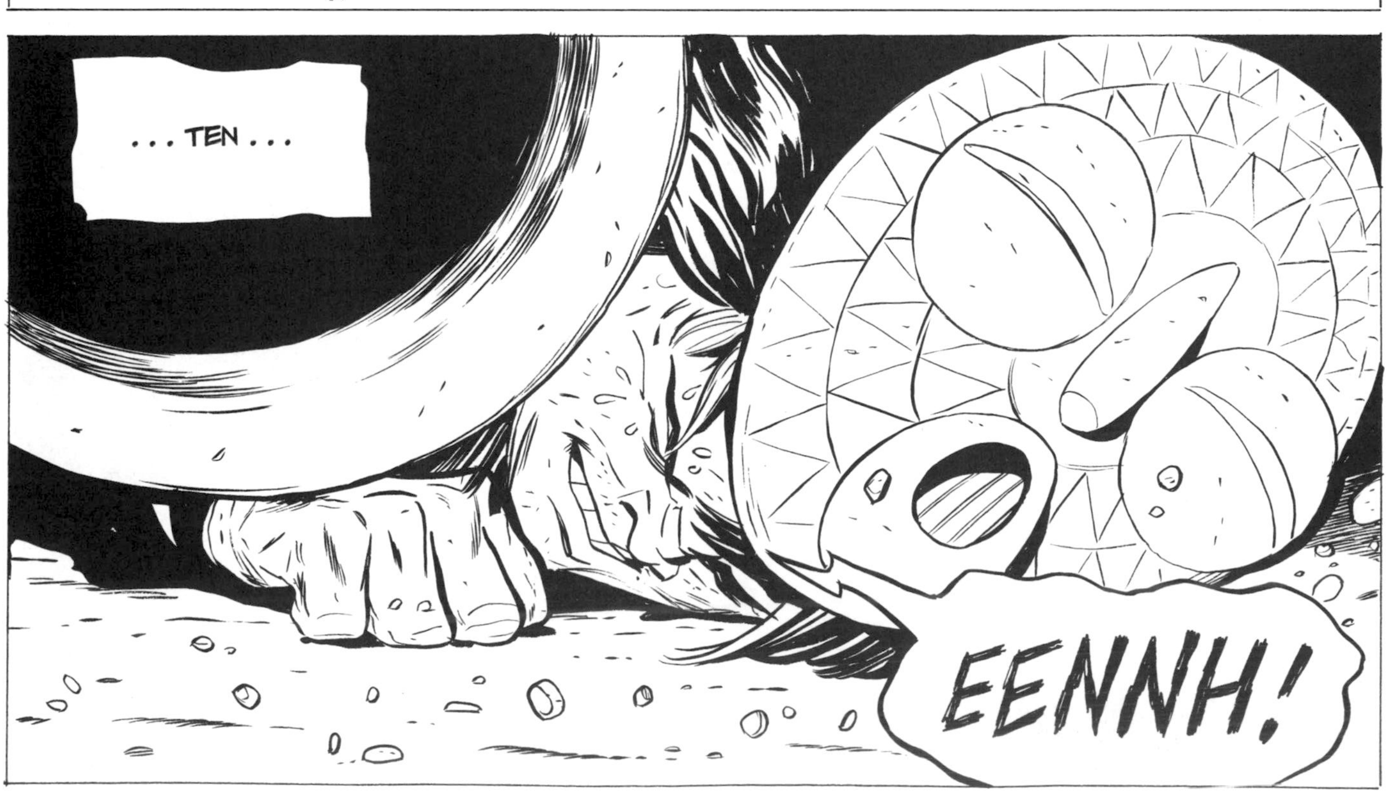
. . . TEN . . .
EENNH!

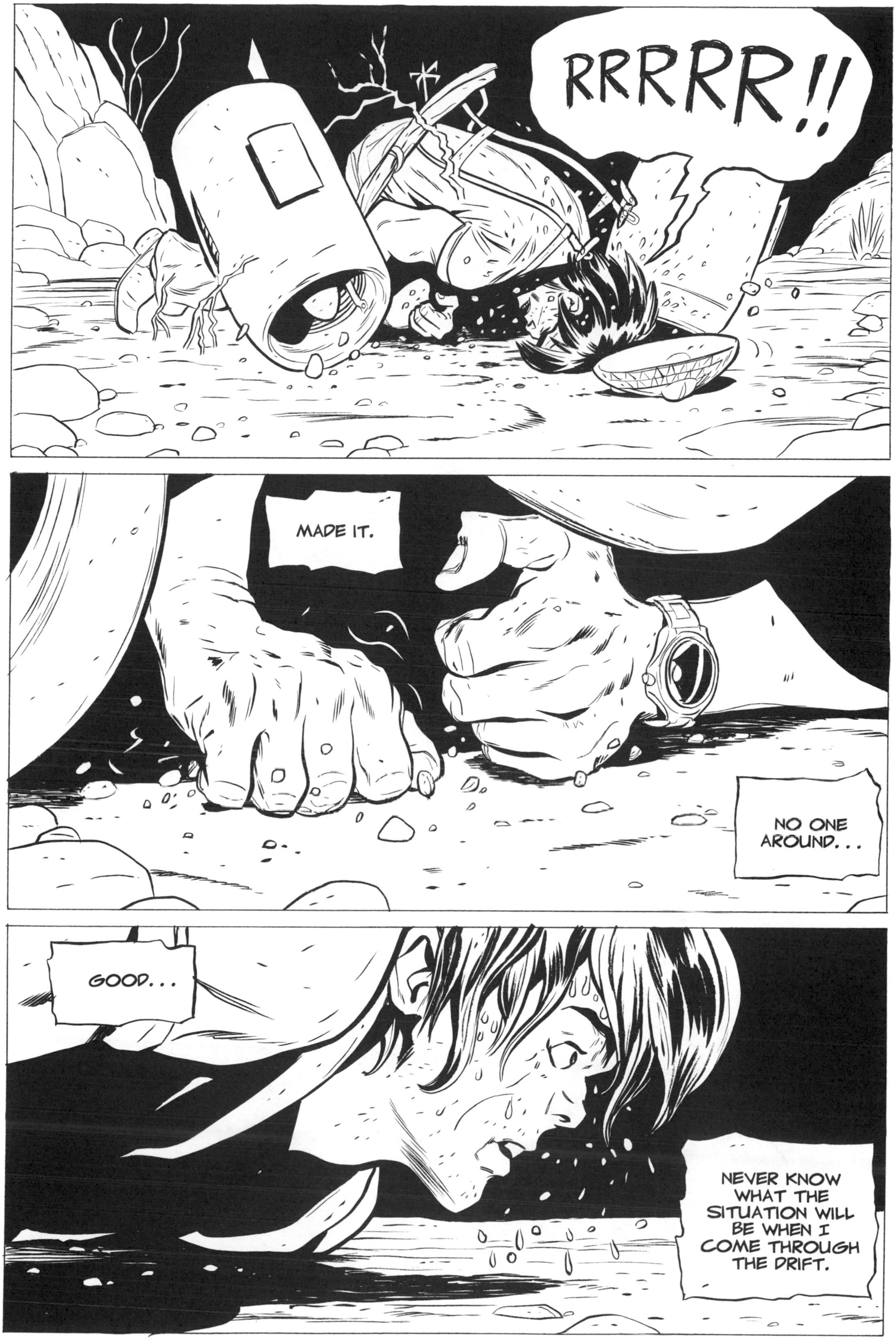
RRRRR!!
MADE IT.
NO ONE AROUND...
GOOD...
NEVER KNOW WHAT THE SITUATION WILL BE WHEN I COME THROUGH THE DRIFT.

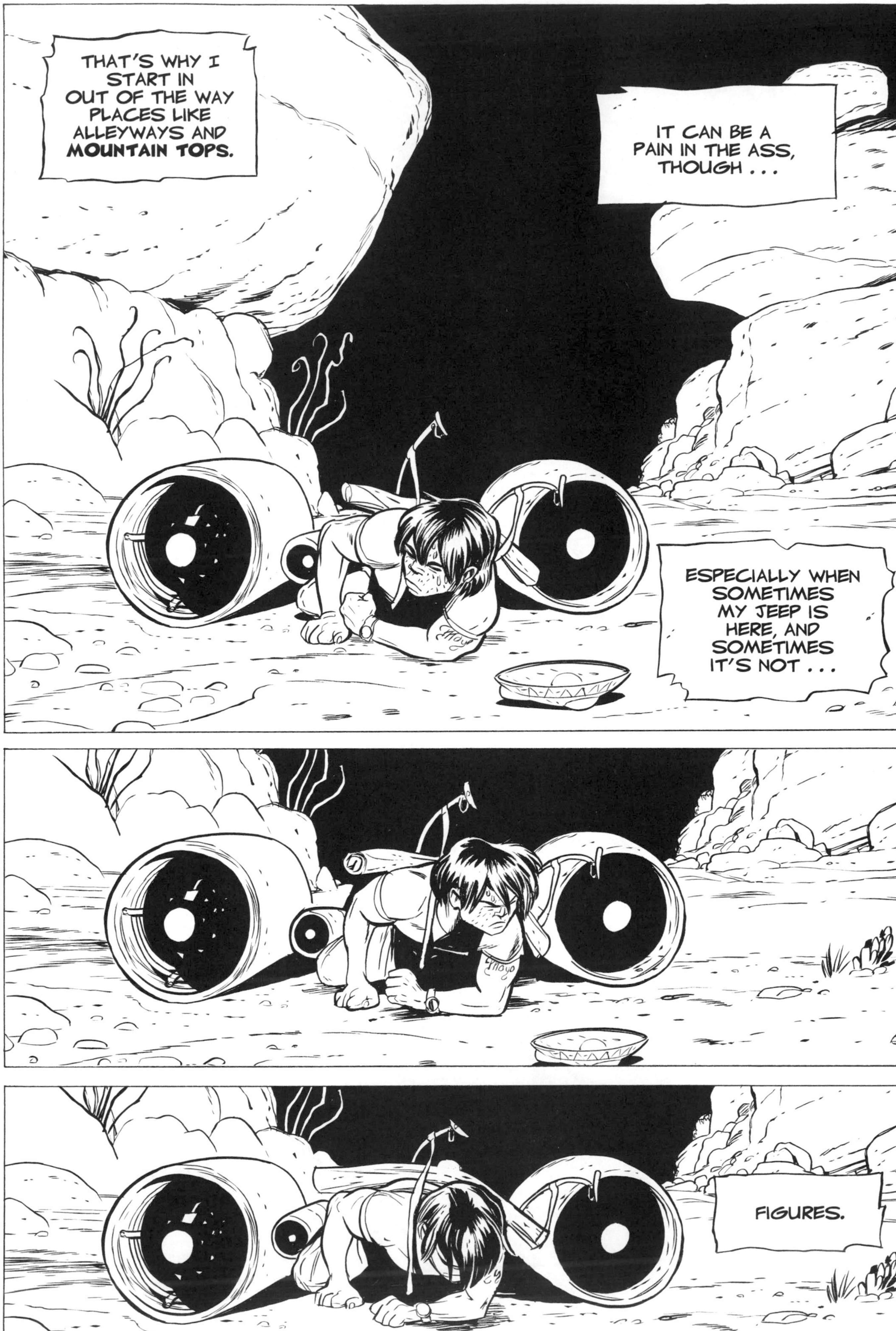
THAT'S WHY I START IN OUT OF THE WAY PLACES LIKE ALLEYWAYS AND **MOUNTAIN TOPS.**
IT CAN BE A PAIN IN THE ASS, THOUGH . . .
ESPECIALLY WHEN SOMETIMES MY JEEP IS HERE, AND SOMETIMES IT'S NOT . . .
FIGURES.

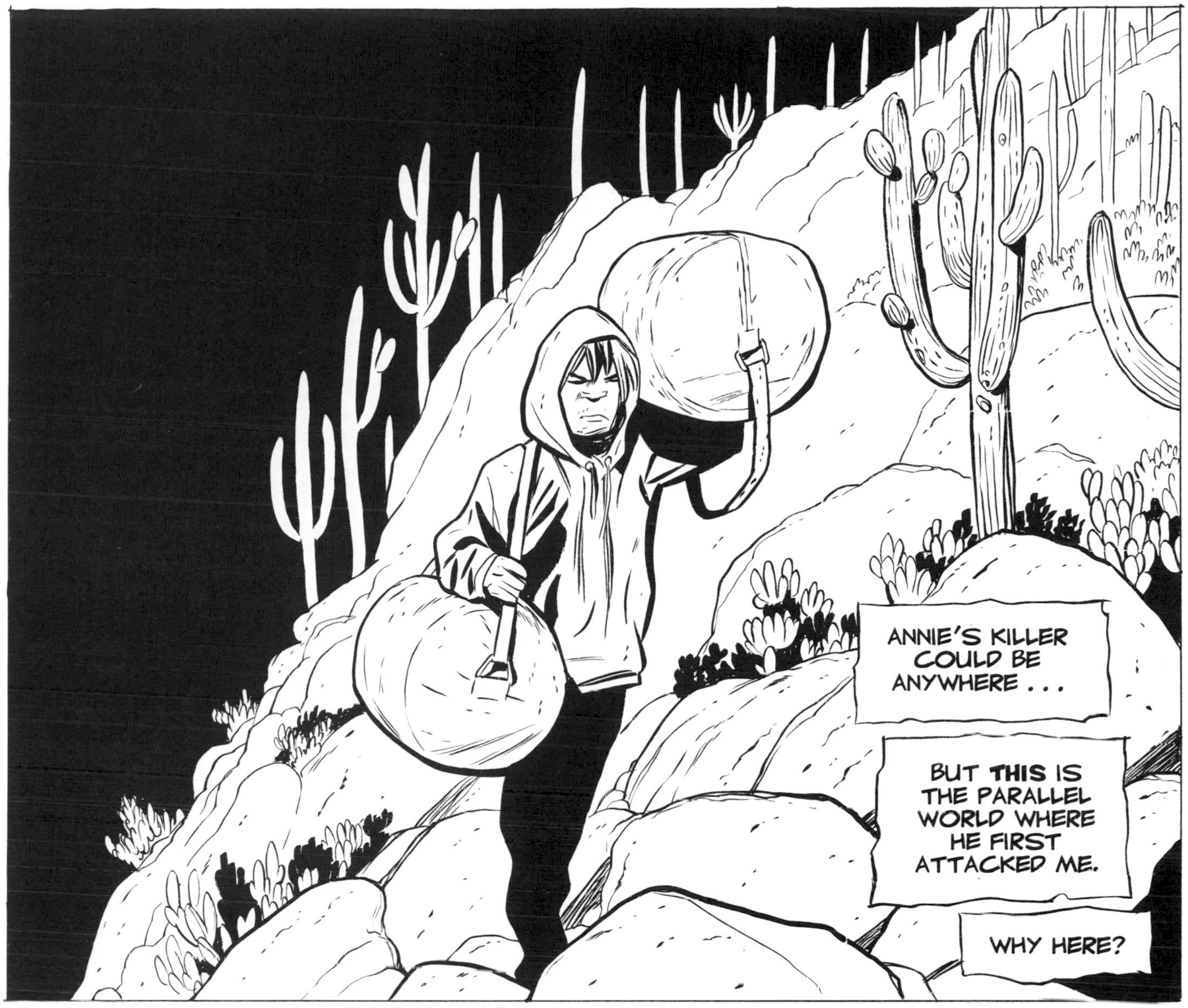
ANNIE'S KILLER COULD BE ANYWHERE . . .
BUT **THIS** IS THE PARALLEL WORLD WHERE HE FIRST ATTACKED ME.
WHY HERE?

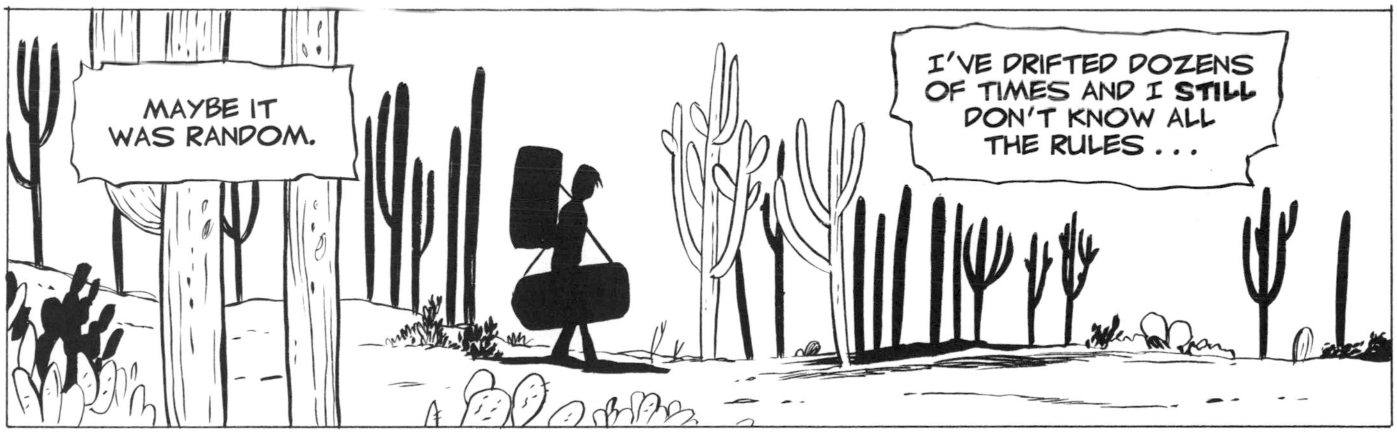
MAYBE IT WAS RANDOM.
I'VE DRIFTED DOZENS OF TIMES AND I **STILL** DON'T KNOW ALL THE RULES . . .

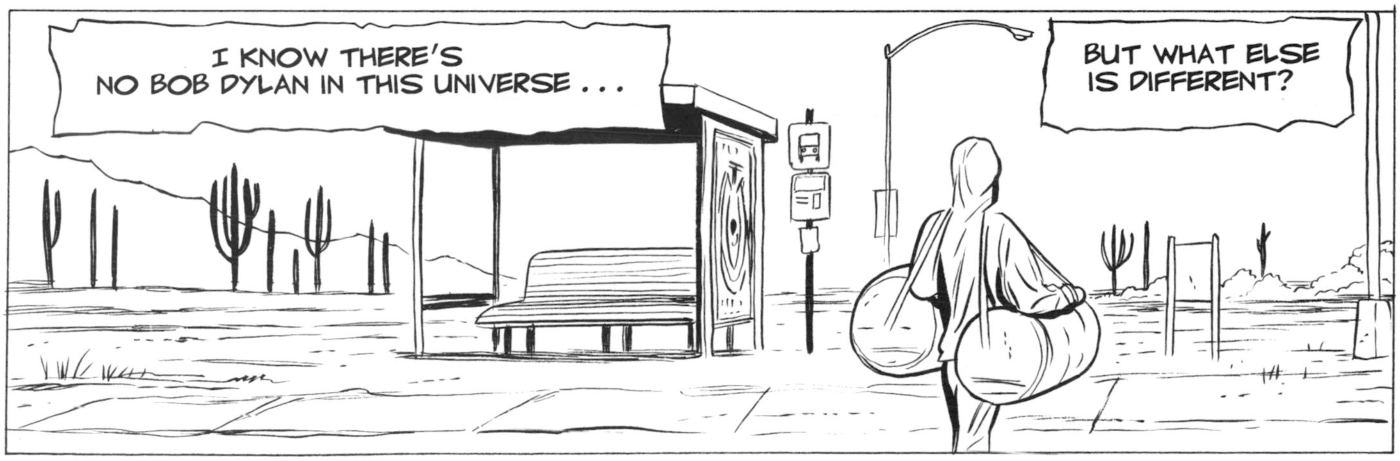
I KNOW THERE'S NO BOB DYLAN IN THIS UNIVERSE . . .
BUT WHAT ELSE IS DIFFERENT?

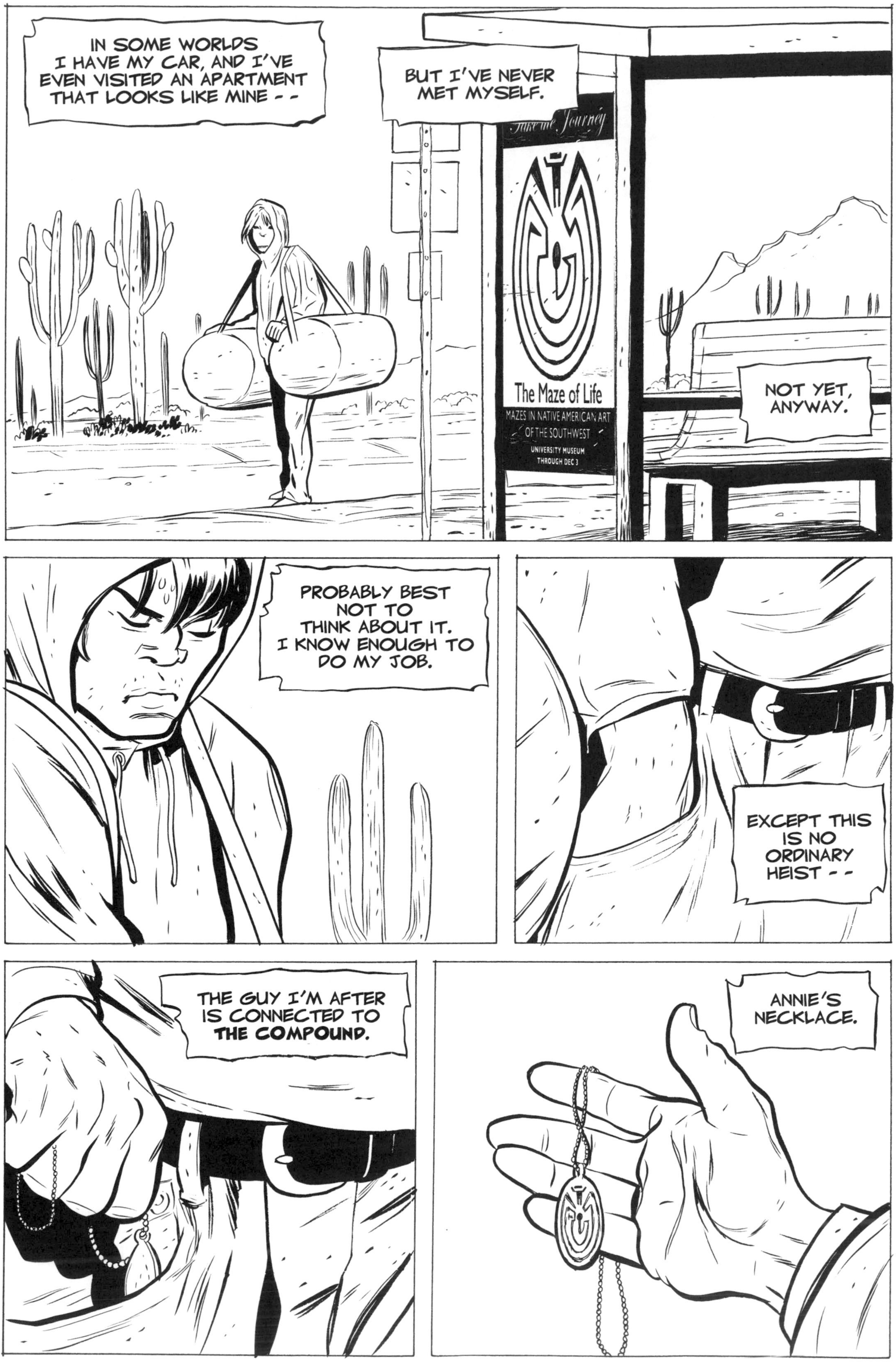

IN SOME WORLDS I HAVE MY CAR, AND I'VE EVEN VISITED AN APARTMENT THAT LOOKS LIKE MINE - -
BUT I'VE NEVER MET MYSELF.
Take the Journey
The Maze of Life
MAZES IN NATIVE AMERICAN ART OF THE SOUTHWEST
UNIVERSITY MUSEUM
THROUGH DEC 3
NOT YET, ANYWAY.
PROBABLY BEST NOT TO THINK ABOUT IT. I KNOW ENOUGH TO DO MY JOB.
EXCEPT THIS IS NO ORDINARY HEIST - -
THE GUY I'M AFTER IS CONNECTED TO **THE COMPOUND.**
ANNIE'S NECKLACE.

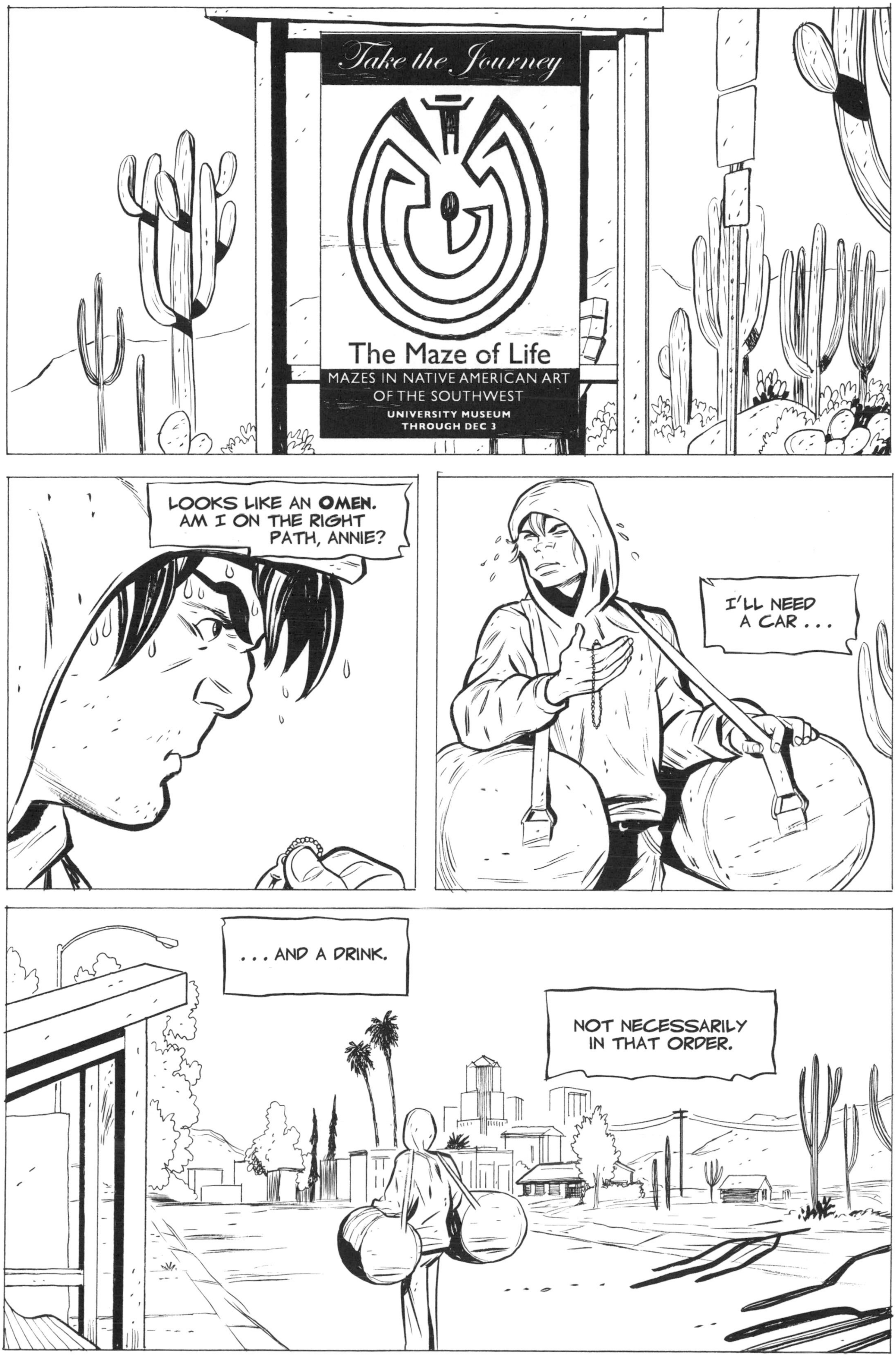

Take the Journey
The Maze of Life
MAZES IN NATIVE AMERICAN ART OF THE SOUTHWEST
UNIVERSITY MUSEUM THROUGH DEC 3
LOOKS LIKE AN OMEN. AM I ON THE RIGHT PATH, ANNIE?
I'LL NEED A CAR . . .
. . . AND A DRINK.
NOT NECESSARILY IN THAT ORDER.

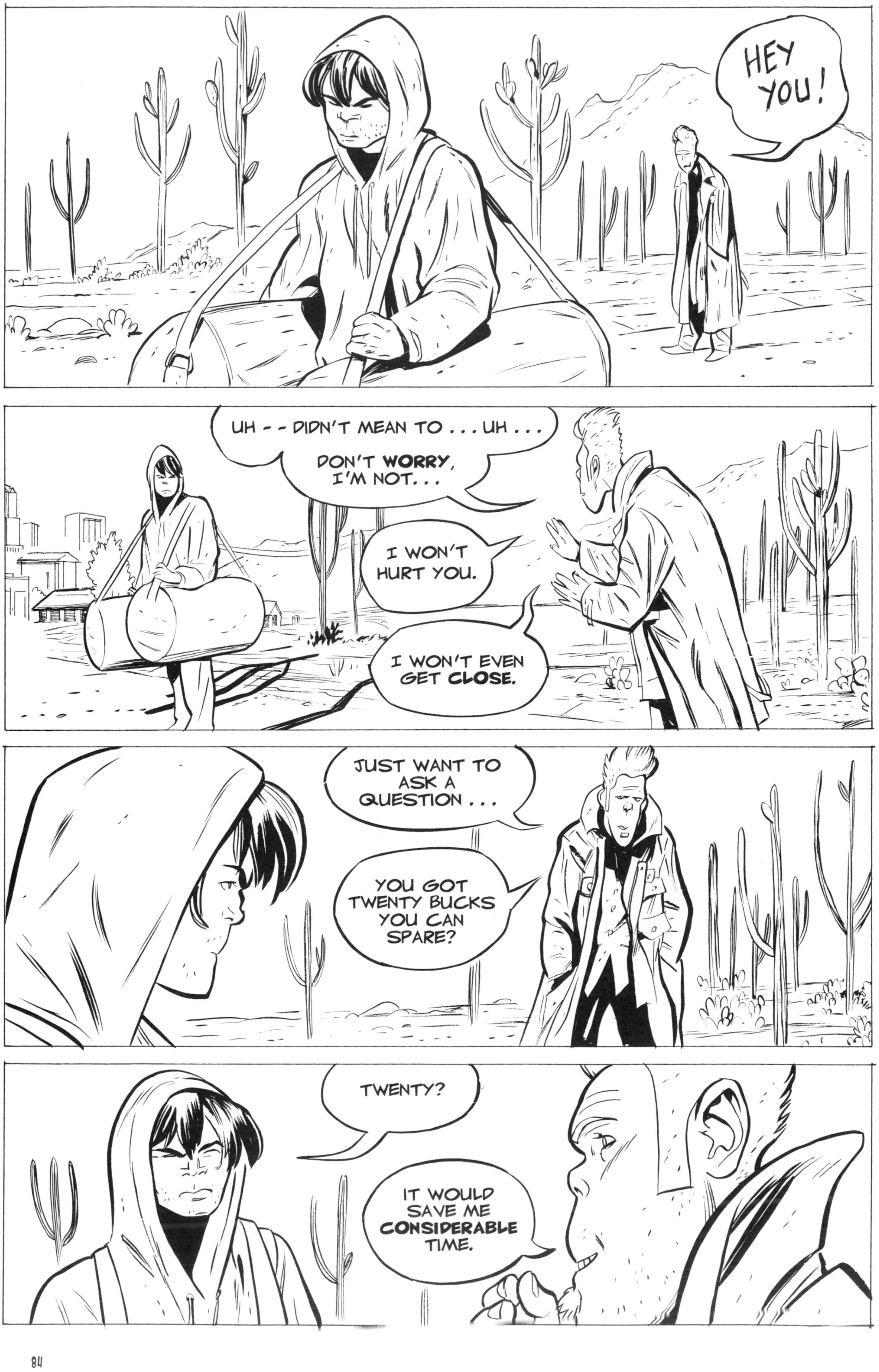
HEY YOU!
UH - - DIDN'T MEAN TO . . . UH . . .
DON'T **WORRY**, I'M NOT. . .
I WON'T HURT YOU.
I WON'T EVEN GET **CLOSE.**
JUST WANT TO ASK A QUESTION . . .
YOU GOT TWENTY BUCKS YOU CAN SPARE?
TWENTY?
IT WOULD SAVE ME **CONSIDERABLE** TIME.

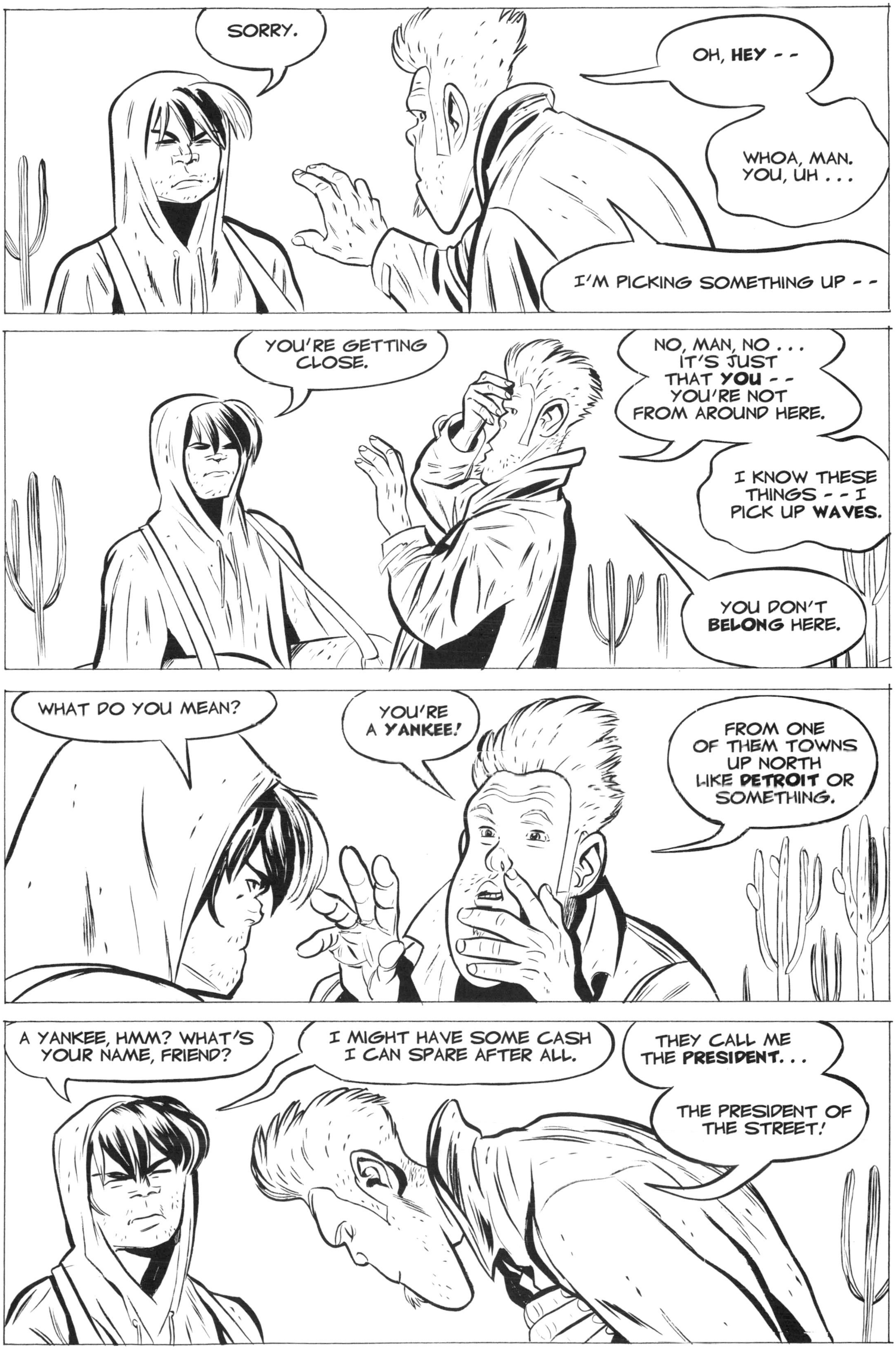
SORRY.
OH, HEY - -
WHOA, MAN. YOU, UH . . .
I'M PICKING SOMETHING UP - -
YOU'RE GETTING CLOSE.
NO, MAN, NO . . . IT'S JUST THAT YOU - - YOU'RE NOT FROM AROUND HERE.
I KNOW THESE THINGS - - I PICK UP WAVES.
YOU DON'T BELONG HERE.
WHAT DO YOU MEAN?
YOU'RE A YANKEE!
FROM ONE OF THEM TOWNS UP NORTH LIKE DETROIT OR SOMETHING.
A YANKEE, HMM? WHAT'S YOUR NAME, FRIEND?
I MIGHT HAVE SOME CASH I CAN SPARE AFTER ALL.
THEY CALL ME THE PRESIDENT. . .
THE PRESIDENT OF THE STREET!

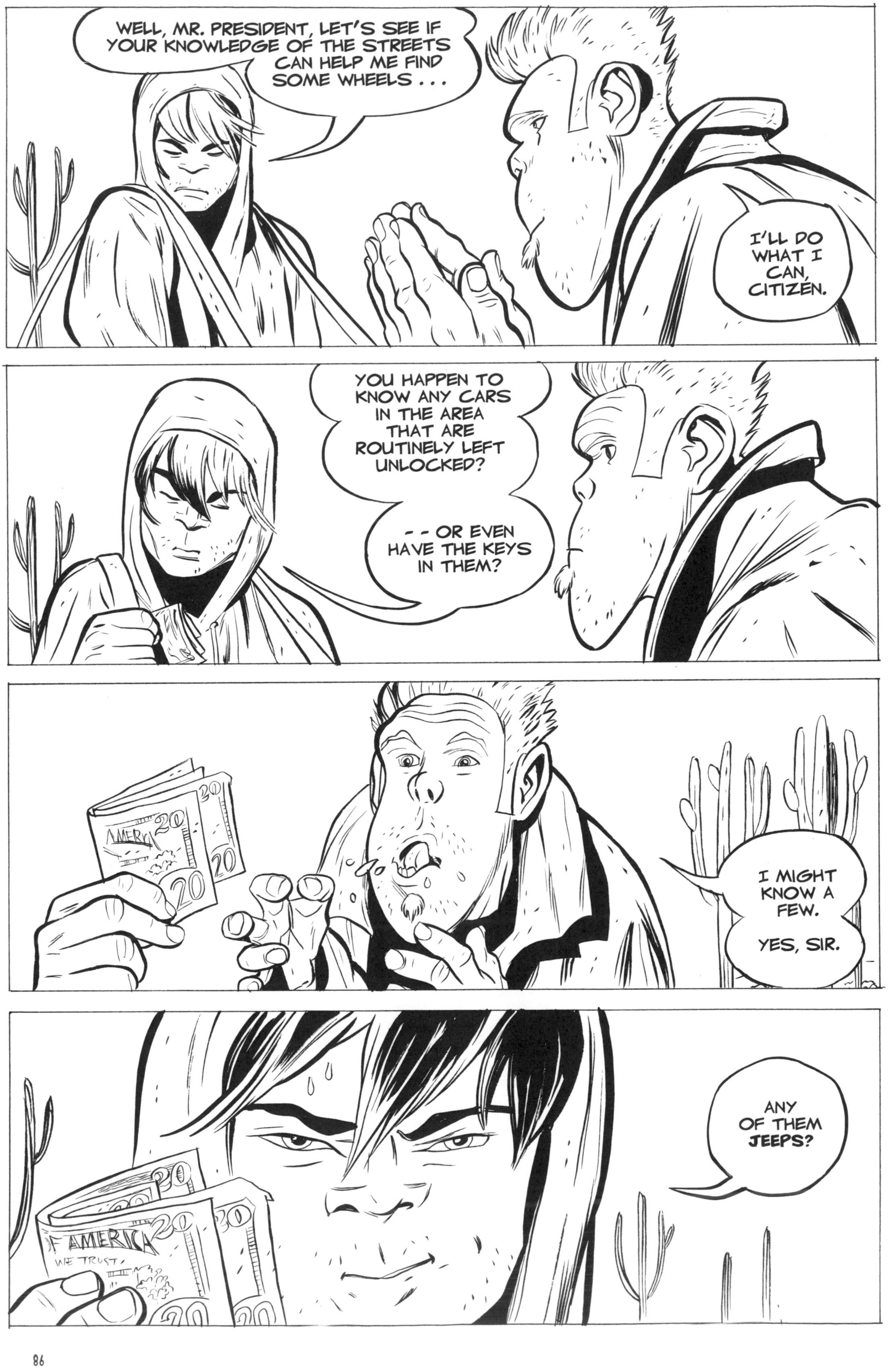
WELL, MR. PRESIDENT, LET'S SEE IF YOUR KNOWLEDGE OF THE STREETS CAN HELP ME FIND SOME WHEELS . . .
I'LL DO WHAT I CAN, CITIZEN.
YOU HAPPEN TO KNOW ANY CARS IN THE AREA THAT ARE ROUTINELY LEFT UNLOCKED?
- - OR EVEN HAVE THE KEYS IN THEM?
I MIGHT KNOW A FEW.
YES, SIR.
ANY OF THEM JEEPS?

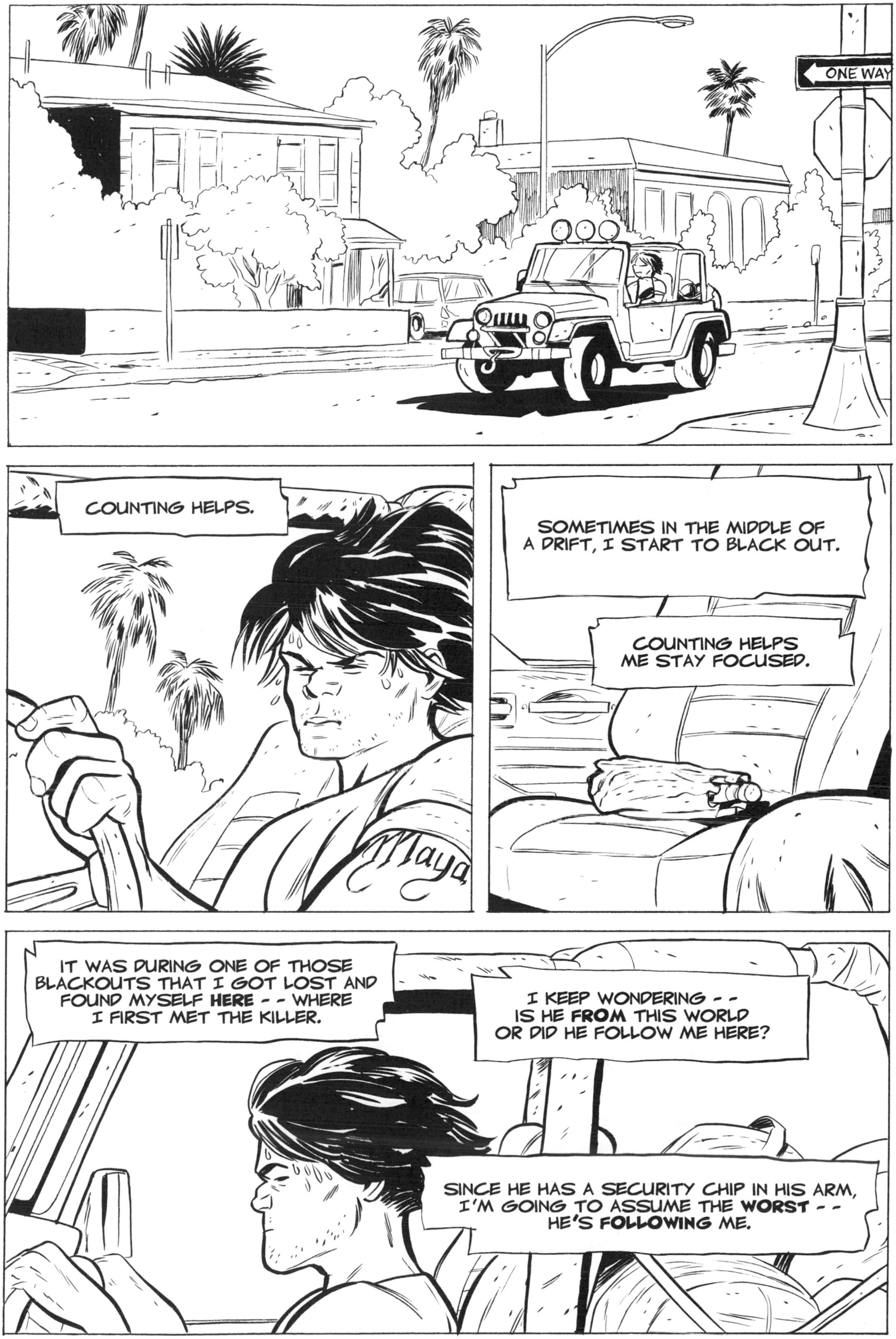
ONE WAY
COUNTING HELPS.
Maya
SOMETIMES IN THE MIDDLE OF A DRIFT, I START TO BLACK OUT.
COUNTING HELPS ME STAY FOCUSED.
IT WAS DURING ONE OF THOSE BLACKOUTS THAT I GOT LOST AND FOUND MYSELF HERE - - WHERE I FIRST MET THE KILLER.
I KEEP WONDERING - - IS HE FROM THIS WORLD OR DID HE FOLLOW ME HERE?
SINCE HE HAS A SECURITY CHIP IN HIS ARM, I'M GOING TO ASSUME THE WORST - - HE'S FOLLOWING ME.

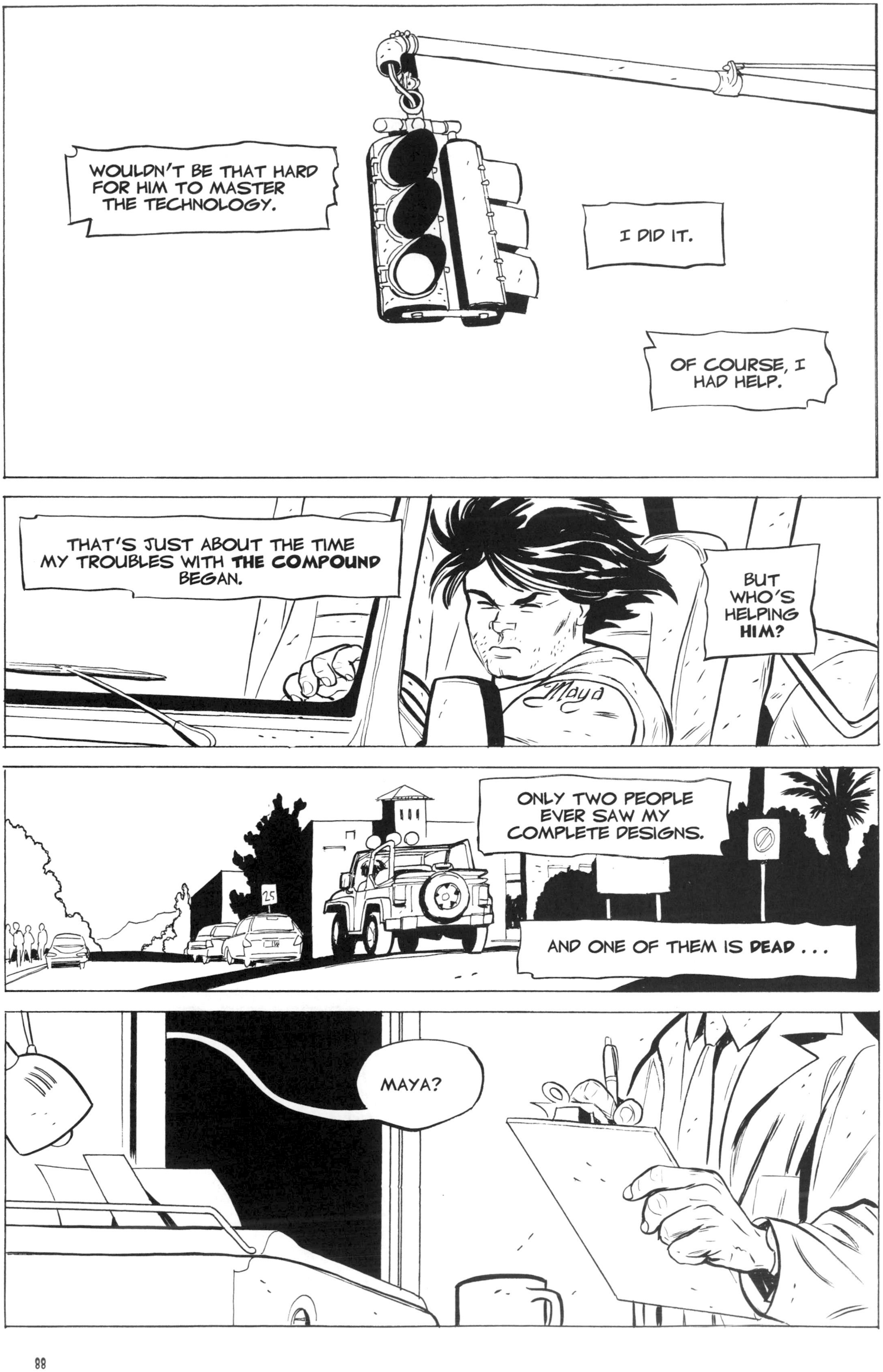
WOULDN'T BE THAT HARD FOR HIM TO MASTER THE TECHNOLOGY.
I DID IT.
OF COURSE, I HAD HELP.
THAT'S JUST ABOUT THE TIME MY TROUBLES WITH **THE COMPOUND** BEGAN.
BUT WHO'S HELPING **HIM?**
Maya
ONLY TWO PEOPLE EVER SAW MY COMPLETE DESIGNS.
25
AND ONE OF THEM IS **DEAD** . . .
MAYA?

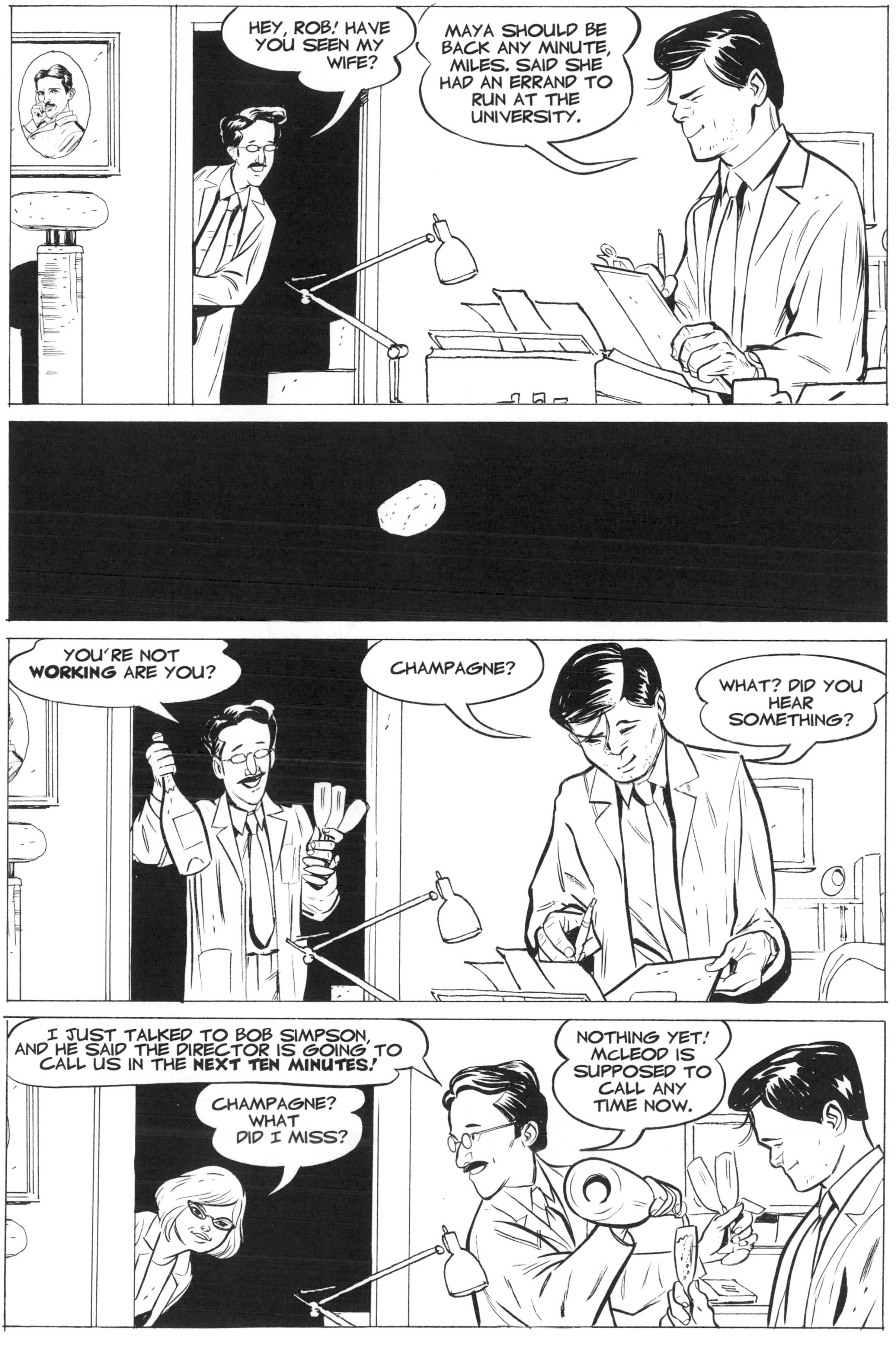
HEY, ROB! HAVE YOU SEEN MY WIFE?
MAYA SHOULD BE BACK ANY MINUTE, MILES. SAID SHE HAD AN ERRAND TO RUN AT THE UNIVERSITY.
YOU'RE NOT **WORKING** ARE YOU?
CHAMPAGNE?
WHAT? DID YOU HEAR SOMETHING?
I JUST TALKED TO BOB SIMPSON, AND HE SAID THE DIRECTOR IS GOING TO CALL US IN THE **NEXT TEN MINUTES!**
CHAMPAGNE? WHAT DID I MISS?
NOTHING YET! McLEOD IS SUPPOSED TO CALL ANY TIME NOW.

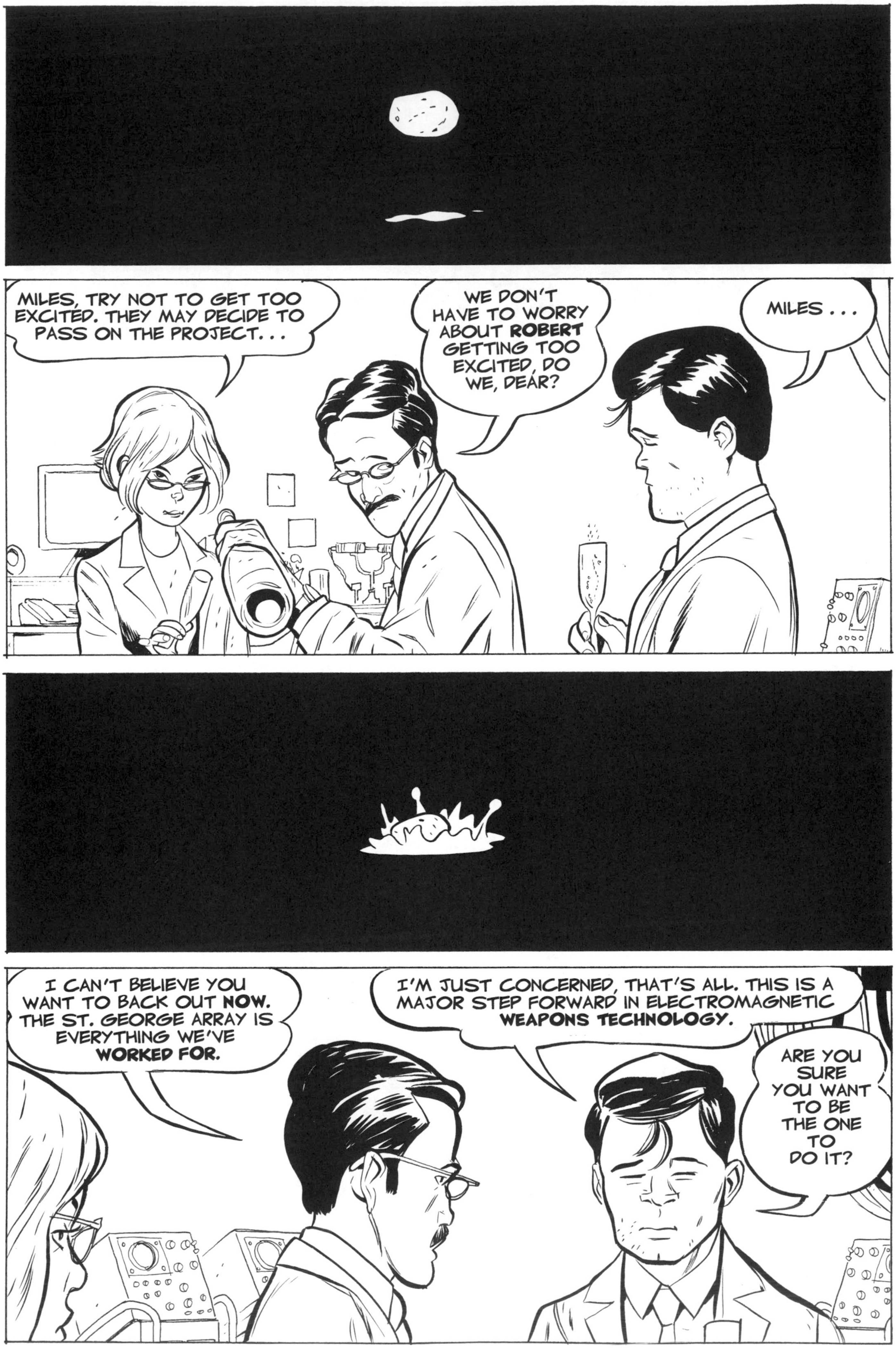
MILES, TRY NOT TO GET TOO EXCITED. THEY MAY DECIDE TO PASS ON THE PROJECT...
WE DON'T HAVE TO WORRY ABOUT **ROBERT** GETTING TOO EXCITED, DO WE, DEAR?
MILES...
I CAN'T BELIEVE YOU WANT TO BACK OUT **NOW**. THE ST. GEORGE ARRAY IS EVERYTHING WE'VE **WORKED FOR.**
I'M JUST CONCERNED, THAT'S ALL. THIS IS A MAJOR STEP FORWARD IN ELECTROMAGNETIC **WEAPONS TECHNOLOGY.**
ARE YOU SURE YOU WANT TO BE THE ONE TO DO IT?

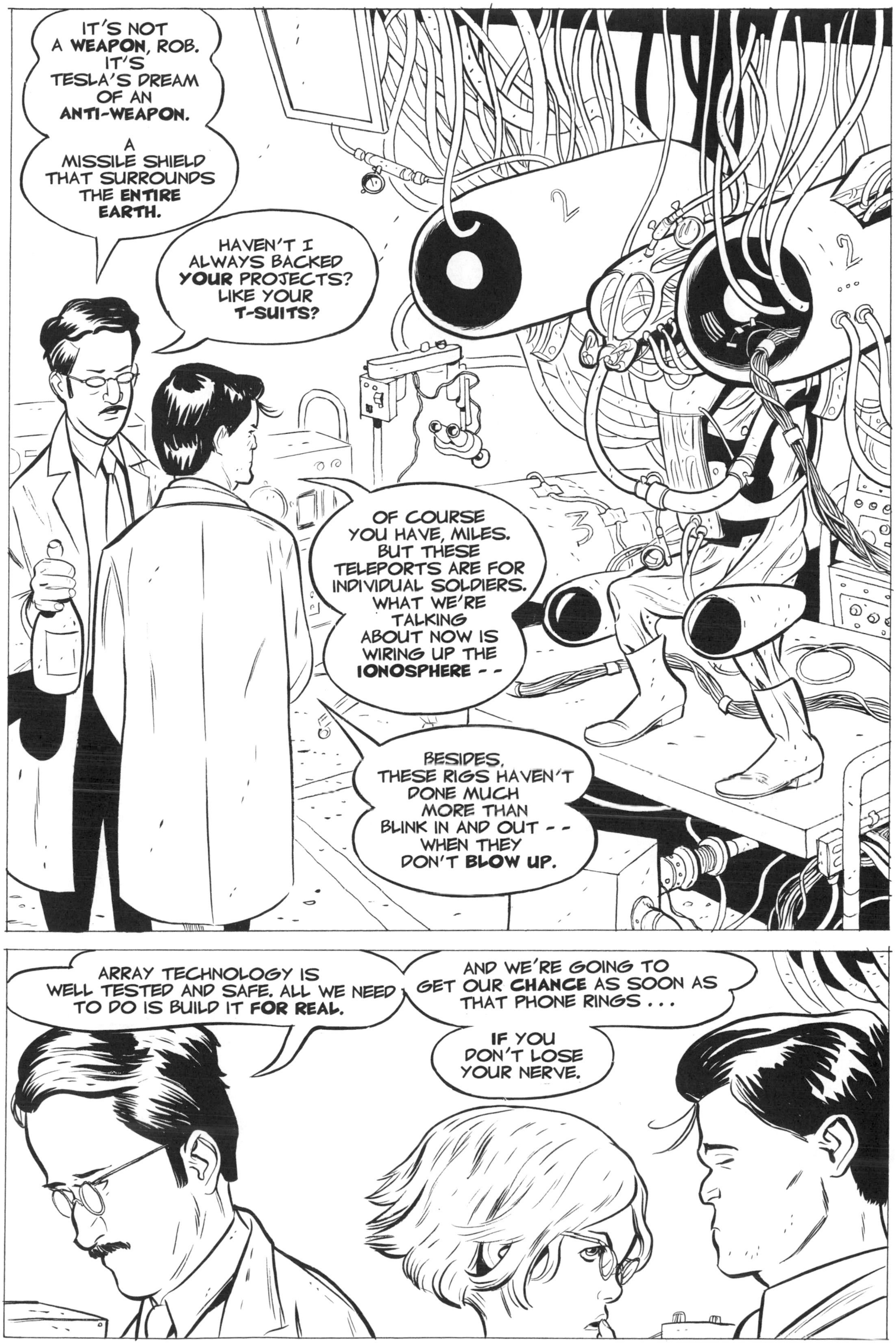
IT'S NOT A WEAPON, ROB. IT'S TESLA'S DREAM OF AN ANTI-WEAPON.
A MISSILE SHIELD THAT SURROUNDS THE ENTIRE EARTH.
HAVEN'T I ALWAYS BACKED YOUR PROJECTS? LIKE YOUR T-SUITS?
OF COURSE YOU HAVE, MILES. BUT THESE TELEPORTS ARE FOR INDIVIDUAL SOLDIERS. WHAT WE'RE TALKING ABOUT NOW IS WIRING UP THE IONOSPHERE - -
BESIDES, THESE RIGS HAVEN'T DONE MUCH MORE THAN BLINK IN AND OUT - - WHEN THEY DON'T BLOW UP.
ARRAY TECHNOLOGY IS WELL TESTED AND SAFE. ALL WE NEED TO DO IS BUILD IT FOR REAL.
AND WE'RE GOING TO GET OUR CHANCE AS SOON AS THAT PHONE RINGS . . .
IF YOU DON'T LOSE YOUR NERVE.

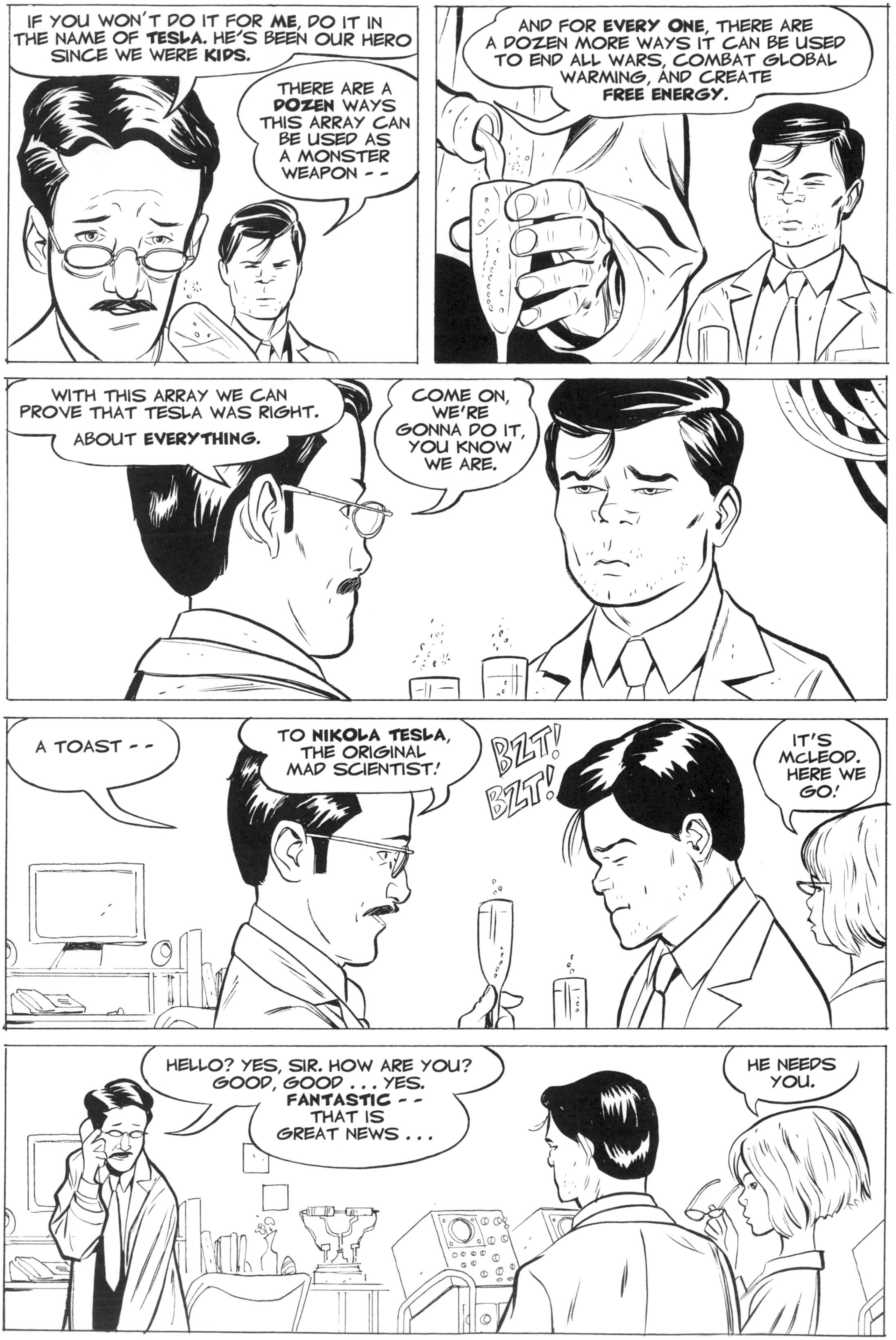
IF YOU WON'T DO IT FOR ME, DO IT IN THE NAME OF TESLA. HE'S BEEN OUR HERO SINCE WE WERE KIDS.
THERE ARE A DOZEN WAYS THIS ARRAY CAN BE USED AS A MONSTER WEAPON --
AND FOR EVERY ONE, THERE ARE A DOZEN MORE WAYS IT CAN BE USED TO END ALL WARS, COMBAT GLOBAL WARMING, AND CREATE FREE ENERGY.
WITH THIS ARRAY WE CAN PROVE THAT TESLA WAS RIGHT.
ABOUT EVERYTHING.
COME ON, WE'RE GONNA DO IT, YOU KNOW WE ARE.
A TOAST --
TO NIKOLA TESLA, THE ORIGINAL MAD SCIENTIST!
BZT! BZT!
IT'S McLEOD. HERE WE GO!
HELLO? YES, SIR. HOW ARE YOU? GOOD, GOOD . . . YES. FANTASTIC -- THAT IS GREAT NEWS . . .
HE NEEDS YOU.

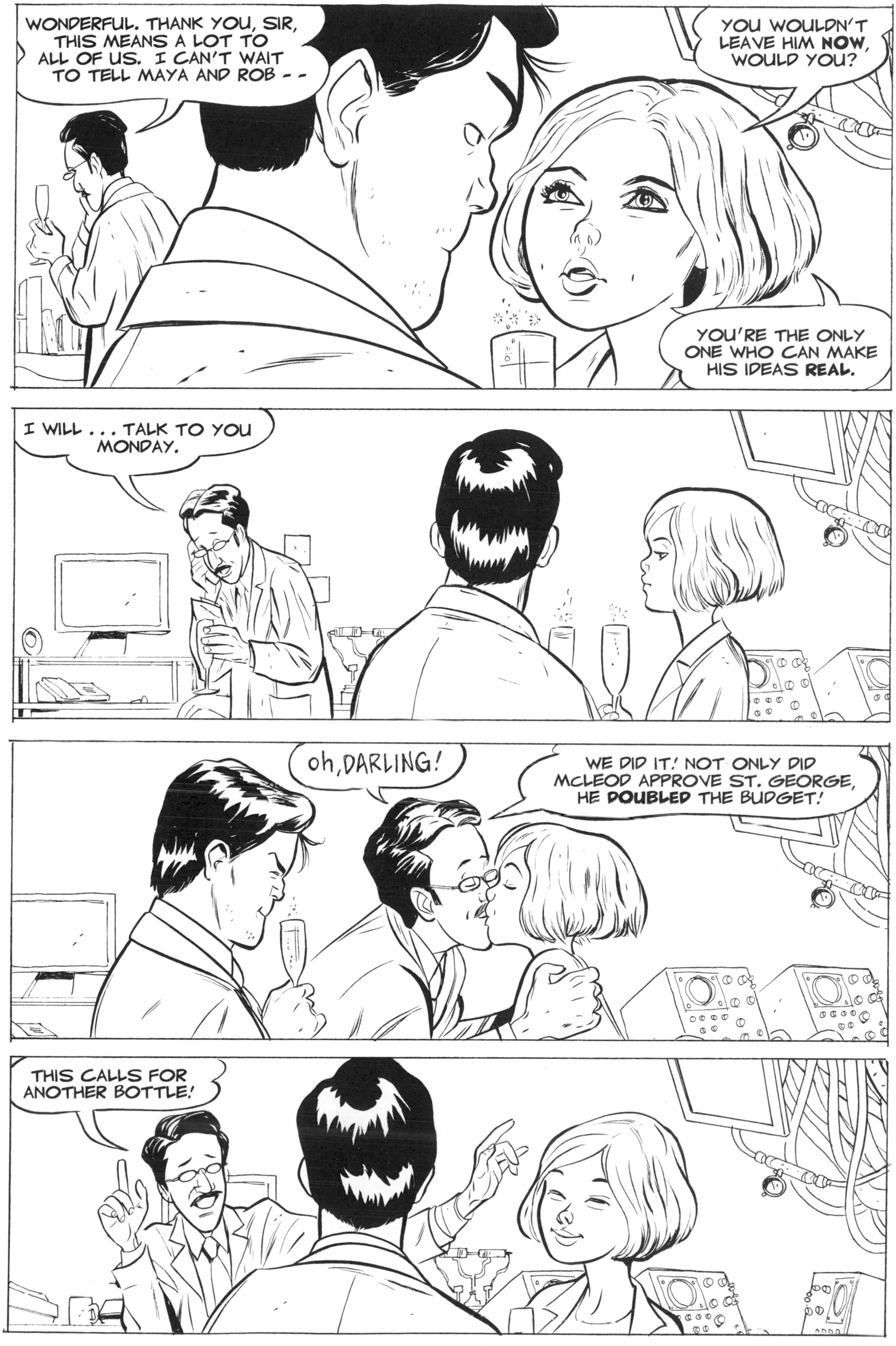
WONDERFUL. THANK YOU, SIR, THIS MEANS A LOT TO ALL OF US. I CAN'T WAIT TO TELL MAYA AND ROB - -
YOU WOULDN'T LEAVE HIM NOW, WOULD YOU?
YOU'RE THE ONLY ONE WHO CAN MAKE HIS IDEAS REAL.
I WILL . . . TALK TO YOU MONDAY.
oh, DARLING!
WE DID IT! NOT ONLY DID McLEOD APPROVE ST. GEORGE, HE DOUBLED THE BUDGET!
THIS CALLS FOR ANOTHER BOTTLE!

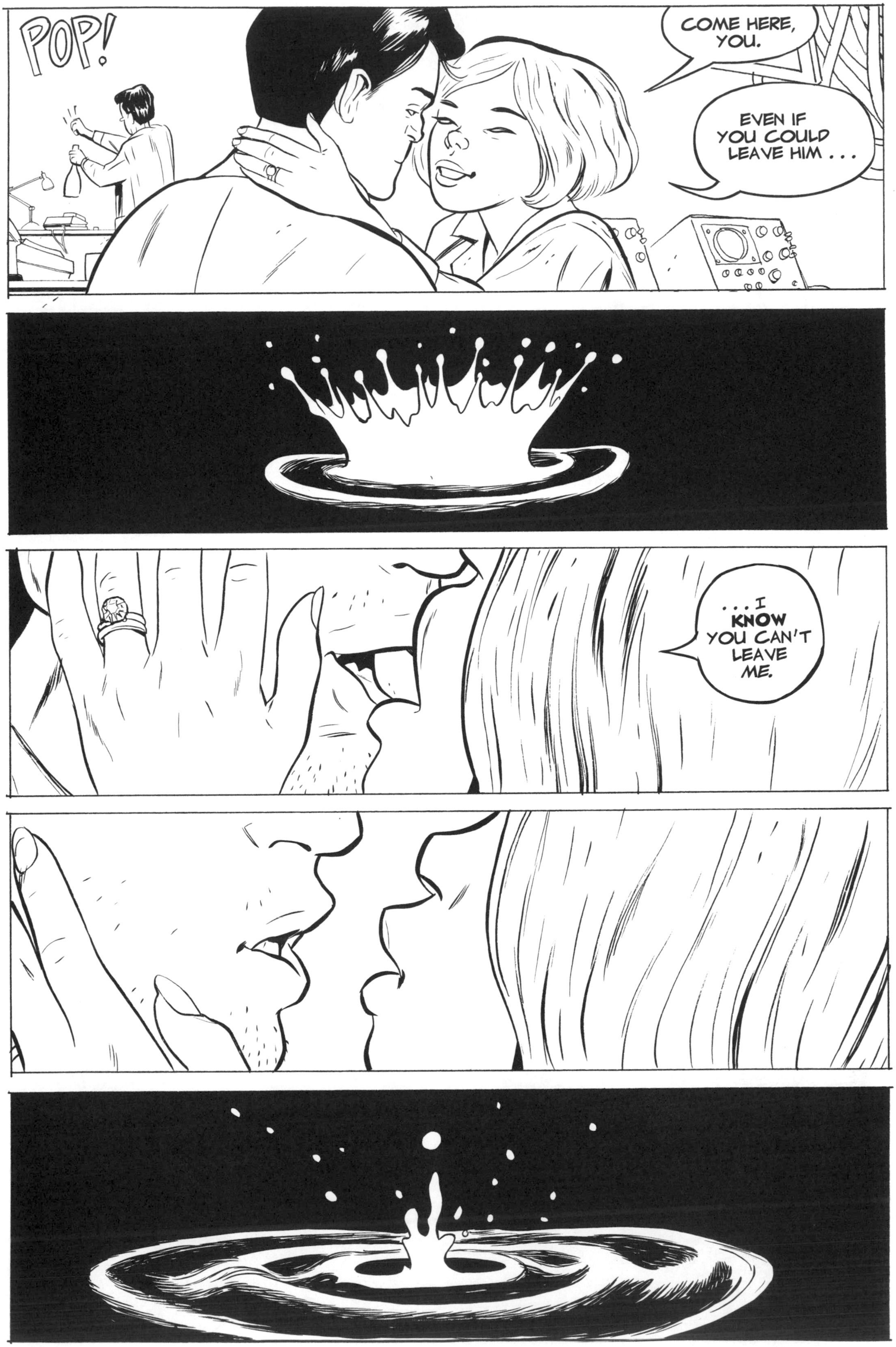
POP!
COME HERE, YOU.
EVEN IF YOU COULD LEAVE HIM . . .
. . . I KNOW YOU CAN'T LEAVE ME.

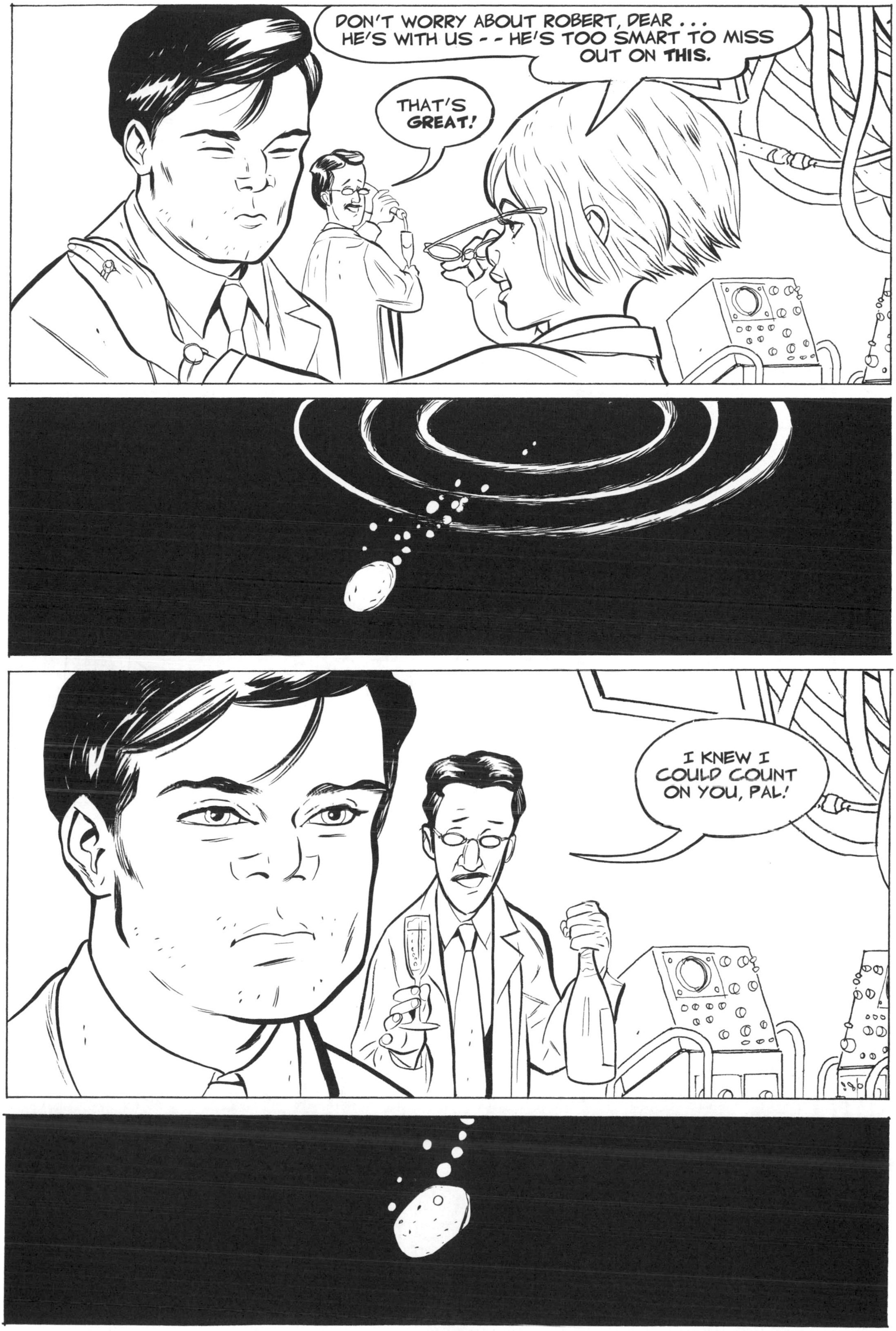
DON'T WORRY ABOUT ROBERT, DEAR . . . HE'S WITH US - - HE'S TOO SMART TO MISS OUT ON THIS.
THAT'S GREAT!
I KNEW I COULD COUNT ON YOU, PAL!

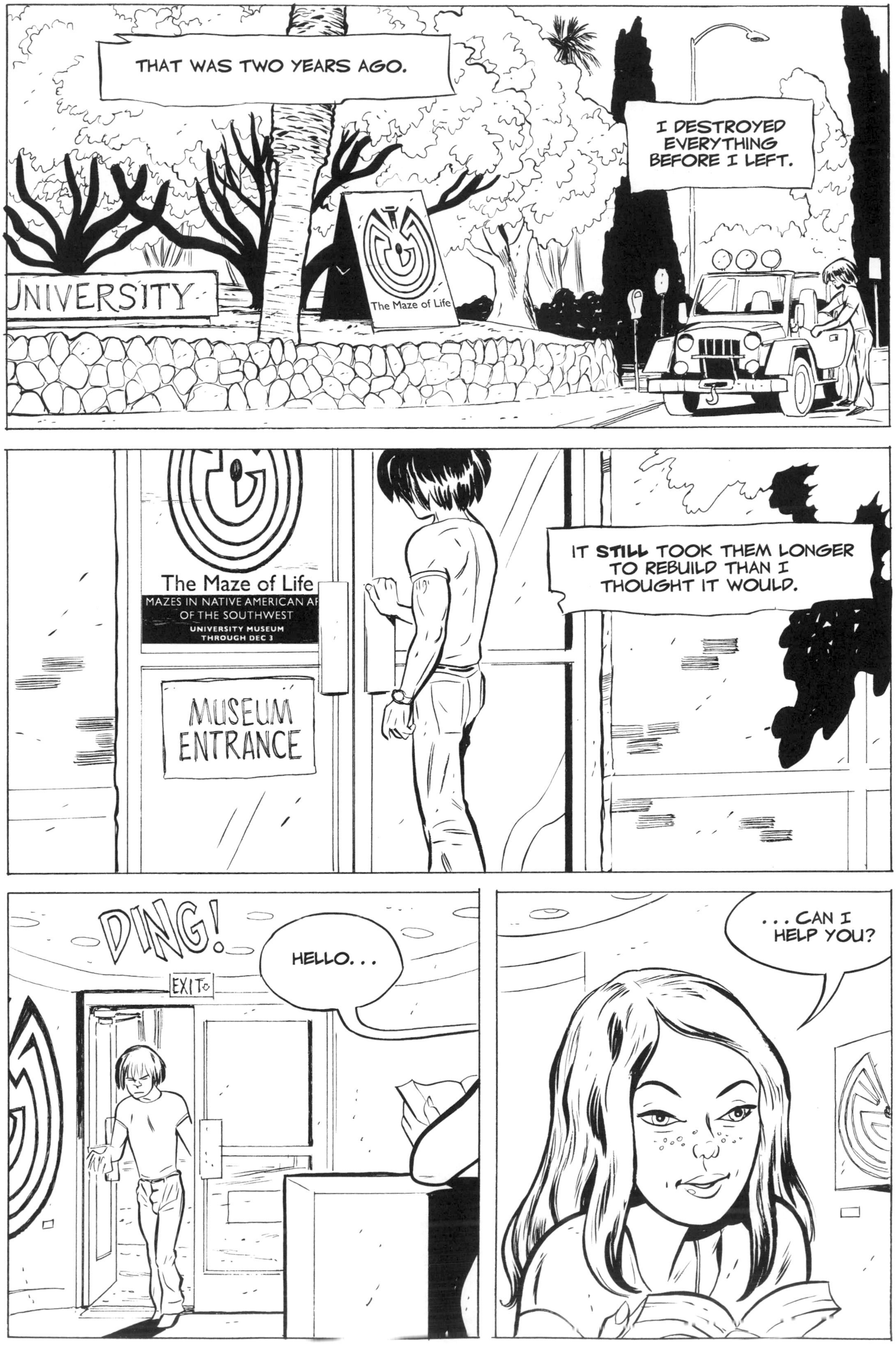
THAT WAS TWO YEARS AGO.
I DESTROYED EVERYTHING BEFORE I LEFT.
UNIVERSITY
The Maze of Life
IT STILL TOOK THEM LONGER TO REBUILD THAN I THOUGHT IT WOULD.
The Maze of Life
MAZES IN NATIVE AMERICAN A
OF THE SOUTHWEST
UNIVERSITY MUSEUM
THROUGH DEC 3
MUSEUM ENTRANCE
DING!
EXIT
HELLO...
...CAN I HELP YOU?

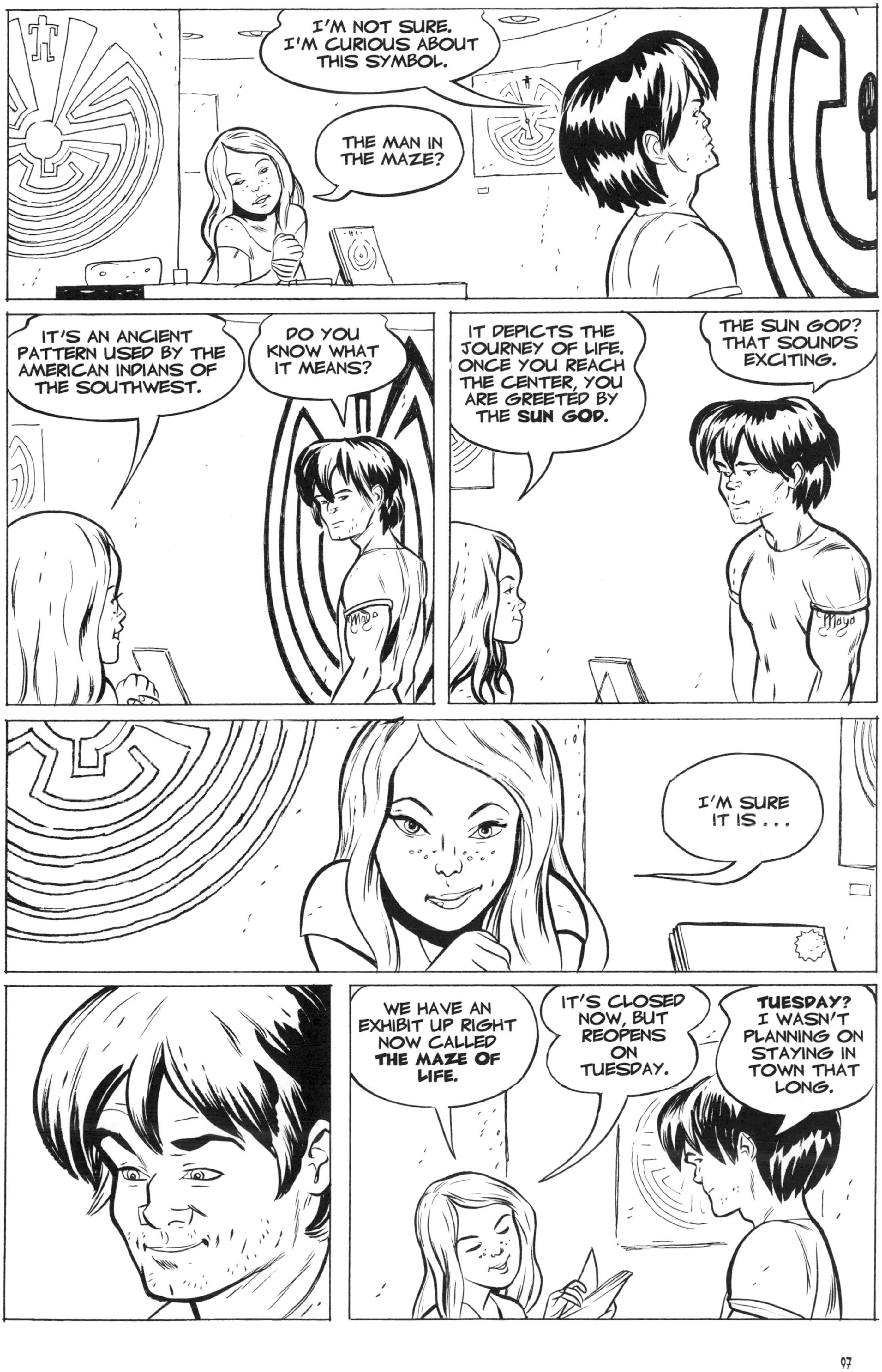

I'M NOT SURE. I'M CURIOUS ABOUT THIS SYMBOL.
THE MAN IN THE MAZE?
IT'S AN ANCIENT PATTERN USED BY THE AMERICAN INDIANS OF THE SOUTHWEST.
DO YOU KNOW WHAT IT MEANS?
IT DEPICTS THE JOURNEY OF LIFE. ONCE YOU REACH THE CENTER, YOU ARE GREETED BY THE **SUN GOD**.
THE SUN GOD? THAT SOUNDS EXCITING.
Maya
I'M SURE IT IS . . .
WE HAVE AN EXHIBIT UP RIGHT NOW CALLED **THE MAZE OF LIFE**.
IT'S CLOSED NOW, BUT REOPENS ON TUESDAY.
TUESDAY? I WASN'T PLANNING ON STAYING IN TOWN THAT LONG.

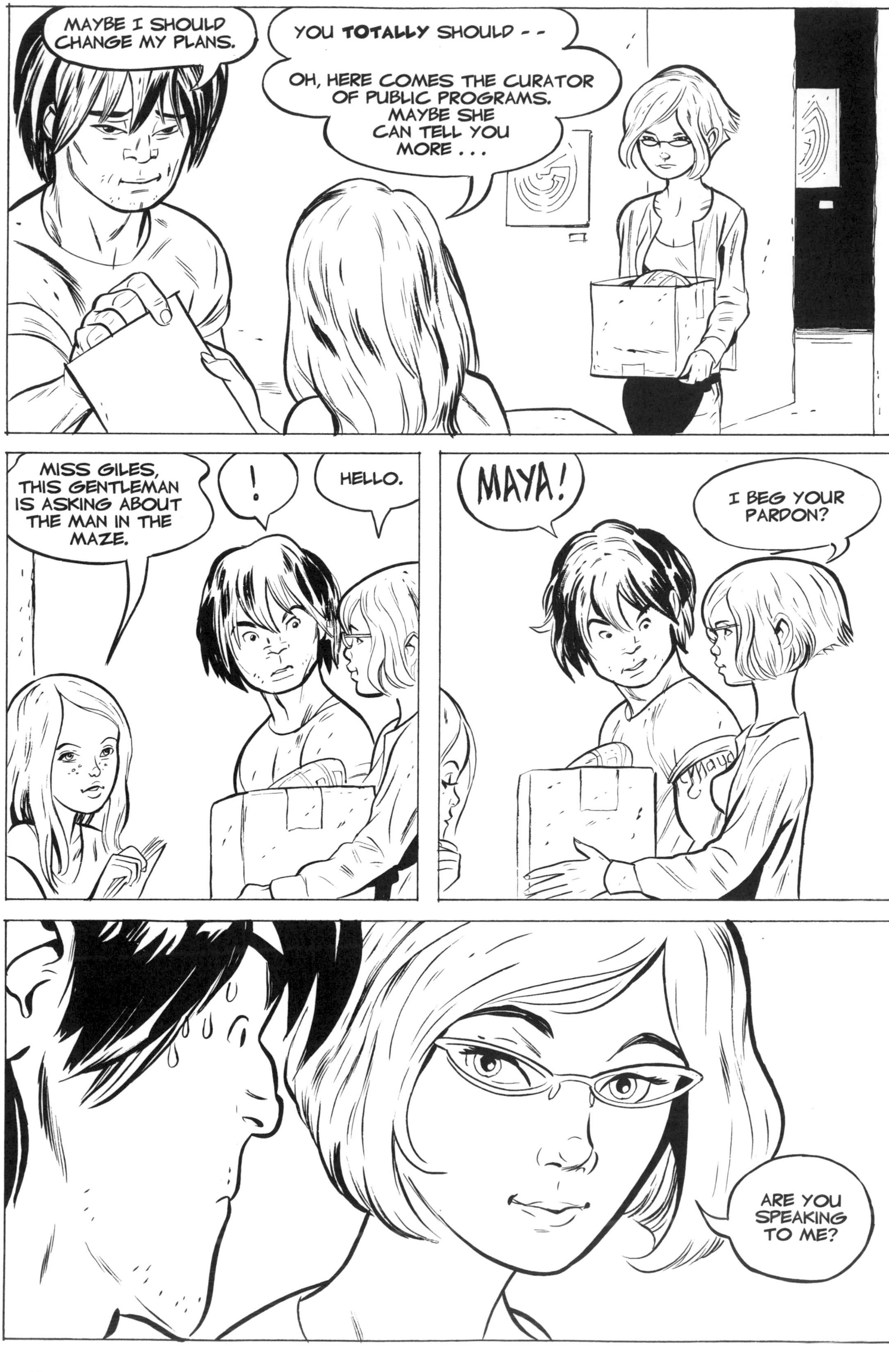
MAYBE I SHOULD CHANGE MY PLANS.
YOU TOTALLY SHOULD - -
OH, HERE COMES THE CURATOR OF PUBLIC PROGRAMS. MAYBE SHE CAN TELL YOU MORE . . .
MISS GILES, THIS GENTLEMAN IS ASKING ABOUT THE MAN IN THE MAZE.
!
HELLO.
MAYA!
I BEG YOUR PARDON?
Maya
ARE YOU SPEAKING TO ME?

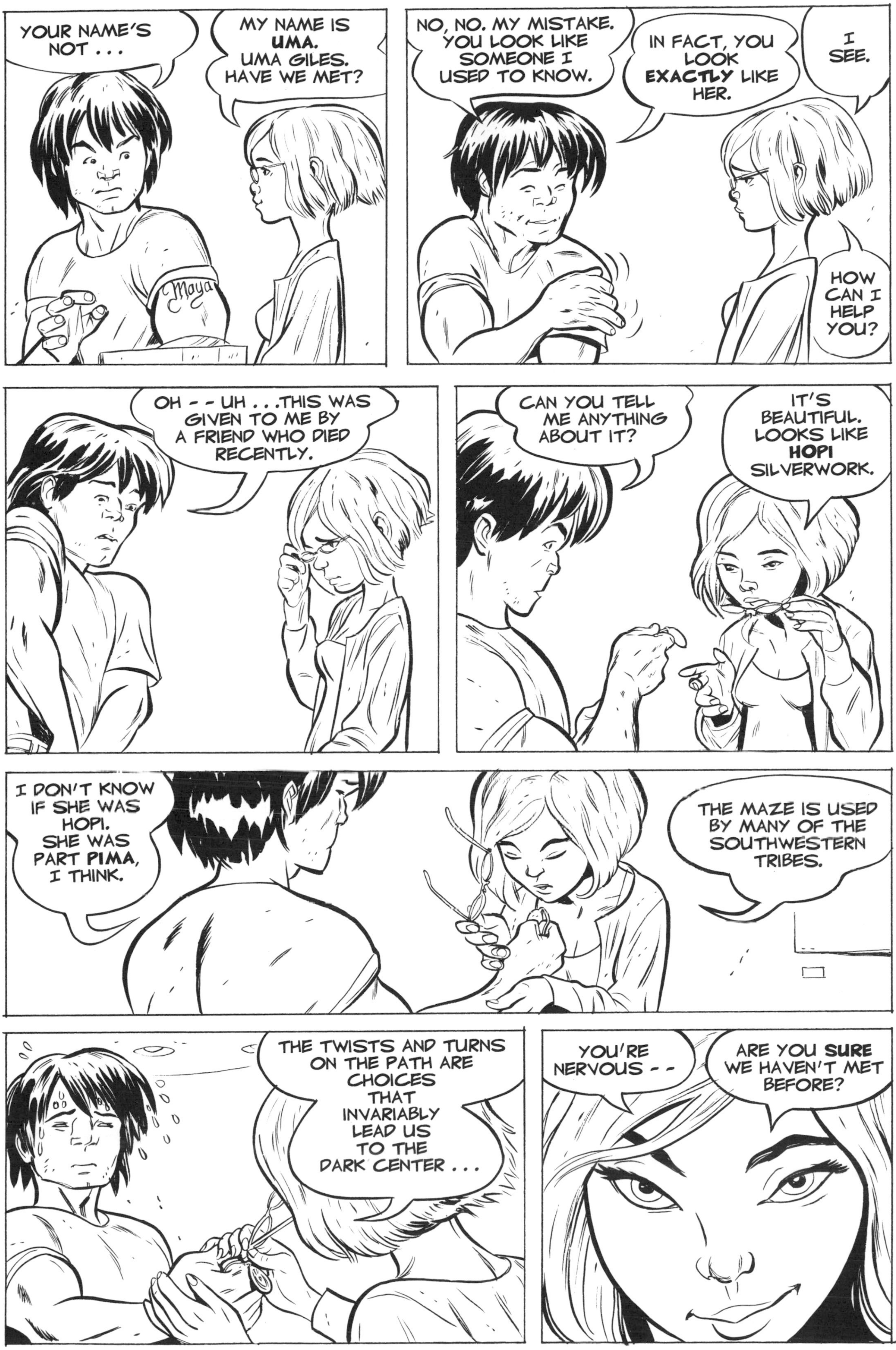
YOUR NAME'S NOT . . .
MY NAME IS UMA. UMA GILES. HAVE WE MET?
NO, NO. MY MISTAKE. YOU LOOK LIKE SOMEONE I USED TO KNOW.
IN FACT, YOU LOOK EXACTLY LIKE HER.
I SEE.
HOW CAN I HELP YOU?
Maya
OH - - UH . . . THIS WAS GIVEN TO ME BY A FRIEND WHO DIED RECENTLY.
CAN YOU TELL ME ANYTHING ABOUT IT?
IT'S BEAUTIFUL. LOOKS LIKE HOPI SILVERWORK.
I DON'T KNOW IF SHE WAS HOPI. SHE WAS PART PIMA, I THINK.
THE MAZE IS USED BY MANY OF THE SOUTHWESTERN TRIBES.
THE TWISTS AND TURNS ON THE PATH ARE CHOICES THAT INVARIABLY LEAD US TO THE DARK CENTER . . .
YOU'RE NERVOUS - -
ARE YOU SURE WE HAVEN'T MET BEFORE?

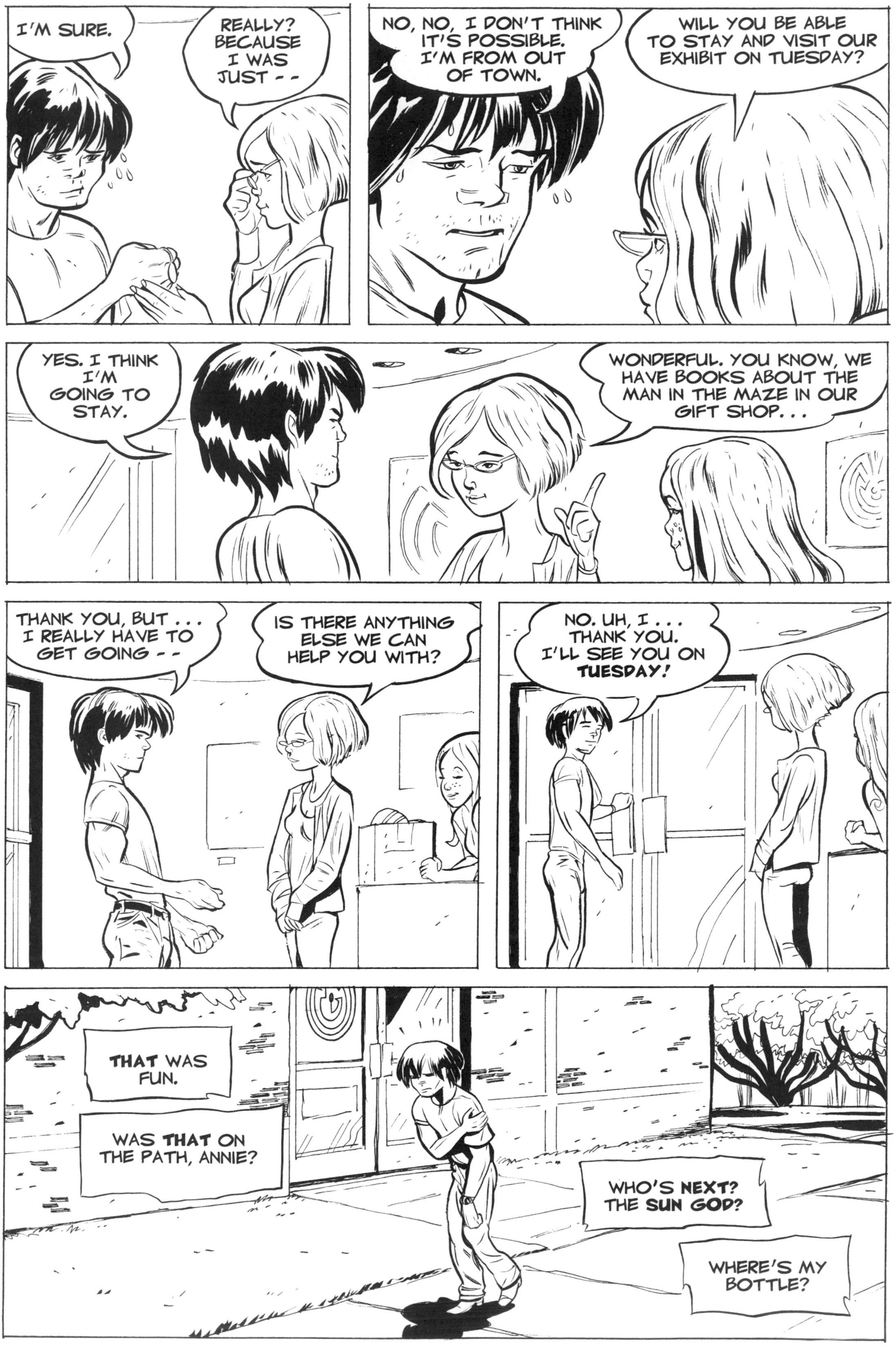
I'M SURE.
REALLY? BECAUSE I WAS JUST --
NO, NO, I DON'T THINK IT'S POSSIBLE. I'M FROM OUT OF TOWN.
WILL YOU BE ABLE TO STAY AND VISIT OUR EXHIBIT ON TUESDAY?
YES. I THINK I'M GOING TO STAY.
WONDERFUL. YOU KNOW, WE HAVE BOOKS ABOUT THE MAN IN THE MAZE IN OUR GIFT SHOP...
THANK YOU, BUT ... I REALLY HAVE TO GET GOING --
IS THERE ANYTHING ELSE WE CAN HELP YOU WITH?
NO. UH, I ... THANK YOU. I'LL SEE YOU ON TUESDAY!
THAT WAS FUN.
WAS THAT ON THE PATH, ANNIE?
WHO'S NEXT? THE SUN GOD?
WHERE'S MY BOTTLE?

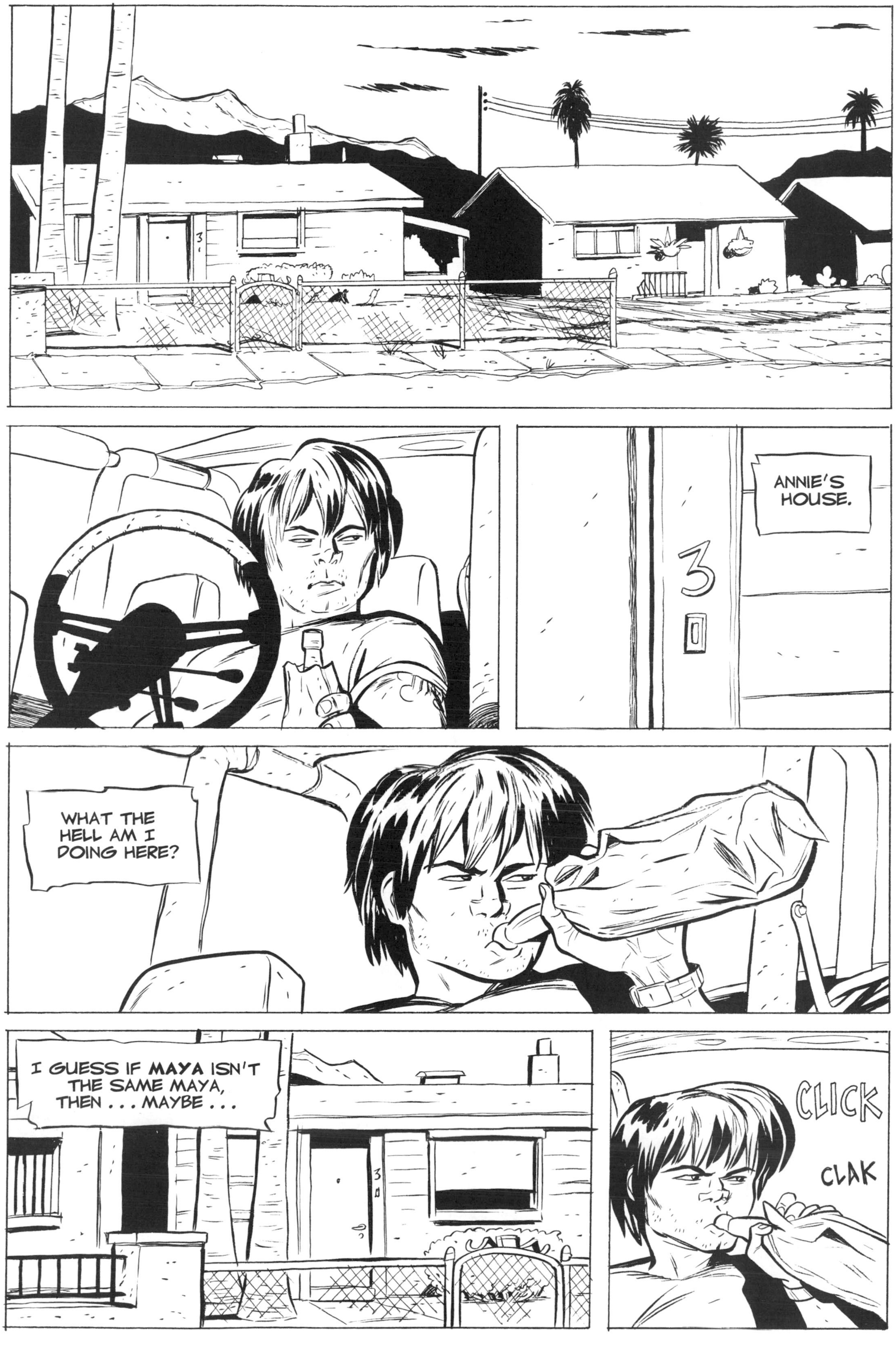
ANNIE'S HOUSE.
WHAT THE HELL AM I DOING HERE?
I GUESS IF MAYA ISN'T THE SAME MAYA, THEN . . . MAYBE . . .
CLICK
CLAK

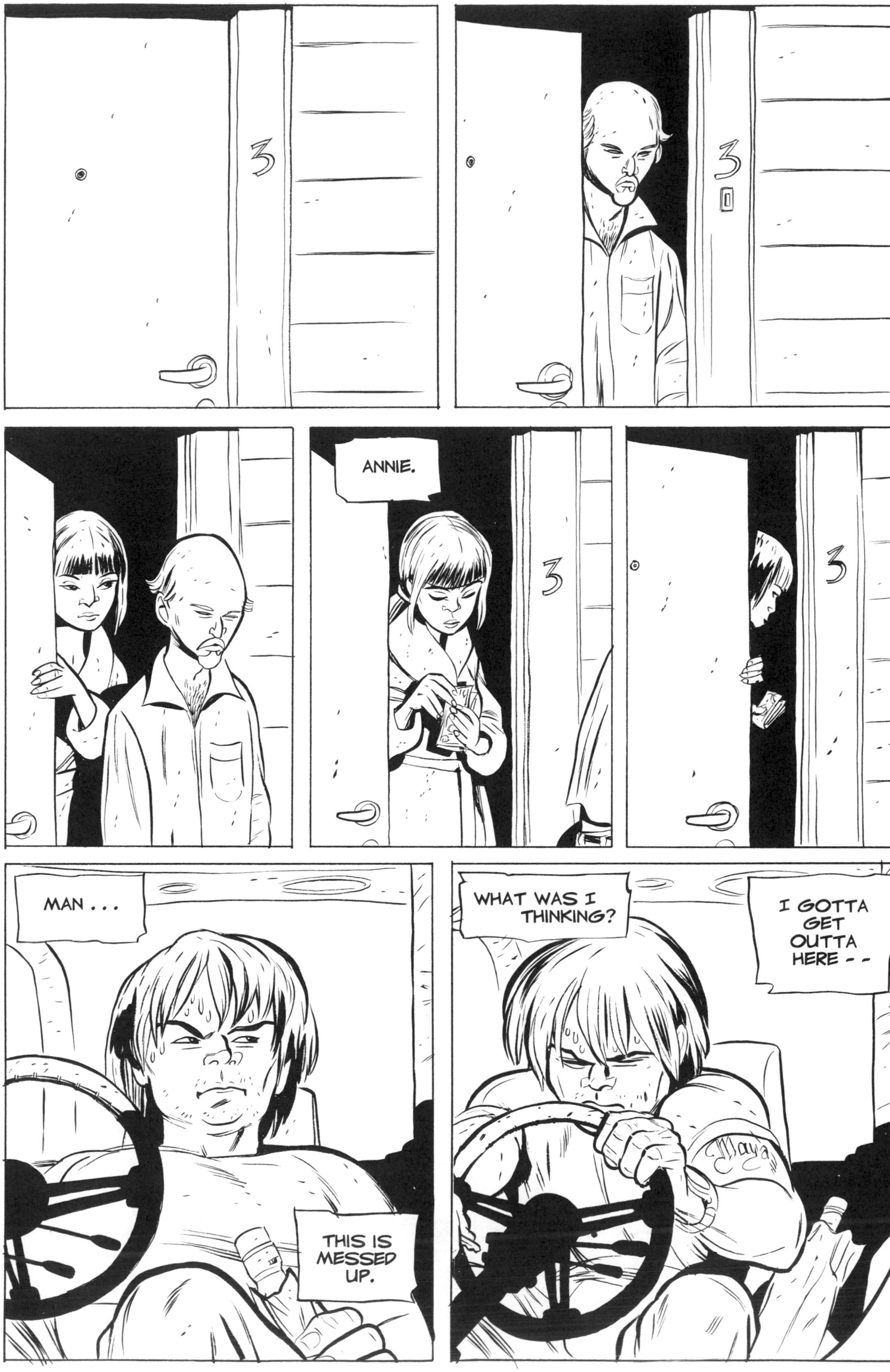
ANNIE.
MAN . . .
THIS IS MESSED UP.
WHAT WAS I THINKING?
I GOTTA GET OUTTA HERE - -

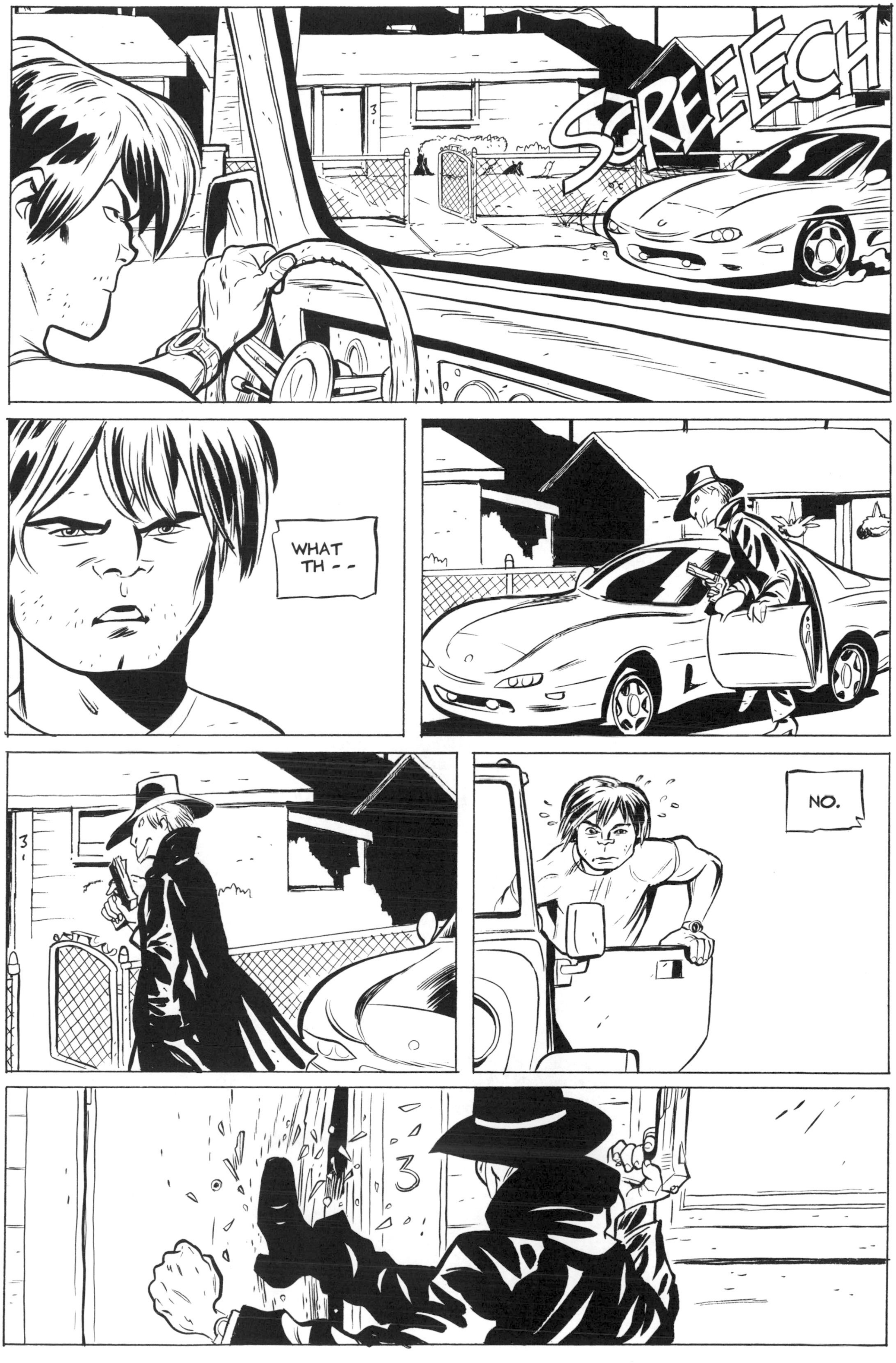
SCREEECH
WHAT TH --
NO.

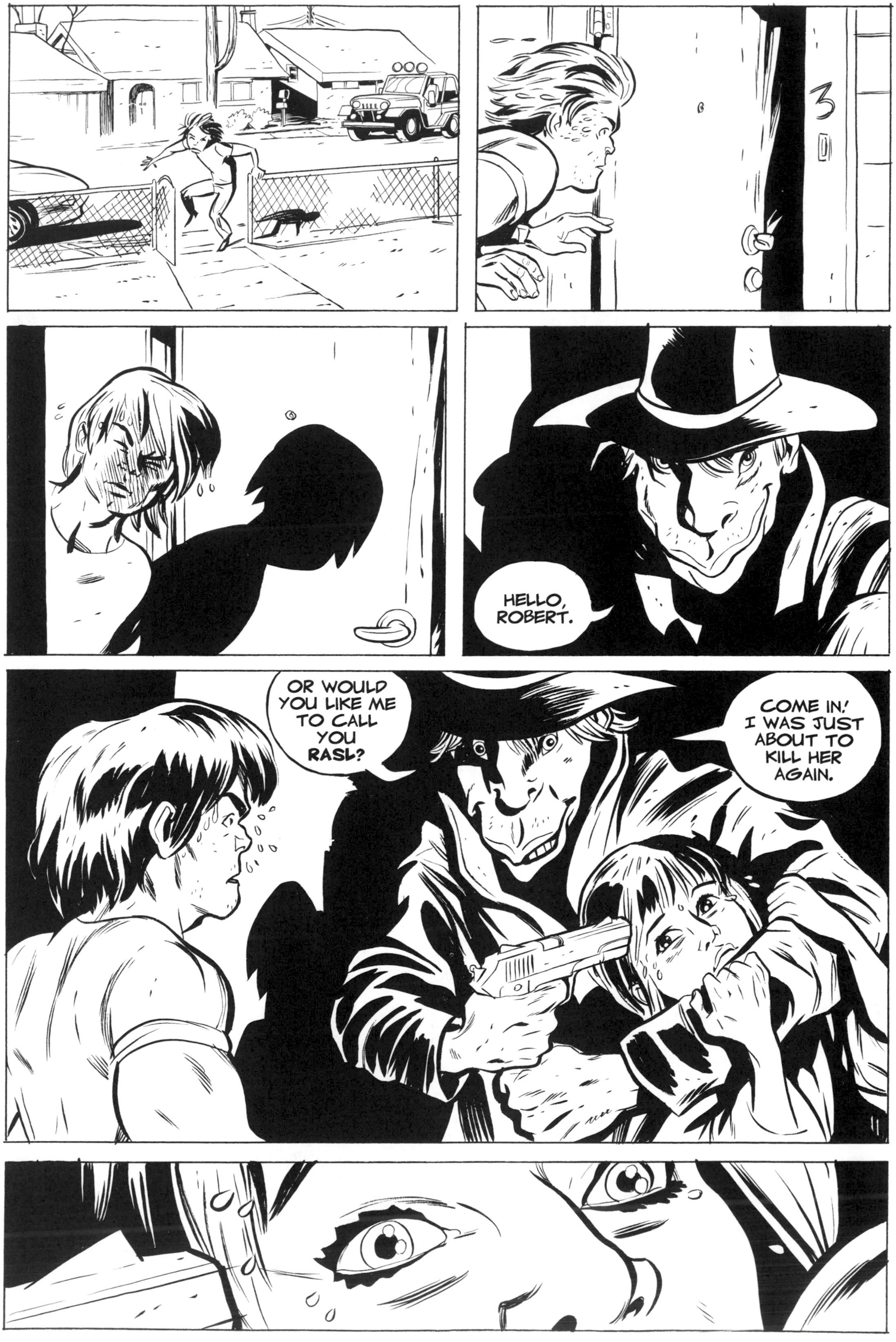
HELLO, ROBERT.
OR WOULD YOU LIKE ME TO CALL YOU RASL?
COME IN! I WAS JUST ABOUT TO KILL HER AGAIN.

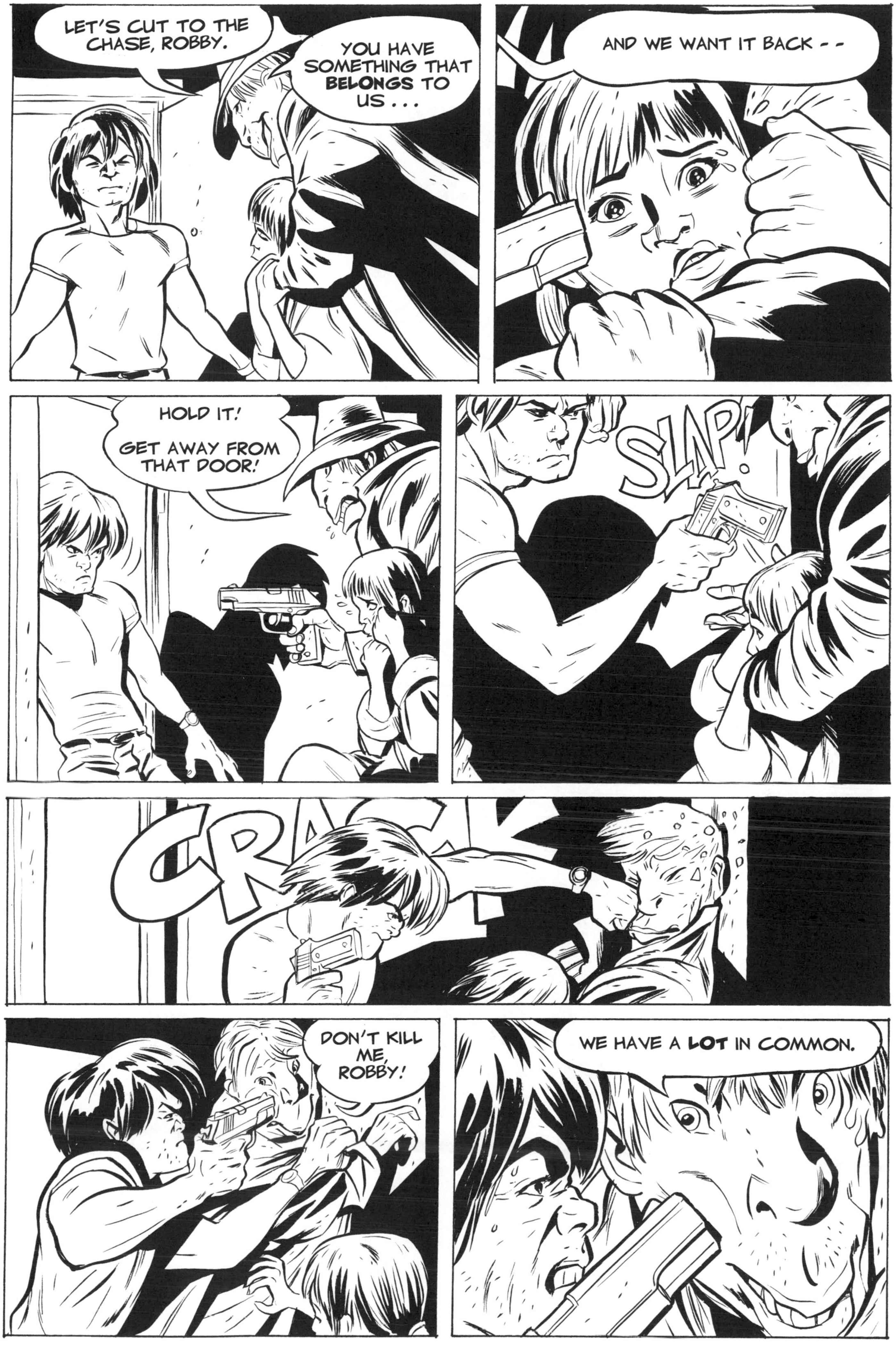
LET'S CUT TO THE CHASE, ROBBY.
YOU HAVE SOMETHING THAT **BELONGS** TO US . . .
AND WE WANT IT BACK - -
HOLD IT!
GET AWAY FROM THAT DOOR!
SLAP!
CRACK
DON'T KILL ME, ROBBY!
WE HAVE A **LOT** IN COMMON.

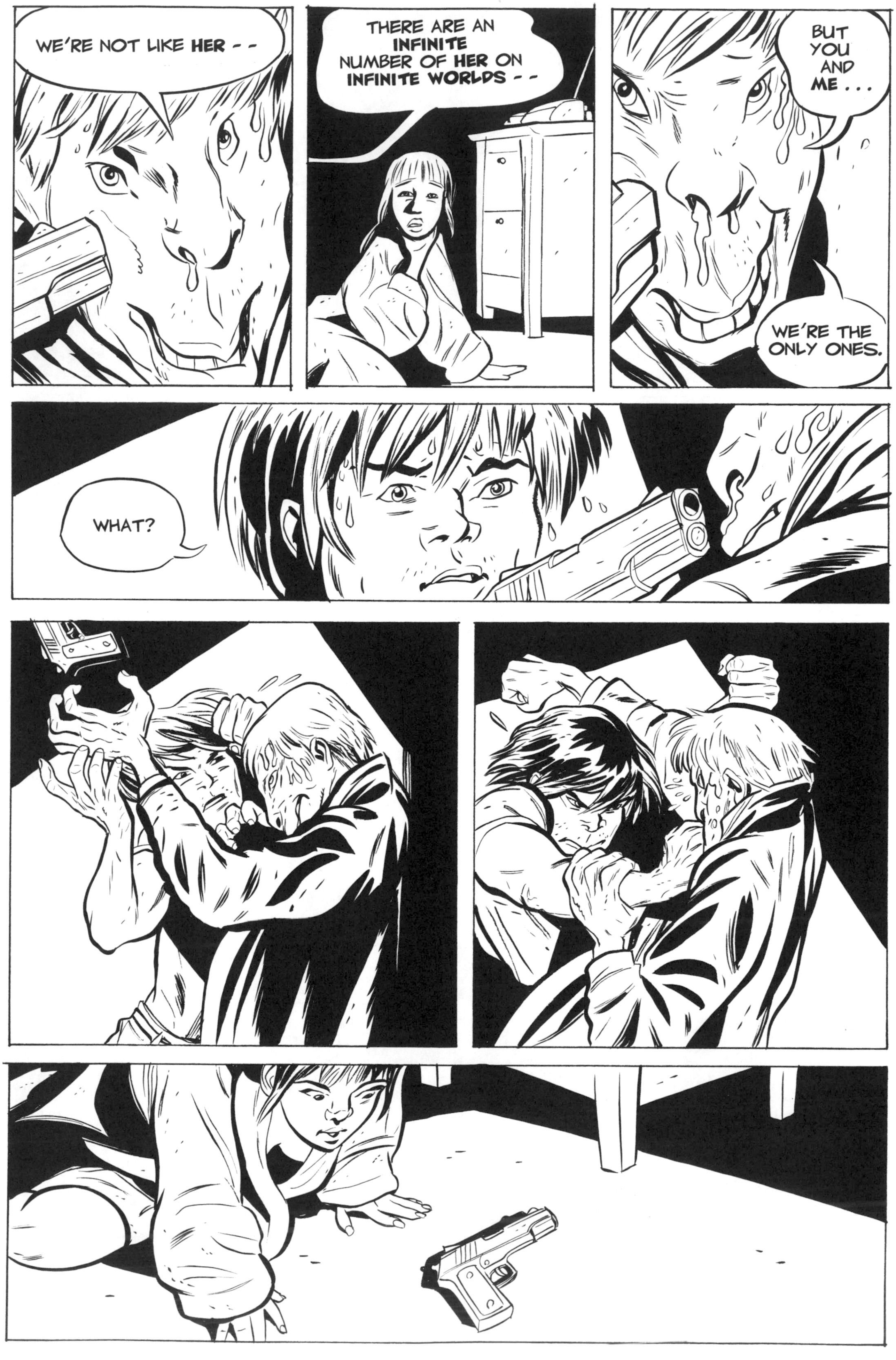
WE'RE NOT LIKE HER - -
THERE ARE AN INFINITE NUMBER OF HER ON INFINITE WORLDS - -
BUT YOU AND ME . . .
WE'RE THE ONLY ONES.
WHAT?

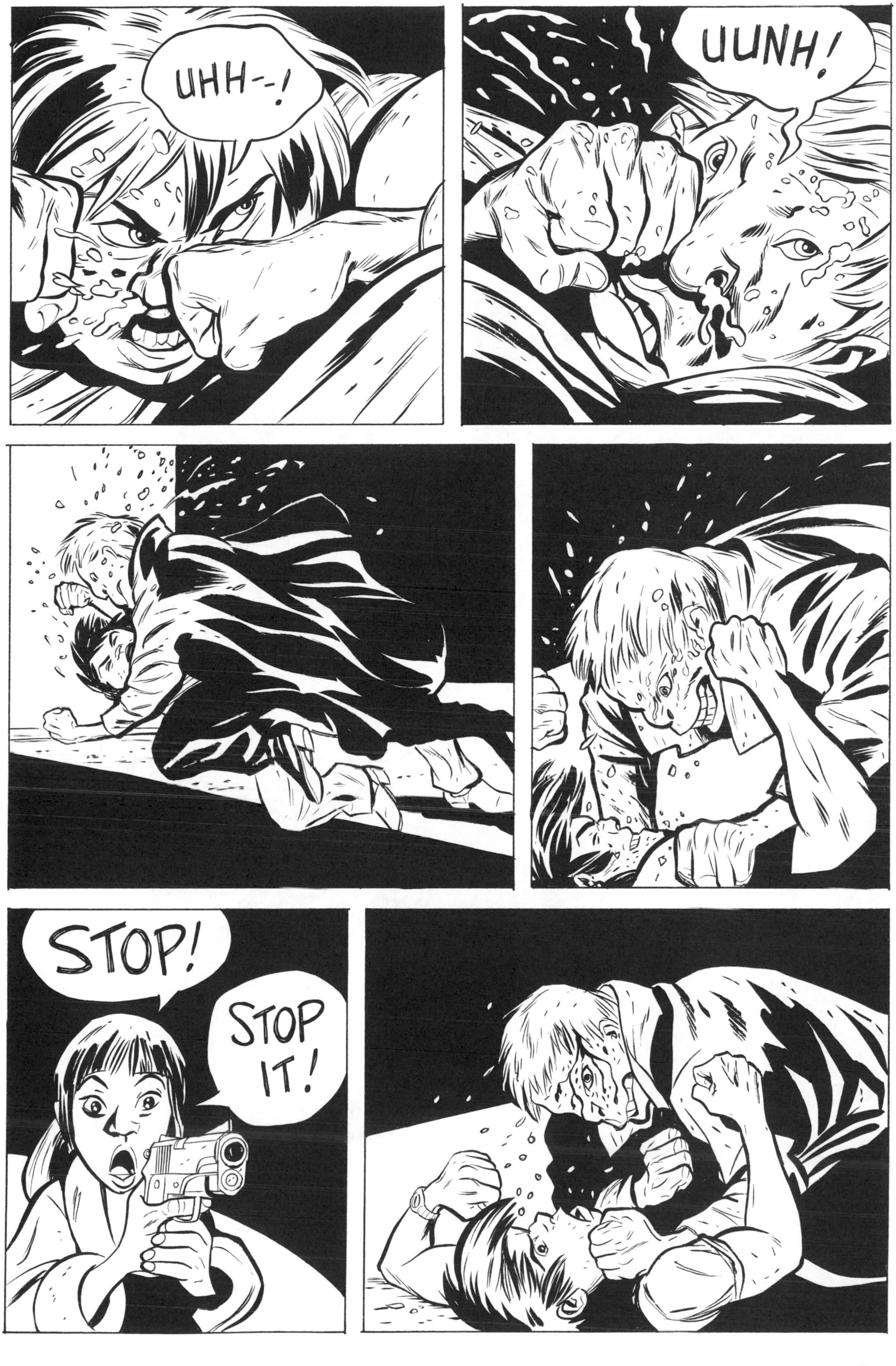
UHH--!
UUNH!
STOP!
STOP IT!

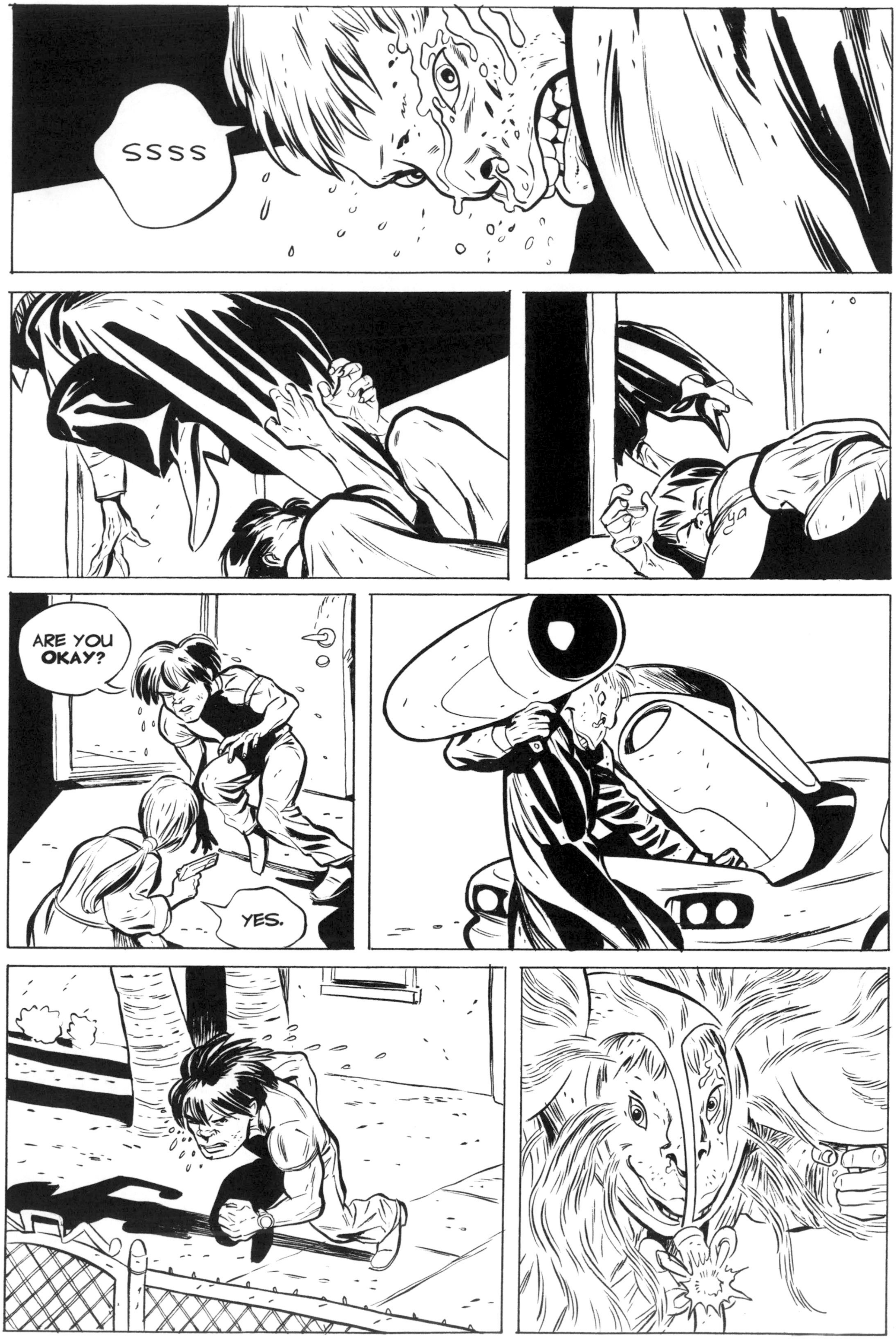
SSSS
ARE YOU OKAY?
YES.

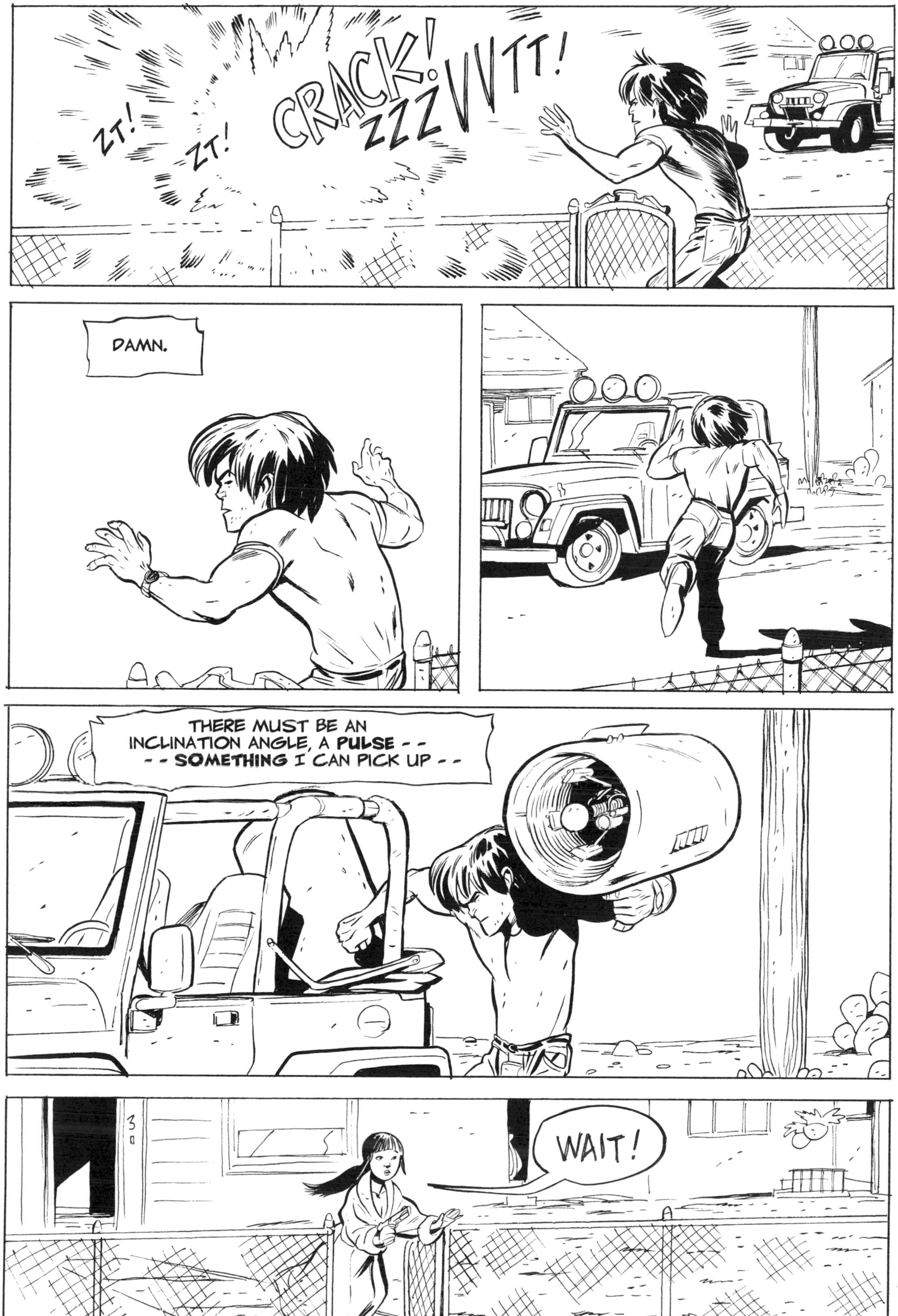
ZT!
ZT!
CRACK!
ZZZVVTT!
DAMN.
THERE MUST BE AN INCLINATION ANGLE, A PULSE - - - - SOMETHING I CAN PICK UP - -
WAIT!

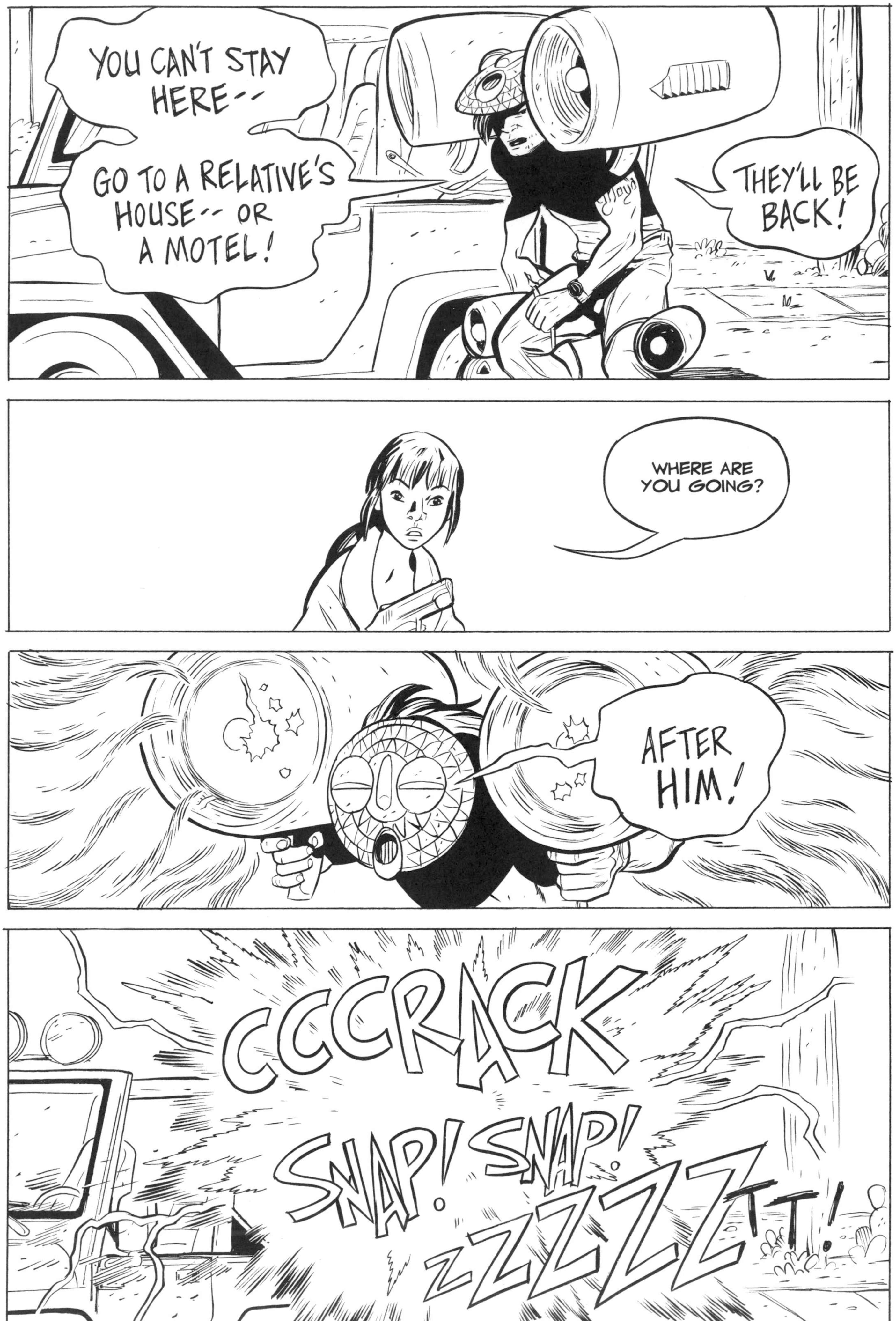
YOU CAN'T STAY HERE--
GO TO A RELATIVE'S HOUSE-- OR A MOTEL!
THEY'LL BE BACK!
WHERE ARE YOU GOING?
AFTER HIM!
CCCRACK
SNAP! SNAP!
ZZZZZZTTT!

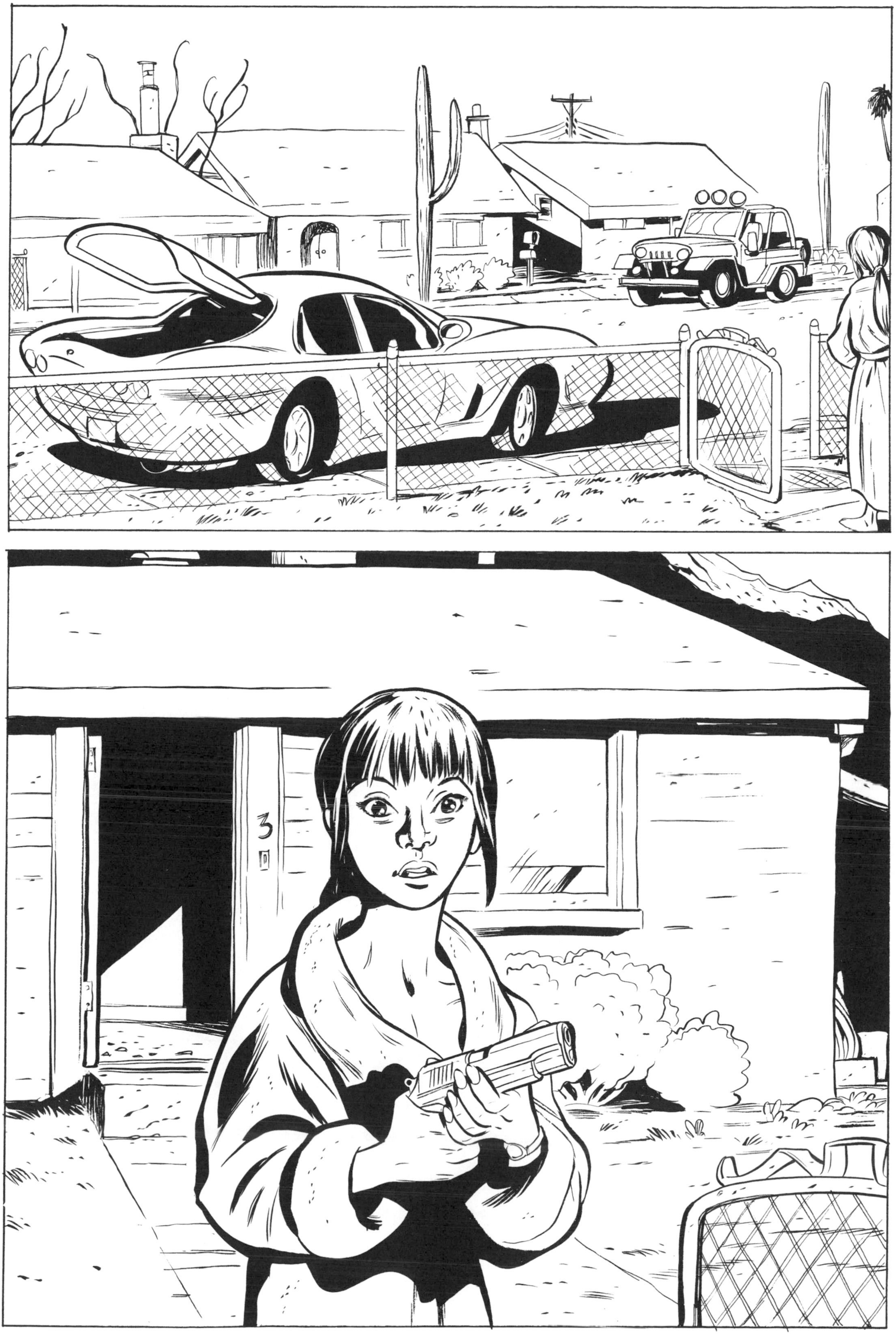
3

TO BE CONTINUED IN
RASL 2: THE FIRE OF ST. GEORGE

SPECIAL THANKS TO
MARTY FULLER, SCOTT GAUDI,
LARRY MEDRANO, JENNIFER OLIVER,
AND LOUIE RIOS FOR SHARING
THEIR KNOWLEDGE, ADVICE
AND PATIENCE.